Science, Gender and the Exploitation of Animals in Britain Since 1945

This book offers an historical analysis of the culture of animal-dependent science in Britain from 1945 to the present, exploring key areas of animal experimentation such as warfare, medical science and law from a gendered perspective. Questioning the nature of knowledge production in this area, and how animal experimentation intersects with broader cultural norms and values concerning sex, and gender, it examines the impact of contemporary forms of capitalism on animal dependent science, its historical trajectory and gendered configuration. With close attention to the broad social context from the creation of the Welfare State and the loss of Empire, to the emergence of neoliberalism in the 1980s and its present day omnipotent manifestation, the author asks how animal experimentation and the use of nonhuman animals in specific areas of science is gendered and has implications for women. Drawing on a variety of sociological, philosophical, feminist and historical theories and engaging with a wealth of primary and secondary materials of scientific research of the time, *Science, Gender and the Exploitation of Animals in Britain Since 1945* contends that there is a persistent, gendered ideology of animal use which remains inscribed within the policies of the British neoliberal state. As such, it will appeal to scholars of sociology, history and philosophy with interests in gender and the treatment of nonhuman animals.

Catherine Duxbury is a LSE Fellow for the LSE100: The LSE Course, at The London School of Economics and Political Science.

Solving Social Problems
Series editor:
Bonnie Berry, Director of the Social Problems Research Group, USA

Solving Social Problems provides a forum for the description and measurement of social problems, with a keen focus on the concrete remedies proposed for their solution. The series takes an international perspective, exploring social problems in various parts of the world, with the central concern being always their possible remedy. As such, work is welcomed on subjects as diverse as environmental damage, terrorism, economic disparities and economic devastation, poverty, inequalities, domestic assaults and sexual abuse, healthcare, natural disasters, labour inequality, animal abuse, crime, and mental illness and its treatment. In addition to recommending solutions to social problems, the books in this series are theoretically sophisticated, exploring previous discussions of the issues in question, examining other attempts to resolve them, and adopting and discussing methodologies that are commonly used to measure social problems. Proposed solutions may be framed as changes in policy, practice, or more broadly, social change and social movement. Solutions may be reflective of ideology, but are always pragmatic and detailed, explaining the means by which the suggested solutions might be achieved.
Also in the series

Culture and Activism
Animal Rights in France and the United States
Elizabeth Cherry

Advocacy for Social Change
Coalitions and the Organizations that Lead Them
Herbert J. Rubin

Everyday Fears of Legal Immigrants with Undocumented Spouses
Under U.S. Immigration Policy
Nina Michalikova

Science, Gender and the Exploitation of Animals in Britain Since 1945
Catherine Duxbury

For more information about this series, please visit: https://www.routledge.com/Solving-Social-Problems/book-series/ASHSER1354

Science, Gender and the Exploitation of Animals in Britain Since 1945

Catherine Duxbury

LONDON AND NEW YORK

First published 2022
by Routledge
2 Park Square, Milton Park, Abingdon, Oxon OX14 4RN

and by Routledge
605 Third Avenue, New York, NY 10158

Routledge is an imprint of the Taylor & Francis Group, an informa business

© 2022 Catherine Duxbury

The right of Catherine Duxbury to be identified as author of this work has been asserted by her in accordance with sections 77 and 78 of the Copyright, Designs and Patents Act 1988.

All rights reserved. No part of this book may be reprinted or reproduced or utilised in any form or by any electronic, mechanical, or other means, now known or hereafter invented, including photocopying and recording, or in any information storage or retrieval system, without permission in writing from the publishers.

Trademark notice: Product or corporate names may be trademarks or registered trademarks, and are used only for identification and explanation without intent to infringe.

British Library Cataloguing-in-Publication Data
A catalogue record for this book is available from the British Library

Library of Congress Cataloging-in-Publication Data
Names: Duxbury, Catherine, author.
Title: Science, gender and the exploitation of animals in Britain since 1945 / Catherine Duxbury.
Description: Abingdon, Oxon ; New York, NY : Routledge, 2021. | Series: Solving social problems | Includes bibliographical references and index.
Identifiers: LCCN 2021015414 (print) | LCCN 2021015415 (ebook) | ISBN 9781138617537 (hardback) | ISBN 9781032081694 (paperback) | ISBN 9780429461644 (ebook)
Subjects: LCSH: Animal experimentation—Great Britain—History. | Animal welfare—Great Britain—History. | Speciesism—Great Britain—History. | Feminism—Great Britain—History. | Feminist theory.
Classification: LCC HV4943.G55 D89 2021 (print) | LCC HV4943.G55 (ebook) | DDC 179/.40941—dc23
LC record available at https://lccn.loc.gov/2021015414
LC ebook record available at https://lccn.loc.gov/2021015415

ISBN: 9781138617537 (hbk)
ISBN: 9781032081694 (pbk)
ISBN: 9780429461644 (ebk)

DOI: 10.4324/9780429461644

Typeset in Times New Roman
by KnowledgeWorks Global Ltd.

Contents

Introduction | 1

Section I
Law, animal welfare and gender | 11

1 British animal experimentation law since 1945: Property, pastoral power and governmentality | 13

2 The march of Thatcherism: Neoliberal laboratory 'care' and the assent of the ASPA, 1981–1986 | 46

3 The power–pain nexus: How women's subjugation subtends speciesism in the legal system | 74

Section II
Scientific intersections: The practice of animal experimentation and its gendered dimensions | 87

4 Animal experimentation at Porton Down: Britain's Military-Animal-Industrial Complex, 1948–1955 | 89

5 Containing the laboratory animal: Laboratory spaces and gendered places, 1947–present | 123

6 Anxious animals, monstrous menstruating women and the science of stress, 1947–present | 157

Section III
Conclusion: 21st century compassion fatigue 201

   Conclusion 203

   Index 211

Introduction

Introduction: Accounting for the more-than-human

I have a confession to make. For almost half of my life, I have been taking drugs that depend on animal testing. I am addicted. Over the years, I have tried to stop taking them, but I suffer tremendously from side effects that leave me unable to function and carry out everyday activities. In case you haven't guessed, I have long-term mental health issues. These drugs keep me relatively sober, and I can at least participate in most human activities for certain periods. Although socialising is something I always struggle with.

Having long-term mental health issues makes you see the world in a very different light. Since I was a little girl, my closest allies were the furry, feathered and scaly critters of the household: dogs, cats, budgies, rabbits guinea-pigs, lizards and an iguana named 'Iggy.' I found safety, comfort and unconditional love from nonhuman animals that people could not provide. My early relationships with animals eventually led to being vegetarian in my teen years and vegan when I turned 20. Couple this with a love of political punk and rock music, making a run for it a university – after several false starts (I have never been 'that bright') and here I am today, wanting to fight with and for nonhuman animals and bring an end to experimentation.

It is no wonder my life experiences have led me to look at the insidious and subtle relationships between women and animals. I am a woman, with chronic mental ill health. I have been sexually harassed, abused and greatly misjudged in my life. Nonhuman animals are my saviours! I owe them. Yet, as I write this, the world is going through a pandemic of epic proportions. This is thanks to a virus known as SARS-CoV-2 or COVID-19. I will still get the COVID-19 vaccination – an injection that required the use of thousands upon thousands of animals. So, my question to you is what is to be done? How can we change the way we relate to nonhuman animals? How can we end entirely unnecessary experimentation? In this book, I hope to highlight the historical formations of animal experimentation in Britain since 1945. It illustrates how laboratory animal science is inherently gendered, and how the bodies of nonhumans of the laboratory are often used as a substitute for us female humans.

DOI: 10.4324/9780429461644-1

2 Introduction

An article published in *The Guardian* newspaper on 13 July 2020 highlights our contradictory and gendered relationships with nonhuman animals of the laboratory.[1] It was an article about the use of mice in the research for a COVID-19 vaccination. The reporter, Rachel Ellison, described researchers as suffering from 'compassion fatigue.' A term first identified by a by Joseph Newsome and his co-authors in the biomedical and veterinary community in 2019.[2] Compassion fatigue is similar to post-traumatic stress disorder (PTSD) and was first identified in nurses but noticed by Newsome *et al.* that it also applies to laboratory animal scientists. The condition can arise after constantly witnessing other living beings in pain:

> Compassion fatigue is a state of exhaustion and biologic, physiologic, and emotional dysfunction resulting from prolonged exposure to compassion stress. Persons who experience compassion fatigue *feel overwhelmed from bearing the suffering of others but typically continue to perform euthanasia in their patients' interest and biomedical research. Factors that may place persons at increased risk for experiencing compassion fatigue include high empathy, low emotional resiliency, a history of traumatic experiences, and the existence of unresolved trauma.* Factors that affect the severity of compassion fatigue are the duration of the incident, the potential for recurrence, exposure to death and dying, and the presence of moral conflicts.[3]

The first thing to note from this definition is that it encompasses subjective states of feeling and experience concerning the continued exposure to killing and death. Second, the risk factors are inadvertently enfolded within the 'feminine' – emotion, empathy, history of traumatic experiences and the existence of unresolved traumas. It is no surprise that in *The Guardian* article, Ellison quotes a female scientist in the first paragraph saying that she 'apologises to mice when she euthanises them.' 'I try to think that they've sacrificed for human health and for science.' The researcher had to 'switch to mice' later in her career due to her 'owning two pet rabbits' and consequently this made her become 'too attached to rabbits she worked with.'[4]

The article by Newsome *et al.* makes recommendations to laboratory animal organisations to recognise human psychosocial factors in the

---

[1] Rachel Ellison, "'It Takes a Toll': Researchers Struggle with Lockdown Cull of Lab Mice," *The Guardian*, 13 July 2020.
[2] Joseph T Newsome; Elizabeth A Clemmons; Dawn C Fitzhugh; Tracy L Gluckman; Michelle A Creamer-Hence; Laura J Tambrallo; Temari Wilder-Kofie, "Compassion Fatigue, Euthanasia Stress, and Their Management in Laboratory Animal Research," *Journal of the American Association for Laboratory Animal Science* 58, no. 3 (2019): 289–292.
[3] Ibid. p. 290. My emphasis.
[4] Rachel Ellison, "'It Takes a Toll': Researchers Struggle with Lockdown Cull of Lab Mice."

workplace.⁵ But, what about nonhuman animals? Again, this welfarist discourse emphasises the very human needs of the use of laboratory animals. In this case, the workers who have to test on animals to meet their research targets.

This welfarist approach advocated by Newsome *et al.* for humans also runs parallel to the development of a welfarist approach to laboratory animals that has occurred since the mid-twentieth century. This book hopes to demonstrate how these discourses of welfare are linked to the omnipotent presence of the economic model of governance known as economic liberalism. Economic liberalism is a mode of thought that vilifies the collective and celebrates the individual. It is characterised by the state's rolling back of its welfare apparatuses to prioritise privatisation, free trade, and individual competition.⁶ Britain was one of the leading nations to export this ideology to pursue world domination at the turn of the nineteenth century. Via the colonisation of lands and its peoples, Britain became one of the world's leading empires. At every turn, it instituted the philosophy of liberalism to gain ascendency in the world and subdue populations.⁷

We are still very much bound by the tight grip of liberalism but in its more radical guise of neoliberalism. Since the late 1970s and 1980s, Britain and the United States have inaugurated a swathe of radical economic reforms summed up by British premier, Margaret Thatcher, as 'there is no society, only individuals.'⁸ This economic revolution in Britain is still with us today. The same old rhetoric is heard coming from most centre and centre-right politicians' mouths: Government is bad, business is good.⁹

Yet, you may ask, what has this got to do with animal experimentation and its gendered intersections? Fair point. However, one only has to look at the history of animal experimental science to appreciate the insidious nature of liberalism and its discontents. British liberalism is expressed in many of the laws and institutions that maintain the Status Quo regarding the regulation of experiments. The ideology of liberalism that emphasises individuals, universality and private property relations was fortified and enfolded into legal rights doctrines concerning people and animals in the twentieth century. Lynn Hunt observes that this internalisation in the legal realm of liberal ideas made 'slow and steady progress' in the nineteenth and twentieth centuries but was integrated into jurisprudence and state establishments.¹⁰ This inculcation of liberal ideologies into law and institutions

---

5 Wilder-Kofie, "Compassion Fatigue, Euthanasia Stress, and Their Management in Laboratory Animal Research." p. 291.
6 Domenico Losurdo, *Liberalism: A Counter-History* (London: Verso, 2014). p. 1.
7 Ibid.
8 Eric Hobsbawm, *The Age of Extremes 1914–1991*, 15th ed. (London: Abacus, 2009). p. 337.
9 Ibid.
10 Lynn Hunt, *The French Revolution and Human Rights : A Brief Documentary History* (Boston: Bedford Books of St. Martin's Press, 1996). p. 30.

in a society profoundly affects nonhuman's and women's bodies. It allows us to still be at the receiving end of many a violent relationship, be that interpersonally, institutionally or culturally.

There is then, an astute denial of the rights of women and animals in contemporary British society. One of the main drivers is the neoliberal ideal that is detrimental to all but the richest white males in our society. The denial of these rights for women and animals is legitimated and rationalised by our science and law institutions. As I hope to show, particular living beings' treatment is linked to liberal modes of violent domination both in its ideological and material practices. I aim to demonstrate its enduring social, political and economic appearances – None-more-so than in the realm of animal experimental science and its legal accoutrements that sustain and perpetuate it. Animal experimentation and its legal implementation need to be mapped historically and from a perspective that recognises intersections of oppression. Britain, amongst other liberal nations, affirms the inferior status of animals and other marginalised groups. States are there to maintain hegemony to suppress any degree of social change. What then is to be done?

What am I doing?

In a small way, I would hope that the spirit of such writer-activists as Naomi Klein and Rob Nixon and many of the great feminist animal studies scholars, Carol J. Adams, Lori Gruen, Linda Birke and Donna Haraway permeate this book.[11] All of whom are incredibly inspiring and link nonhuman animals' treatment, nature and environmental degradation to the discrimination experienced by women and other marginalised groups. The book emerges from the work I completed for my PhD in Sociology at the University of Essex and insights gained from my ever-patient supervisor and friend, Professor Colin Samson. The writing is also accrued from my role as an Educator, gaining ideas from students and texts taught across many disciplines I teach in this now precarious world of Higher Education. A lot of the inspiration for this book comes from teaching the third-year undergraduate Liberal Arts module 'Dangerous Ideas: Essays and Manifestos as Social Criticism' in the School of Philosophy and Art History at the University of Essex. To be free of disciplinary shackles and work with students on ideas that provoke and encourage creativity in the classroom is a

---

11 Naomi Klein, *This Changes Everything: Capitalism Vs Climate* (London: Penguin Books, 2014); Rob Nixon, *Slow Violence and the Environmentalism of the Poor* (Cambridge, Massachusetts & London, England: Harvard University Press, 2011); Carol Adams, *The Sexual Politics of Meat* (Oxford, UK: Polity Press, 1990); Lori Gruen, *Ethics and Animals: An Introduction* (Cambridge, UK: Cambridge University Press, 2018); Lori Gruen, Fiona Probyn-Rapsey, ed., *Animalmaladies: Gender, Animals, and Madness* (New York & London: Bloomsbury Academic, 2019); Lynda Birke, *Feminism, Animals and Science: The Naming of the Shrew* (Buckingham, UK: Open University Press, 1994).

rarity in the age of the neoliberal university. To them, and all my students, I owe an enormous amount of gratitude.

My bias then is towards seeing academia as one that should not aspire to be emotionally detached from the world. Instead, it embraces feelings and emotionality, reaches out to all living beings with care and empathy. I am often reminded here of the feminist educator bell hooks, who claims that we should 'teach to transgress.'[12] Yes, we should, but we should also sin our way through the pretentious world of academia! On that note then, in this book, I refuse to be bound by the myopic ties of monodisciplinary frameworks and give a thorough 'literature review' or dogmatic recipe for my 'methodology.' I find this limits creative expression and curtails writers' (and readers') imaginative insights gained from traversing texts and sources from various backgrounds.[13] I do not trawl the literature and review popular opinions on the subject matter. While many scholars are mentioned, I do not intend to provoke lethargy on the reader by reviewing those whose ideas are similar or different. Instead, this is a book that exemplifies disciplinary disregard and theoretical confusion. And, why not, eh?

Michel Foucault and Donna Haraway are great examples of this transcendence of academic myopia. Their work is filled with 'pick and mix' theoretical insights that establish connections between the lifeworld and the academy's abstract ivory tower. You will find that my writing draws heavily on both great thinkers, especially Foucault. I very much embrace Haraway's' methodological metaphor of writing as playing a game 'cat's cradle.'[14] With this, she hopes to create a methodological approach that is a 'toolkit' for a 'constitutively interactive, collaborative process of trying to make sense of the natural worlds we inhabit and that inhibits us.'[15] Therefore, she aims to 'queer' the natural in the hope to make liveable worlds. In other words, she aims for destabilising the normal. Her metaphor of the cat's cradle helps to accentuate this notion of plurality, interrelationship and complexity:

> Cat's cradle is about patterns and knots; the game takes great skill and can result in some serious surprises. One person can build up a large repertoire of string figures on a single pair of hands; but the cat's cradle figures can be passed back and forth on hands of several players, who add new moves in the building of complex patterns.[16]

---

12 bell hooks, *Teaching to Transgress: Education as the Practice of Freedom* (London: Routledge, 1994).
13 Colin Samson, *The Colonialism of Human Rights: Ongoing Hypocrisies of Western Liberalism* (Cambridge: Polity Press, 2020). p. 6.
14 Donna Haraway, "A Game of Cat's Cradle: Science Studies, Feminist Theory, Cultural Studies," *Configurations* 2, no. 1 (1994): 59–71.
15 "A Game of Cat's Cradle: Science Studies, Feminist Theory, Cultural Studies," *Configurations* 2, no. 1 (1994): p. 66.
16 Ibid. pp. 69–70.

6 *Introduction*

For Haraway, the game of cat's cradle is a metaphor for using more than one approach in research, to recognise the complexity of the worlds we inhabit and, as she says, those we 'inhibit.' To do this, we must *understand* technoscience to change it and our relationship to the 'natural.' To do this is to embrace plurality and 'knot' together approaches to address technoscience's destructive impulses.[17]

By no means, what follows is a comprehensive history of animal experimentation in Britain, and nor did I want it to be that. Readers who want more detail and overview of the topic need to consult further works. I will have missed out a lot, but hopefully, there will be aspects you find interesting to read. The book is split into three sections, with section one on legal regulation of animal experimentation and its interconnections to the jurisprudence of laws primarily relating to women. Section 2, we take a hike through the laboratory's material spaces and analyse the historical transformation of housing experimental animals, the psychological dimensions to confinement of animals of the laboratory and their gendered configurations. Section 3 concludes the book and gives a summative overview.

Chapters 1 and 2: The first two chapters of Section 1 are devoted to the historical development of animal experimental law in Britain. Taking as our starting point, the review of the 1876 Cruelty to Animals Act in 1965, chapter 1 examines the primary debates about the then-current law and theorises using Michel Foucault's notion of Pastoral Power.[18] An insidious form of power over living beings that disguises control as welfare.

In this chapter, I document the first serious discussions to take place by various governmental and scientific actors about the psychological experiences of nonhuman animals of the laboratory. Here, we focus on how these multiple actors rationalised emotion to press for the continuing practice of vivisection.

Chapter 2 follows this and analyses the assent of the Animals (Scientific Procedures) Act, 1986 to its present-day manifestation. This Act superseded the 1876 Act and was the first piece of legal regulation to include psychological wellbeing into legal definitions of pain. European Union legislation is also discussed alongside Britain's role in creating such a widely applicable form of legal control. Chapter 2 follows in the same Foucaultian vein as Chapter 1 but extends the notion of Pastoral Power to Governmentality[19] – total biopolitical regulation of nonhuman bodies in the liberal era. Brexit is then discussed and analysed from the perspective of legal laboratory rights and its implications for nonhuman animals.

17 Ibid. p. 60.
18 Michel Foucault, "Omnes Et Singulatim: Toward a Critique of Political Reason.," in *Power*, ed. J. D. Faubion (London: Penguin, 2002).
19 Michel Foucault, "Governmentality," in *The Foucault Effect: Studies in Governmentality*, ed. Colin Gordon Graham Burchell, Peter Miller (Chicago: University of Chicago Press, 1991).

Chapter 3: To conclude the section on law and animal experimentation, Chapter 3 is devoted to a theoretical exploration into women's rights and legal jurisprudence. Using the important work of such feminists like Catharine MacKinnon and Wendy Brown,[20] I document the intersections between women and animals in the legal realm regarding the experience of pain, systemic violence and the liberal state. I end by proposing a tentative concept to encapsulate women and animals' experiences of institutionalised violence at the hands of capitalist socio-legal politics called the Power–Pain Nexus.

Chapter 4: The first chapter of the second section outlines the research conducted at Porton Down in the 1950s, Britain's leading top-secret military research establishment. After the Second World War atrocities and the start of the Cold War, Britain invested heavily in the research and production of biological and chemical weapons. Thousands of animals were used to test these weapons of mass destruction. Although nuclear power was on the rise, the government still provided a significant amount of funding to investigate such weapons. This chapter focuses on the top-secret biological weapons trials conducted by Porton scientists from 1948 to 1955. I analyse how scientists used nonhuman bodies and how the role of the post-mortem examination on their bodies became a theatrical routine that wouldn't be amiss in a horror film.

Chapter 5: This chapter focuses on the laboratory's material spaces and how animal welfare became a key signature of the lab's spatial layouts. I take a theoretical juxtaposition here and investigate the historical development of laboratory animal spaces using feminist psychoanalysis. Here, I argue that containment is a metaphor for the female body and simultaneously, this is an exercise of patriarchal power and symbolic exploitation of the female.

Chapter 6: We remain firmly in the laboratory for this final empirical chapter. We explore the historical establishment of the experience of stress and psychological ill-health in animals of the laboratory. I show how the discourses of stress intersected and ran parallel to the discourses of mental ill-health in women regarding the gradual medicalisation of pre-menstrual syndrome. In this chapter, we are not dealing with animals' welfare in terms of the lab's material spaces, but rather their psychological wellbeing and how the laboratory accounts for this. I use Fiona Probyn-Rapsey and Lori Gruen's work and their term 'animaladies' to demonstrate how 'animals,' 'maladies' and 'ladies' are deeply entangled in laboratory animal research.[21]

Chapter 7: I conclude the book by bringing together the main themes to emerge from the book's historical journey. I also give a brief argument about how to end animal experiments.

---

20 Catharine MacKinnon, "Of Mice and Men: A Feminist Fragment on Animal Rights," in *Women's Lives, Men's Laws*, ed. Catharine MacKinnon (Boston MA: Harvard University Press, 2007); Wendy Brown, *States of Injury: Power and Freedom in Late Modernity* (Princeton, NJ: Princeton University Press, 1995).
21 Probyn-Rapsey, *Animalmaladies: Gender, Animals, and Madness*.

A note on terminology

For most of this book, I use the word animal to designate the more-than-human being. I acknowledge that this is a vast generalisation, which eschews subjectivity of sentience, and places nonhuman animals, in all their individuality, into the very binary modes which this thesis tries to address and overcome. However, I am using the historical referential 'animal' by using language used in the archival documents.

Nonhuman animals have been generalised for the most part, with specific species being discussed in relation to the particular experiment in the narrative. Despite this, I take stock from Derrida, in his paper '*The Animal That Therefore I Am (More To Follow)*,' who examines 'the animal' with particular reference to his cat but also acknowledges the singularity of species:

> If I say "it is a real cat" that sees me naked this is in order to mark its unsubstitutable singularity. When it responds in its name, it doesn't do so as the exemplar of a species called "cat", even less so of an "animal" genus or kingdom. It is true that I identify it as a male or female cat. But even before that identification, it comes to me as *this* irreplaceable living being that one day enters my space, into this place where it can encounter me, see me, even see me naked. Nothing can ever rob me of the certainty that what we have here is an existence that refuses to be conceptualised.[22]

I too, acknowledge this 'unsubstitutable singularity.' For historical purposes, to avoid anachronism, I use the term 'animal' in places.

On gender

As this book addresses the intersectional nature of animals, science and gender, it is also pertinent to discuss what I mean when referring to gender. Here, I use Judith Butler's idea of the performativity of gender, to suggest that one's learned performance of gendered behaviour (masculine or feminine) is something we act out, a performance.[23] This is imposed upon us by normative heterosexual standards (also, as I later argue through the construction of scientific knowledge via the use of nonhuman animals in experiments).

---

22 Jacques Derrida, *The Animal That Therefore I Am*, ed. John Caputo (New York: Fordham University Press, 2008). p. 9.
23 Judith Butler, "Performative Acts and Gender Constitution: An Essay in Phenomenology and Feminist Theory," in *Performing Feminisms: Feminist Critical Theory and Theatre*, ed. Sue-Ellen Case (Baltimore: Johns Hopkins University Press, 1990). p. 270.

Butler argues that gender is not a natural 'thing' and therefore does not exist, she writes 'gender reality is performative which means, quite simply, that it is real only to the extent that it is performed.'[24] I take Butler's idea of gender, as one that is a social construction, open to change and contestation.

> Because there is neither an 'essence' that gender expresses or externalises nor an objective ideal to which gender aspires; because gender is not a fact, the various acts of gender creates the idea of gender, and without those acts, there would be no gender at all. Gender is, thus, a construction that regularly conceals its genesis.[25]

Moreover, there is no dividing line between sex and gender, but rather, following Butler, I assume that our gendered performances affect people in material, corporeal ways, which in turn are affected by social constructions. Following Butler, I take the idea of sex not as 'a bodily given on which the construct of gender is artificially imposed, but…a cultural norm which governs the materialisation of bodies.'[26] Rather than embrace radical constructivism, it is important to note how materialisation of bodies (human and nonhuman) happens through discourse and social conventions. This involves a consideration of materiality and consists of a turn to 'matter, not as a site or surface, but as *a process of materialisation that stabilises overtime to produce the effect of boundary, fixity, and surface we call matter.*'[27]

Bibliography

Adams, Carol. *The Sexual Politics of Meat*. Oxford, UK: Polity Press, 1990.
Birke, Lynda. *Feminism, Animals and Science: The Naming of the Shrew*. Buckingham, UK: Open University Press, 1994.
Brown, Wendy. *States of Injury: Power and Freedom in Late Modernity*. Princeton, NJ: Princeton University Press, 1995.
Butler, Judith. *Bodies That Matter*. 2nd ed. Oxon, UK: Routledge, 2011.
———. "Performative Acts and Gender Constitution: An Essay in Phenomenology and Feminist Theory." In *Performing Feminisms: Feminist Critical Theory and Theatre*, edited by Sue-Ellen Case, 270–282. Baltimore: Johns Hopkins University Press, 1990.
Derrida, Jacques. *The Animal That Therefore I Am*. Edited by John Caputo. New York: Fordham University Press, 2008.
Ellison, Rachel. "'It Takes a Toll': Researchers Struggle with Lockdown Cull of Lab Mice." *The Guardian*, 13 July 2020.

---

24 Ibid. p. 278.
25 Ibid. p. 273.
26 Judith Butler, *Bodies That Matter*, 2nd ed. (Oxon, UK: Routledge, 2011). pp. 2–3.
27 Ibid. p. xviii.

Foucault, Michel. "Governmentality." In *The Foucault Effect: Studies in Governmentality*, edited by Colin Gordon, Graham Burchell, and Peter Miller, 87–104. Chicago: University of Chicago Press, 1991.
———. "Omnes Et Singulatim: Toward a Critique of Political Reason." In *Power*, edited by J.D. Faubion, 298–325. London: Penguin, 2002.
Gruen, Lori. *Ethics and Animals: An Introduction*. Cambridge, UK: Cambridge University Press, 2018.
Haraway, Donna. "A Game of Cat's Cradle: Science Studies, Feminist Theory, Cultural Studies." *Configurations* 2, no. 1 (1994): 59–71.
———. "A Game of Cat's Cradle: Science Studies, Feminist Theory, Cultural Studies." *Configurations* 2, no. 1 (1994): 59–71.
Hobsbawm, Eric. *The Age of Extremes 1914–1991*. 15th ed. London: Abacus, 2009.
hooks, bell. *Teaching to Transgress: Education as the Practice of Freedom*. London: Routledge, 1994.
Hunt, Lynn. *The French Revolution and Human Rights: A Brief Documentary History*. Boston: Bedford Books of St. Martin's Press, 1996.
Klein, Naomi. *This Changes Everything: Capitalism Vs Climate*. London: Penguin Books, 2014.
Losurdo, Domenico. *Liberalism: A Counter-History*. London: Verso, 2014.
MacKinnon, Catharine. "Of Mice and Men: A Feminist Fragment on Animal Rights." In *Women's Lives, Men's Laws*, edited by Catharine MacKinnon. Boston MA: Harvard University Press, 2007.
Nixon, Rob. *Slow Violence and the Environmentalism of the Poor*. Cambridge, Massachusetts & London, England: Harvard University Press, 2011.
Probyn-Rapsey, Fiona, Lori Gruen, ed. *Animalmaladies: Gender, Animals, and Madness*. New York & London: Bloomsbury Academic, 2019.
Samson, Colin. *The Colonialism of Human Rights: Ongoing Hypocrisies of Western Liberalism*. Cambridge: Polity Press, 2020.
Wilder-Kofie, Temari, Joseph T Newsome, Elizabeth A Clemmons, Dawn C Fitzhugh, Tracy L Gluckman, Michelle A Creamer-Hence, Laura J Tambrallo. "Compassion Fatigue, Euthanasia Stress, and Their Management in Laboratory Animal Research." *Journal of the American Association for Laboratory Animal Science* 58, no. 3 (2019): 289–292.

Section I
Law, animal welfare and gender

1 British animal experimentation law since 1945

Property, pastoral power and governmentality

The European Union (EU) Directive 2010/63 on the Protection of Animals used for Scientific Purposes came into effect in the United Kingdom in January 2013.[1] Recital 12 of the Directive declares 'animals have an intrinsic value which must be respected.' They are 'sentient creatures,' whose use should be restricted to 'areas which may ultimately benefit human or animal health, or the environment.' Not only that, the Directive stipulates that scientific procedures must be conducted in such a way that they involve 'animals with the lowest capacity to experience pain, suffering, distress or lasting harm.'[2] This broadening of the definition of the *experience* of pain in (some) nonhuman animals under experiment, to include *psychological* notions of wellbeing, also links to the heavy emphasis placed in the Directive on the welfare of these animals. Recital 31 states that 'animal welfare considerations should be given the highest priority.'[3] This acknowledgement of both sentience and the need for the care of experimental animals may seem surprising to the reader. This aspect of animal experimentation law has a long historical trajectory and is dependent on a series of intricate and complex power relations formed between state, scientific actors and animal welfare bodies over a specific time.

In a lot of ways, this first section of this book maps out the theoretical and philosophical purview of the rest of the chapters: animal welfare, power and its gendered implications from historical perspective. This first chapter addresses key regulatory measures transposed into law since the post-Second World War era. It analyses the consequences this has had and continues to have, for nonhuman animals themselves. For it was after the Second World War that laboratory scientists, politicians and lawmakers started to take the

---

1 Darren Calley, "The Aggregation of Suffering in the Regulatory Context: Scientific Experimentation, Animals, and Intrinsic Value," *Journal of Animal Ethics* 7, no. 1 (2017): 1–30.
2 Council of the European Union, "Directive 2010/63/EU of the European Parliament and of the Council of 22 September 2010 on the Protection of Animals Used for Scientific Purposes," *Official Journal of the European Union* (2010), L276/33.
3 Ibid.

welfare of nonhuman animals seriously.[4] I examine key debates of animal experimentation law, from 1947 to the present day. The EU Directive 2010/63, of which the United Kingdom falls under in the guise of the 1986 Animals (Scientific Procedures) Act (ASPA),[5] frames the contemporary legal obligations scientists and scientific organisations have to obey to carry out their researches. This chapter traces the historically contingent origins of ASPA with a specific focus on the complex discourses which evolved on and about animal pain and welfare. It is through this review of British animal experimental law that I shall be investigating the epistemological status of the animal body, questioning the origins of knowledge relating to animals and directing attention to the social practices that define the animal body in experimental research. In order to analyse this epistemological shift of nonhuman animals, for Chapter 1 I shall be using Michel Foucault's ideas of Pastoral Power and for Chapter 2, governmentality.[6]

My argument has several interrelated components which help us to track the origins of current legislated welfarist discourses of care in experimental animals. Initially, I argue that during the first post-Second World War review of the 1876 Act in 1965, pastoral power operated under the guise of animal welfare. Pastoral power acted as an ideological precursor to the establishment of modes of governance (governmentality) over nonhuman laboratory life made manifest in the ASPA, 1986. Second, this power over nonhuman life contributes to the maintenance of the legal attribution of animals as objects of property, despite the recent attribution of sentience afforded them in EU Directive 2010/63. This designation of sentience is historically contingent, and it helps to reinforce and mediate modes of governmentality (welfare practices) and the discourses circulating concerning animals' experiences of pain. The incorporation of welfare into animal experimentation is used by animal-dependent scientists and lawmakers to facilitate the continued exploitation and domination of nonhuman bodies.

British animal experimentation law

British animal experimentation law has a long and convoluted history.[7] Its origins began in the latter half of the nineteenth century when the

---

4 Catherine Duxbury, "Animals, Science and Gender: Animal Experimentation in Britain, 1947–1965" (PhD, University of Essex, 2017).
5 Until its departure from the EU on 31 October 2019.
6 Michel Foucault, "Omnes Et Singulatim: Toward a Critique of Political Reason," in *Power*, ed. J. D. Faubion (London: Penguin, 2002); "Governmentality," in *The Foucault Effect: Studies in Governmentality*, ed. Colin Gordon Graham Burchell, and Peter Miller (Chicago: University of Chicago Press, 1991).
7 See for example, Richard D. French, *Antivivisection and Medical Science in Victorian Society* (Princeton, New Jersey: Princeton University Press, 1975); Nicolaas Rupke, ed. *Vivisection in Historical Perspective* (London: Routledge, 1990).

Parliament passed its first law for vivisection.[8] The 1876 Cruelty to Animals Act regulated the practice of vivisection and introduced a compulsory licensing system for scientists who wanted to conduct experiments on living animals.[9] All scientists who used animals in their research were subject to control under this law. This was until its complete revision in the late twentieth century under the guise of the Animals (Scientific Procedures) Act 1986 (ASPA).[10]

The ASPA 1986 came about as a result of various non-governmental, state and supranational organisations. Within Britain itself, pressure came from activists and animal welfare groups, as well as politicians.[11] Extraneous to Britain was the role played by the Council of Europe (CoE) and the EU, of which Britain had been a member since 1975.[12]

Both the CoE and EU issued documents on the care and use of laboratory animals. In 1986, they produced the European Treaty Series 123. Britain had a substantial input in formulating this document.[13] As such the CoE treaty series was not legally binding but was influential in the formation of the 1986 EU Directive 86/609/EEC. This is a legally binding document for those countries who are members of the EU, and this included Britain.[14]

Britain transposed much of Directive 86/609/EEC into their ASPA law.[15] This included widening the definition of the experience of pain, alongside stipulating the legal requirement for the care and welfare of laboratory animals.[16] In 2010, the EU updated Directive 86/609 into Directive 2010/63. This happened alongside the revision of Appendix A of the CoE European Treaty Series 123, intending to make congruent the legislative framework across the EU member states. Not only that, the update placed even greater emphasis on the welfare of laboratory animals, including the classification of the severity of procedures and the likely impact on the psychological and

---

8 Harriet Ritvo, *The Animal Estate: English and Other Creatures in the Victorian Age* (London, UK: Penguin Books Ltd, 1990).
9 Ibid.
10 Dan Lyons, *The Politics of Animal Experimentation* (Hampshire: Palgrave Macmillan, 2013).
11 Richard Ryder, *Animal Revolution: Changing Attitudes Towards Speciesism*, 2nd ed. (Oxford & New York: Berg, 2000); Lyons, *The Politics of Animal Experimentation*.
12 Jan-Bas Prins Javier Guillén, Bryan Howard, Anne-Dominique Degryse, Marcel Gyger, "The European Framework on Research Animal Welfare Regulations and Guidelines," in *Laboratory Animals: Regulations and Recommendations for the Care and Use of Animals in Research*, ed. Javier Guillén (London: Elsevier, 2018).
13 Hansard, Animal Experiments: Council of Europe Convention, House of Lords [HL] Deb 05 June 1981 vol 420 cc1509-10WA.
14 {Javier Guillén, 2018 #354} Also see The National Archives (forthwith TNA) T 489/69 Animal Experiments: Proposals to Amend the Cruelty to Animals Act and the European Convention on Proposals on Animal Experiments.
15 Javier Guillén, "The European Framework on Research Animal Welfare Regulations and Guidelines."
16 "Animals (Scientific Procedures) Act" (1986).

physical health of nonhuman laboratory animals.[17] This was in addition to a revision of their accommodation and care, including cage sizing, diet and exercise.[18] In 2012, Britain transposed Directive 2010/63 by updating the ASPA.[19] In this chapter, the main focus will be on the ASPA and its latest revisions. This includes discussions recently held in Parliament by politicians about animal experimentation, animal sentience and the impact Brexit will have on such researches.

The legal strategy of sentience: Desubjectification through inclusion

If we refer back to the opening paragraph of the chapter, we can see that EU Directive 2010/63 construes nonhuman laboratory animals as 'sentient' and needing care and welfare. The Directive stipulates a broad definition of pain to encapsulate nonhuman animals' psychological as well as physical wellbeing.[20] This idea of avoiding unnecessary physical *and* psychological pain, as well as according sentience to nonhuman laboratory animals, is only a recent phenomenon.

Historically, animals were not considered sentient beings under British law. This is why EU Directive 2010/63 may come as a shock to readers. It begs the questions: if nonhuman laboratory animals are lawfully considered sentient, then why still use them in scientific procedures? Moreover, why are they still classed as property?[21] One line of argument I take throughout this book is that nonhuman laboratory animals may have been accorded sentient status, but, they are still *objectified*. They are constructed as 'active objects' rather than active *moral* agents. For this reason, nonhuman animals are still secondary to the human 'entitlement' to use.[22] Legal regulations and laws *still* render nonhuman animals as objects of property.[23] Nonhuman animals are still held within human-centred hierarchies of dominance and power.

---

17 Council of the European Union, "Directive 2010/63/EU of the European Parliament and of the Council of 22 September 2010 on the Protection of Animals Used for Scientific Purposes."
18 Javier Guillén, "The European Framework on Research Animal Welfare Regulations and Guidelines."
19 HM Government, "Animal Testing and Research" https://www.gov.uk/guidance/research-and-testing-using-animals#animals-scientific-procedures-act-1986.
20 Council of the European Union, "Directive 2010/63/EU of the European Parliament and of the Council of 22 September 2010 on the Protection of Animals Used for Scientific Purposes."
21 Animal-Law, "Brexit, Article 13, and the Debate on Recognising 'Animal Sentience' in Law," in *A-Law expert legal briefing note* (The UK Centre for Animal Law, 2017).
22 Dinesh Joseph Wadiwel, *The War against Animals* (Leiden & Boston: Brill Rodopi, 2015); Kay Peggs, "Nonhuman Animal Experiments in the European Community: Human Values and Rational Choice," *Society and Animals* 18, no. 1 (2010): 6.
23 Ian Robertson, *Animals, Welfare and the Law* (Abingdon & New York: Routledge, 2015).

Gary Francione, a prominent animal rights scholar, outlines the confusing connotations associated with the legal definition of property. He indicates that it is defined as a set of relations between persons governing the use of 'things' and the 'incidents of ownership,' which come with various rights and obligations associated with that ownership.[24] These rights of ownership are intrinsically tied to the market system. Animals are assigned prices; they are an economic commodity to be bought and sold in the interests of the owner. Animals in law are assigned a use-value according to their specific commodified purpose, whether that be as pets, for food or for scientific experiments. Moreover, owning an animal is no different from owning other sorts of personal property.[25] This leads to a form of utilitarianism, which Francione defines as 'legal welfarism.' It positions nonhumans as an object in relation to their human use-value. Animal welfare, in this instance, becomes an economic imperative rather than one stemming from genuine moral concern.[26]

Although Francione is right in asserting that the status of animals as property shapes welfare concerns, he doesn't question the epistemological construction of nonhuman animals enshrined in animal experimentation law.[27] In other words, what power-knowledge relations construct the nonhumans as property, and how does this link to discourses about their welfare? As the subsequent text will demonstrate, the ideology promulgated by the CoE, EU, UK governmental and scientific organisations in the formulation of ASPA is influenced by the recognition of animals as sentient beings. But this recognition rests on an insidious set of philosophical suppositions that in the end renders nonhumans' experience of pain as relative to and undercut by humans' experiences. This leads one to conclude that the influence of the scientific idea of welfare is much more complicated than Francione admits.

It is here where the analyses conducted by socio-legal researcher Dinesh Joseph Wadiwel are most useful.[28] Wadiwel extends the writings of Francione by using a Foucauldian biopolitical framework to explore violence towards animals. Where biopolitics is defined as power over life and death, through the regulation of a population's health and welfare, Wadiwel argues that this also extends to nonhuman animals through the concept of sovereignty.[29]

For Wadiwel, human dominance (sovereignty) over nonhuman animals is the result of the consolidation of individual, institutional and epistemic forces. This inevitably includes legalised forms of violence towards them, such as vivisection. Property rights established in animals endorse the human right of

---

24 Gary L. Francione, *Animals, Property and the Law*, 2nd ed. (Philadelphia: Temple University Press, 2007). p. 33.
25 Gary Francione, *Animals as Persons: Essays on the Abolition of Animal Exploitation*. (New York: Columbia University Press, 2008). p. 44.
26 Francione, *Animals, Property and the Law*. p. 35.
27 Francione, *Animals as Persons: Essays on the Abolition of Animal Exploitation*.
28 Wadiwel, *The War against Animals*.
29 Ibid. p. 24.

liberty at the expense of nonhumans' right to life.[30] As a result, a biopolitical tension between the human and nonhuman occurs where:

> Biopolitics expresses a contestation between human and animal, this war can only take place within the context of a sovereign order that seeks to reproduce conflict, an authorising system of rationality and truth that tells us that violence against animals is either justifiable or, at its most diabolical, a knowledge system that denies that this violence is occurring.[31]

Human domination is ontologically secured by a social structure that authorises what counts as 'knowledge' and 'truth.' This systemically renders nonhuman animals inferior before any ethical concerns about their treatment occur. Consequently, engendering a sharp epistemic and material division between those who are deemed to be subjects of a life, and those who are objectified.[32] For Wadiwel, the articulation of violence towards animals is both legitimated by a legal system that naturalises human dominance hierarchies, and an episteme (scientific knowledge, especially in this respect) that promulgates this domination. The biopolitical violence that Wadiwel articulates is illustrated throughout Directive 2010/63. As stated previously, this EU regulation is the linchpin for the institutionalisation of contemporary laboratory animal welfare in Britain via the ASPA. For instance, Recital 31 clearly emphasises that '… animal-welfare considerations should be given the highest priority in the context of animal keeping, breeding and use ….'[33] This demonstrates the assimilation of biopolitical forms of welfare into laboratory life. It helps to justify further the harm caused to nonhuman animals – in the end, regulating human use but not the human right to use. Biopolitical legal welfarism evidences the de-subjectification of nonhuman laboratory animals. It also shows how their granted sentient status is intrinsically tied to the logic of a capitalist market system.

Not only that, it is essential to note at this juncture that EU and UK law defines what is considered to be an 'animal' and consequently, *who* is deemed to be sentient. Article 2 of Directive 86/609/EEC's categorises laboratory nonhuman animals as 'protected animals.' They are those animals who are used for experimentation and must not succumb to 'unnecessary suffering' in experimental practices.[34] Directive 86/609/EEC defines a

---

30 Ibid. p. 23.
31 Ibid. p. 27.
32 Ibid. p. 156.
33 European Union, "Directive 2010/63/EU of the European Parliament and of the Council of 22 September 2010 on the Protection of Animals Used for Scientific Purposes." p. 36.
34 "Council Directive of 24 November 1986 on the Approximation of Laws, Regulations and Administrative Provisons of the Member States Regarding the Protection of Animals Used for Experimental and Other Scientific Purposes," (1986).

'protected' animal as 'any live non-human vertebrate, including free-living larval and/or reproducing larval forms, but excluding foetal or embryonic forms.'[35] The revised Directive 2010/63 was transposed into ASPA in 2012,[36] and it broadens this category of the 'animal' to include cephalopods, foetal and embryonic forms. It also accords nonhumans with the sentient status thus far discussed.[37]

As I will show, welfare helps to mediate between animals-as-objects (property) and animals-as-sentient-beings (how they feel and experience pain). By presenting a veneer of respectability between law and animal experimentation, welfare contributes to a perpetuation of a logic of rationality. This logic inscribes the nonhuman with sentience but of having no decision-making power.[38] Humans conceptualise and classify nonhuman experiences because of a presumed hierarchy of difference. The hierarchy materialises as human domination over nonhumans and in turn, construes laboratory animals as those most suitable for use (humans are *immunised* from the threat of use as a result of this differentiation).[39] As well as being seen as the object of use, which is the most economically efficient:

> The choice of methods and the species used have a direct impact on both the numbers of animals used and their welfare. *The choice of methods should therefore ensure the selection of the method that is able to provide the most satisfactory results* and is likely to cause the minimum pain, suffering or distress. The methods selected should use the minimum number of animals that would provide reliable results and require the use of species with the lowest capacity to experience pain, suffering, distress or lasting harm that are optimal for extrapolation into target species.[40]

Species-specific testing is encouraged and the method used must ensure valid and reliable results. Pain and suffering are a 'necessary' part of experimentation and not questioned, just defined from a human-centric standpoint. Consequently, nonhumans are still objects of property. It is here where Foucault's ideas on governmentality can help understand the historically

---

35 Ibid. p. 1.
36 HM Government, "The Animals (Scientific Procedures) Act 1986 Amendment Regulations 2012," (2012).
37 Council of the European Union, "Directive 2010/63/EU of the European Parliament and of the Council of 22 September 2010 on the Protection of Animals Used for Scientific Purposes." Articles 8–9, p. 34.
38 Peggs, "Nonhuman Animal Experiments in the European Community: Human Values and Rational Choice." p. 13.
39 For discussions on immunity, see Wadiwel, *The War against Animals*.
40 Council of the European Union, "Directive 2010/63/EU of the European Parliament and of the Council of 22 September 2010 on the Protection of Animals Used for Scientific Purposes." Recital 13, p. 34.

contingent decree of 'sentience' in lab animals. Governmentality can also help us track the historical emergence of these discourses of welfare – discourses, which help to reinforce speciesism and the continued exploitation of nonhuman animals.

Theorising pain: Property and pastoral power

Foucault states that Western modernity is marked by a transformation in the exercise of power by states: from one of sovereignty, which took as its object a territory, to government, focused on populations.[41] Foucault marks these non-linear transitions of power of Western societies in his genealogical method.[42] Such a genealogy of power relations is analysed via an array of concepts: pastoral power, discipline, security and biopower.[43] 'Governmentality' is thus the confluence of these well-known concerns of Foucault. Pastoral power characterises the rise of a Christian pastorate as a technology of power and its transition to a secular statist enterprise of the *raison d'État*.[44] Governmentality signifies the shift in power relations, from one concerned with maintaining sovereign rule, to one that intervenes in the lives of people at the minutest level (their health and welfare). This is to develop a nation's economy. It is a set of practical relations concerned with the body politic to establish a government's political economy.[45]

For Foucault, pastoral power preceded governmentality in the development of the modern liberal state. Where pastoral care was once the responsibility of the Christian church in looking after the sick and needy, gradually the government took over this responsibility.[46] However, both pastoral power and governmentality are not neatly delineated concepts in Foucaudian histories. It is in this chapter where I demonstrate the intermingling of these concepts at a judicial level and the level of laboratory relations between human and nonhuman animals. Following Wadiwel, I argue that the two ideas are interdependent. This is to ensure complete human domination over nonhuman life. This power of nonhuman life via the judiciary runs parallel to forms of patriarchal domination over women, discussed in the final chapter of this section.[47] 'Modern' forms of pastoral power act

---

41 Foucault, "Governmentality."
42 Ibid.
43 Ben Golder, "Foucault and the Genealogy of Pastoral Power," *Radical Philosophy Review* 10, no. 2 (2007): 157–176.
44 Ibid.
45 Foucault, "Governmentality."
46 *Security, Territory, Population (Michel Foucault: Lectures at the Collège De France)*, ed. Arnold Davidson, Graham Burchell, 2nd ed. (Basingstoke; New York: Palgrave Macmillan, 2009).
47 Dinesh Joseph Wadiwel (2015: 116) proposes an alternative model of Governmentality. His model describes pastoral power as an entry point for human domination over other humans.

as a contemporary biopolitical tool of domination over both human and nonhuman life.[48] This modern 'benign' technique of biopower encapsulates governmentality in the 'liberal age.' Modern forms of pastoral power are encapsulated within contemporary forms of biopolitical sovereignty. This, in turn, has produced a refinement of governmental modes of power over human and nonhuman populations.[49]

The modern pastorate: Pastoral power of the state

According to Foucault, pastoral power was analogous to the shepherd guiding his flock, knowing them both collectively and individually.[50] Pastoral power was a way to explain the role of the state and its ability to simultaneously have totalising control and individualised care over populations. For Foucault, pastoral power is a form of biopolitics, a way to regulate and control people (precisely, individuals within communities) through particular and seemingly benign forms of treatment given by public institutions such as hospitals and schools.[51] In this respect, what is outstanding about British animal experimentation law is how scientists and government, over time, have managed to conflate care and control in a particularly compelling way.

According to Foucault, this totalising and yet individual form of power allows for the delivery of specific kinds of welfare to individuals within a given population while at the same time increasing disciplinary control over them.[52] This 'strange technology of power'[53] in which certain institutions assumed a caring role over the lives of people, had four dimensions to it which shaped both the 'shepherd' and their 'flock.' First, *responsibility*, referring to the duty of care the shepherd has to their flock as a whole and towards individuals within it.[54] Second, the flock must be *submissive* – the sheep must be obedient to their leader and the members of the flock actively decide to submit to the will of the shepherd. Third, *individualised knowledge*, the shepherd knows each member of their flock, the minutia of each being's existence.[55] Fourth, *self-mortification*, the flock renounce their chance of any existence beyond the group, a depreciation of life extraneous to their current existence. For Foucault, this was a '… a kind of everyday death.'[56] What I argue in this chapter is that pastoral care is both an arm of governmentality, but also a precursor to it, in light of the 1965 Littlewood review of the 1876 Act.

---

48 Wadiwel, *The War against Animals*. p. 118.
49 Ibid. p. 116.
50 Foucault, "Omnes Et Singulatim: Toward a Critique of Political Reason."
51 Ibid.
52 Ibid.
53 Ibid. p. 231.
54 Ibid. p. 236.
55 Ibid. p. 237.
56 Ibid. p. 239.

Power

It is worth noting here Foucault's definition of power.[57] He distinguishes power relations from specific 'states of domination' and violent interactions. For Foucault, power is relational, and it works both ways – by those who are exercising it and those who respond to its implementation. In other words, there is always a degree of recalcitrance coming from the exploited subject, and power relations are dynamic and reversible. On the other hand, domination, for Foucault, is a use of force against someone, and there is no room for resistance. States of domination are fixed and stable.[58] This then poses a problem for the use of the concept of pastoral power, as it inevitably implies that nonhuman laboratory animals have the liberty to exercise their disdain. Following Clare Palmer,[59] I contend that it is crucial to accept that animal oppression is held within totalising structures of domination. This total domination over nonhuman animals is also a result of a specific and varied set of discourses and 'micropractices.' As Palmer argues '… it is these discourses and practices on which we should focus.'[60] In this sense, an analysis of the history of laboratory animal legislation using Foucauldian notions of governmentality is appropriate. It acknowledges a totalising state of domination; and those micropractices that may allow for the possibility of some degree of recalcitrance from nonhuman laboratory animals.

By looking at this specific incidence of nonhuman oppression, and its manifestation through discourses of welfare, we can study the very *microphysics* of power which Foucault was so keen to highlight.[61] By focussing on the development of this particular historical conjunction in animal experimental law, it offers us a way of understanding how power manifests and operates in specific contexts, instances and relations. This consideration of nonhuman animals as *feeling beings* was a turning point in animal experimentation law. It was the first time welfarist discourses became subsumed into jurisprudential concerns.

This chapter is split into several parts and its general premise is to map out the development of legal discourses of care and welfare, which became embedded in the ASPA. I start the chapter in 1947 when anti-vivisection societies called for a third Royal Commission into the workings of the 1876 Cruelty to Animals Act. I then move on to discuss the Littlewood Report of 1965. The Littlewood Report was commissioned by the government to consider whether

---

57 Michel Foucault, "The Subject and Power," in *Power: The Essential Works of Michel Foucault 1954–1984:Volume 3: Power V.* ed. James D Faubion, Paul Rabinow, Robert Hurley, 3rd ed. (London: Penguin Books, 2001).
58 Ibid. p. 340.
59 Clare Palmer, "'Taming the Wild Profusion of Existing Things?' A Study of Foucault, Power, and Human/Animal Relationships," *Environmental Ethics* 23, no. 4 (2001): 339–358.
60 Ibid. pp. 350–351.
61 Ibid.

or not the 1876 Act needed to be revised. Here, it will be shown that this was the first time that the welfare and care of nonhuman laboratory animals were legally acknowledged as being important. The final section of the chapter discusses the implementation of the ASPA 1986, including an analysis of the influence of European bodies in the formation of the Act.

The 1876 Cruelty to Animals Act

Up until the ASPA 1986, British scientists and organisations conducting animal experiments would have fallen under the 1876 Cruelty to Animals Act (briefly mentioned above). It is worth stipulating the main clauses of this Act before moving on to its review.

It was in 1876 the government introduced a Bill to prevent the infliction of cruelty on experimental animals. The General Medical Council and other medical organisations lobbied hard, and the Bill was significantly changed in favour of the scientists. It was to allow for the 'gaining of abstract knowledge and of saving life or alleviating suffering in animals as well as human beings.'[62] The law states that:

> The experiment must be performed with a view to the advancement by new discovery of physiological knowledge or of knowledge which will be useful for saving or prolonging life or alleviating suffering.[63]

Provision was also added requiring the scientists to hold a license. The Secretary of State granted the licence once it had been signed by a prominent member of the scientific community.[64] The license prevented experimenters from carrying out tests on animals without anaesthetics, and the law ordered nonhumans to be killed after the experiment, so they would not suffer any 'unnecessary pain.'[65] Inspectors were employed to visit institutions that conducted experiments on animals. These inspectors would observe practices including the actual experiments.

Despite the imposition of these sanctions, there were still ways and means around them, especially concerning the licensing system, and the classification of experiments. One could be granted a license, but for specific researches, a certificate had to be attained. Certificates were labelled from A to F, with A being required if experiments were to be done without anaesthetics. 'B' allowing for investigations to be conducted, which kept the animal alive after the anaesthetic had ceased. Certificate 'E', contra to the

---

62 Sydney Littlewood, "Report of the Departmental Committee on Experiments on Animals," ed. Home Office (London: Her Majesty's Stationery Office, 1965). pp. 5–6.
63 "1876 Cruelty to Animals Act." p. 2.
64 Littlewood, "Report of the Departmental Committee on Experiments on Animals." p. 6, p. 222; "1876 Cruelty to Animals Act." p. 4.
65 "1876 Cruelty to Animals Act." p. 2.

Act, allowed a scientist to perform experiments on cats and/or dogs without anaesthetics, and this must be granted with certificate 'A.' Certificate 'F' was for experiments on horses and donkeys without anaesthetics, and this also had to be accompanied by certificate A.[66]

It was clear that scientists were free to conduct any form of experiment while at the same time being seen to be regulated under the gaze of the Secretary of State. This chapter's primary focus is the legal regulation of animal pain. In the 1876 Act, this came under the 'Pain Condition.' It is worth noting, in full, the stipulations of this clause, as I will be referring to it throughout this chapter. It states:

a   If an animal at any time is found to be suffering pain which is either severe or is likely to endure, and if the main result of the experiment has been attained, the animal shall forthwith be painlessly killed.
b   If an animal at any time during any such experiment is found to be suffering severe pain which is likely to endure, such an animal shall forthwith be painlessly killed.
c   If an animal appears to an inspector to be suffering considerable pain, and if the inspector directs such an animal to be destroyed, it shall forthwith be painlessly killed.[67]

It is evident then that the definition of pain followed by animal experimenters was highly subjective. The decision as to if and when an animal was in pain relied heavily on the scientists themselves, or one of 'Her Majesty's Inspectors.' Although, as is demonstrated throughout this chapter, the contestation of pain in the animal by the scientific profession, and government actors, was a highly subjective and dynamic phenomenon. The definition of pain shifted dramatically over the twentieth century to encompass aspects of psychological distress. This would legitimate further, the practice of vivisection.

The Act had a significant impact on scientific research using animals, but it was not until after the First World War that vivisection in Britain increased significantly. Between 1920 and 1940, licensed animal experiments increased from 70,000 to approximately 1 million. The anti-vivisection movements' supporters became silent observers to the practice of animal experimentation, as public support seemed to grow in favour of it.[68] Some authors argue that in the immediate post-war years, the anti-vivisection movement became almost invisible. There was no serious challenge towards the abolition of animal experimentation.[69] Richard Ryder claims that due to the mental distress of

66 Littlewood, "Report of the Departmental Committee on Experiments on Animals." pp. 225–237.
67 Ibid. p. 55.
68 Richard Ryder, *Victims of Science: The Use of Animals in Research* (London, UK: National Anti-Vivisection Society, 1983). Ibid. p. 163.
69 Ibid. pp. 142–145.

the First World War, the anti-vivisection movement stagnated. Ryder argues this is because survivors of the war 'turned their attention to the welfare of their species.' The animal welfare movement was 'dominated by middle-class women,' failing to achieve as much public support as they used to. Incidentally, he claims, because of the tragedies of the War, the movement appeared 'faintly ridiculous ... and it seemed that the period from the mid-1920s until the 1960s represents a gap in the progress of the movement.'[70]

According to Ryder, nothing of particular note happened in the 1950s and 1960s concerning the animal welfare movements, apart from the efforts of a few 'middle-class women.'[71] However, as I shall demonstrate, the call for a third Royal Commission on Vivisection, and a review of the 1876 Act provided the impetus for the revival of anti-vivisection organisations in post-War Britain. It also was an antecedent for the dawn of the animal rights movements in the latter half of the twentieth century. Articles and letters critical of vivisection appeared in the columns of the daily newspapers between the period 1947–1965, and scientific societies began to convene public lectures specifically focussed on animal experimentation. Scientists came under increasing public scrutiny regarding their experiments.[72] In response, pro-vivisection societies, such as the Universities Federation for Animal Welfare (UFAW) promulgated a welfare perspective towards the treatment of nonhuman animals under experiment. They published a wide array of documents to substantiate this approach.[73] As will be shown, the UFAW became the central and most influential pro-vivisection organisation in Britain. They established a whole host of recommendations and regulations concerning laboratory animal welfare. They created the now internationally practised 'Three R's': Replacement, Reduction and Refinement.[74]

*

POST-WAR ANTI-VIVISECTION REVIVAL AND THE LITTLEWOOD ENQUIRY: THE BEGINNINGS OF A PASTORAL *'RAISON D'ÉTAT'* FOR ANIMALS, 1947–1965

It is worth noting here the substantial increase in experiments on animals in the post-War period in Britain. In 1939, 954,691 experiments had been registered by the Home Office, after the war in 1950, this number increased to 1,779,215 with a substantial increase in 1960, bringing the number to

---

70 Ibid. p. 142.
71 This is in itself a heavily loaded gendered statement.
72 Duxbury, "Animals, Science and Gender: Animal Experimentation in Britain, 1947–1965."
73 Ibid.
74 Nuffield Council on Bioethics, "The Ethics of Research Involving Animals" (London: Nuffield, 2005).

3,701,184.[75] This exponential growth in animal experiments was fuelled by the economic imperatives of the government, with the introduction of the welfare state, including the provision of free healthcare under the National Health Service. This political impetus for a healthy population and active workforce helped to channel funding towards medical research, especially into the burgeoning pharmaceutical companies.[76] Alongside research for civilian purposes, the government increased defence spending, funding military research into the chemical and biological weapons of warfare.[77] This too required the use of unprecedented amounts of nonhuman animals in the experiments for these weapons of mass destruction.[78]

With this dramatic increase in animal experiments, the anti-vivisection movements began their campaigns for a change in legislation.[79] A 1948 Deputation to the Home Secretary, James Chuter Ede, urged him to review the Act. The Deputation represented a broad range of anti-vivisection societies from across Britain. The National Anti-Vivisection Society (NAVS) and the British Union for the Abolition of Vivisection (BUAV) were such groups that made contributions to the Deputation's Report. In continuity with the composition of the Victorian movements,[80] these representatives were mainly from the British upper classes, including the Duchess of Hamilton and Miss Louise Lind-af-Hageby.[81] The Deputation invoked a nationalistic and moral discourse about the health of society. This moral discourse did not address human dominion over nonhuman animals, nor their status as objects of property. Instead, the Deputation placed the moral health and welfare of the nation as primary, while questioning animal utility second.[82] As Lind-af-Hageby remarked, 'the cause of humanity to animals is a vital part of civilisation and social development. The Society [Antivivisection and Animal Defence Society] regards all cruelty as an evil

---

75 Littlewood, "Report of the Departmental Committee on Experiments on Animals." p. 253.
76 Lyons, *The Politics of Animal Experimentation*.
77 David Edgerton, *Warfare State: Britain, 1920–1970* (Cambridge, UK: Cambridge University Press, 2006).
78 Duxbury, "Animals, Science and Gender: Animal Experimentation in Britain, 1947–1965."
79 The National Archives [Forthwith TNA], HO45/25867, Antivivisection Deputation to the Home Secretary, Animals Defender Magazine, 1948. British Union for the Abolition of Vivisection (BUAV), *Animals Defender Magazine*, 1948. p. 47.
80 For a very good overview of the Nineteenth Century Vivisection and Anti-Vivisection movements, see: French, *Antivivisection and Medical Science in Victorian Society*; Rupke, *Vivisection in Historical Perspective*; Ritvo, *The Animal Estate: English and Other Creatures in the Victorian Age*; Hilda Kean, *Animal Rights: Political and Social Change in Britain since 1800* (London, UK: Reaktion Books Ltd, 1998); "The 'Smooth Cool Men of Science': The Feminist and Socialist Response to Vivisection," *The History Worshop Journal*, 40, no. 1 (1995): 16–38.
81 TNA, HO45/25857, Note of A Deputation from the Anti-Vivisection Societies Received at the Home Office on 23rd February 1948. p. 1.
82 Ibid.

which is socially disruptive and degrading to the perpetrators ....'[83] Dr Wilfred Tyldesly additionally noted how: 'this nation will never be healthy while vivisection is permitted to uphold the monstrous pretence.'[84] Despite the abolitionists seeking understanding from the Home Secretary, they were ultimately denied a review of the Act. Chuter Ede, in a letter to Ronald Chamberlain Esq, M.P. on 9 June 1948, stated that there was 'no sufficient case' concerning the law or its administration to 'justify [him] in recommending the appointment of a fresh Royal Commission.'[85]

With a revived anti-vivisection movement calling for another Royal Commission, it was the turn of the scientists to reinvigorate their defence of vivisection. With their requests, they hoped to counter the concerns of the anti-vivisectionists by pressuring the government into a review that disqualified non-scientific opinion. Their chief weapon here was the work and propaganda of the UFAW.

To infinity and beyond: The UFAW and its continuing role in shaping laboratory animal welfare

Major C.W. Hume formed the UFAW in 1926. They sought to approach nonhuman laboratory animals in ways that absented the 'emotional or sentimental' yet served the interests of science by building a 'realistically humane policy based on objective fact.'[86] They often publish books and pamphlets for animal-dependent scientists, offering advice about animal welfare in the laboratory. Their most notable publication was the *Handbook on the Care and Management of Laboratory Animals* (1947), edited by scientist Alastair Worden.[87] This book offered advice on the housing of animals in laboratories, their handling, treatment and even their death. The Handbook also delved into discussions surrounding nonhumans' psychology, arguing; 'there appears to be room for a good deal of research into the psychological conditions that make a happy and contented stock.'[88] The Handbook is still in existence today and is currently in its 8th edition.[89]

---

83 TNA, HO45/25867 Antivivisection Deputation to the Home Office: Speech by Miss Lind-Af-Hageby, 23 February 1948. p. 1.
84 TNA, HO45/25867, Antivivisection Deputation speech by Wilfred Tyldesley, 23 February 1948. pp. 2–3.
85 TNA, HO45/25867, Letter Addressed to Chamberlain from Home Secretary Chuter Ede, 9 June 1948. p. 1.
86 Alastair N. Worden, ed. *The UFAW Handbook on the Care and Management of Laboratory Animals*, 1st ed. (London: Bailliere, Tindall And Cox, 1947).
87 Ibid.
88 Ibid. p. 19.
89 Robert Hubrecht; James Kirkwood, ed. *The UFAW Handbook on the Care and Management of Laboratory and Other Research Animals*, 8th ed. (Chichester: John Wiley & Sons, 2010). See Chapters 4 and 5 for further discussion of these UFAW handbooks.

For the UFAW, it was the 1950s, with its change in government from Labour to Conservative (left-wing to more right-wing), that seemed to be most fruitful for the organisation. In this decade, they appeared to cement their reputation as *the* non-governmental body to consult. Alliances were made between the members of the organisation and both the Research Defence Society (RDS) and the Medical Research Council (MRC).[90] It is interesting to note that there were two members of the RDS who had secure connections to the UFAW. Dr Baker, author of UFAW's The Scientific Basis of Kindness to Animals at the time of its 3rd edition, and Dr Lane-Petter, who edited the second edition of the Handbook in 1957. Lane-Petter was also the Director of the Laboratory Animals Centre, an organisation dedicated to the regulation and breeding of laboratory animals.[91] Elite networks of scientists were integral to the perpetuation of animal experimentation.

In the post-War period of the 1950s, the RDS, in public speeches, co-opted the rhetoric of the UFAW to convince the general public of the benefit of animal experimentation for medicine, and the safety, welfare and health of the animals used in experiments. This promulgation of pro-animal experimentation ideology was particularly evident in this decade, explicitly emanating from Sir Henry Dale and Lord Cohen of Birkenhead in their public speeches for the RDS. In the 1955 Paget Memorial Lecture entitled 'Humanity's Rising Debt to Medical Research,' Sir Henry Dale gave an impassioned speech about the benefits of animal experimentation for the development and progression of medical science.[92] He profoundly adopted the rhetoric of the UFAW, in the hope of countering, what was to him, the 'ignorance and muddleheadedness' of the anti-vivisectionists.[93] This also proved that the two organisations were in ideological alignment and collaboration. Yet, it wasn't until 1957, that the then Conservative Government promised to place the Act under review at some point. It was the moderate Royal Society for the Protection of Animals (RSPCA) which managed to convince the government to lead a formal enquiry.

Between 1959 and 1961, the RSPCA applied continuous pressure onto the government for another review of the Act.[94] They led public campaigns as well as wrote letters to the Home Secretary regularly.[95] The RSPCA were vociferous in stressing that they were not an anti-vivisection society. Instead,

---

90 The RDS was a British pro-animal experimentation lobby group and scientific society founded in 1908. The MRC funds medical research in the UK.
91 Robert G.W. Kirk, '"Wanted-Standard Guinea Pigs': Standardisation and the Experimental Animal Market in Brtain Ca. 1919–1947," *Studies in the History, Philosophy, Biology and Biomedical Science* 39, no. 3 (2008): 280–281.
92 TNA: Cabinet Office Registered Papers (CAB124): CAB124/1638, Paget Memorial Lecture by Sir Henry Dale "Humanity's Rising Debt to Medical Research," 1955.
93 Ibid. p. 17.
94 Lyons, *The Politics of Animal Experimentation*.
95 TNA, CAB124/1638, RSPCA Experiments on Animals, Cruelty to Animals Act 1876, n.d. pp. 2–4.

they argued for changes to the administration of the Act, rather than complete abolition of animal experiments.[96] The RSPCA wanted to make it clear that they were not 'radicals.' In the BUAV's Branches Newsletter in 1962, it claimed they had 'discovered, quite by accident' that the RSPCA 'had written to the Home Secretary on the matter' of the law in relation to experiments on animals. The BUAV declared that despite offering solidarity, the RSPCA nevertheless 'stuck to their decision not to cooperate' with them.[97] Instead, the RSPCA sided with UFAW on the issue of welfare for experimental animals. They often quoted the organisation in their letters to medical journals and the press.[98] This welfarist stance taken by the RSPCA and their public awareness campaign on vivisection helped to facilitate a governmental review of the 1876 Act.[99] With this, in 1962, Sir Stanley Littlewood formed a committee of enquiry into the workings of the 1876 Act.

The beginnings of the consideration of stress, distress and psychological pain in nonhuman laboratory animals

In July 1963, Sir Sydney Littlewood published a letter in the *British Medical Journal* (BMJ) entitled 'Cruelty to Animals Act, 1876.' He asked scientific researchers in the British medical profession to provide evidence about experiments on live animals in light of a forthcoming review of the 1876 Act. He stated that 'the committee's terms of reference are: to consider the present control over experiments on living animals and to consider whether, and if so what, changes are desirable in the law or its administration.' '[I]f any person has information or comment that will help,' he went on to state, 'send it in writing to the ... Home Office.'[100] The letter suggested the establishment of an enquiry into the Act's relevance and application to scientific research and development of the time. Littlewood emphasised that 'it is no part of the committee's task to consider the questions – previously reviewed by two Royal Commissions – whether experiments on animals are justified or have had any useful results.'[101] He sent this request out to other public bodies and newspapers asking for evidence about the practical implications of the Act. At the same time, a committee was appointed to consider its administration and the testimony from witnesses.

During their investigations, the committee visited 29 establishments. This was to view animals before, during and after experiments, and to talk to employees. Visiting these establishments involved some 27 private meetings,

---

96 Ibid. p. 1.
97 Hull History Centre [forthwith HHC], BUAV Papers, (U DBV2): DBV2/18/6, BUAV Branches Newsletter No. 8. n.d.
98 R. F. Rattray, "Rspca Campaign," *British Medical Journal* 1, no. 5282 (1962): 946.
99 Robert Garner, *Political Animals: Animal Protection Politics in Britain and the United States* (Basingstoke: Macmillan Press Ltd, 1998).
100 Sydney Littlewood, "Cruelty to Animals Act, 1876," *British Medical Journal* 2, no. 5351 (1963): 256.
101 Ibid.

taking 83 accounts from witnesses representing 26 organisations.[102] In their investigations, the Advisory Committee asked members of these establishments about animal pain and the 1876 Act's Pain Condition. The notion that an animal could suffer psychological distress was something that scientists had begun to acknowledge in the early twentieth century.[103] It was this enquiry, alongside the publications of the UFAW, which contributed to a broader redefinition of animal pain. It is here that we can observe how the description and purpose of animal experimentation were under contestation. It was a challenge which ultimately revolved around the idea of pain and suffering, with the Committee stating: 'our review of the past left us in no doubt that the principal objects of control have been to prevent the infliction of unnecessary suffering and to limit unavoidable pain ....'[104]

The whole idea of animal experimental law was, and still is, to prevent 'unnecessary suffering.' For the Littlewood Committee, this was their principal objective when reviewing the 1876 Act. This view of unnecessary suffering automatically qualified the animal used in experiments to be open to some degree of pain. In agreement with Wadiwel, pain has a biopolitical character to it. It at once objectifies the experience of suffering that nonhumans endure, and also imposes regulation upon the animal body, within a human dominance hierarchy.[105] It is evident with the definitions laid out in the Pain Condition that human dominance is a priori to any ethical consideration of the nonhuman animal in pain. Human dominance is very much *naturalised* in this aspect of animal experimentation law, so much so that it is not even considered. In other words, animals will always suffer in experimentation because of their property status. In this sense, pain is imposed within set limitations attributable to the maximisation of the nonhumans' value in the experiment.[106] For the enquiry, this was evident in their explication of the Pain Condition, and the further recommendations received about nonhuman experimental animals' experiences of pain.

As will be recalled, the original Pain Condition stipulated that an animal shall be immediately killed during or after an experiment, and if an inspector saw them suffering unnecessarily.[107] The post-War period in British history was the era of stress, and the study of psychological 'disturbances' in both nonhuman and human animals, which were taken more seriously by the scientific professions.[108] This broader concept of the Pain Condition

---

102 Littlewood, "Report of the Departmental Committee on Experiments on Animals." p. 1.
103 Otniel E. Dror, "The Affect of Experiment: The Turn to Emotions in Anglo-American Physiology, 1900–1940," *Isis* 90, no. 2 (1999): 205–237.
104 Littlewood, "Report of the Departmental Committee on Experiments on Animals." p. 54.
105 Wadiwel, *The War against Animals*.
106 Ibid. p. 163.
107 Littlewood, "Report of the Departmental Committee on Experiments on Animals." pp. 235–237.
108 Duxbury, "Animals, Science and Gender: Animal Experimentation in Britain, 1947–1965."

encapsulated individualised knowledge over nonhuman animals.[109] The report related the notion of pain and psychological distress to the individual animal, rather than referring to animals in the plural. For instance, affirming that pain should comprise 'any interference with or departure from the animal's normal state of health or well-being.'[110] This also placed upon the experimenter a greater degree of responsibility coupled with individualised knowledge over each animal in their laboratory[111]; 'if he [sic] is familiar with the animal concerned the practised observer can readily detect when it is "out of sorts" or "off colour" and take steps to discover and remedy the cause.'[112] Each animal must become known to the experimenter, to ascertain their healthiness and wellbeing. For Foucault, this form of pastoral power included being informed about the needs of each member of the flock and to 'provide for them when necessary.'[113] In this case, the scientists would provide for nonhuman animals when necessary if they seemed to be 'out of sorts,' thus highlighting the endowment of responsibility for their 'flock.'

This extension of the Pain Condition involved a reconfiguration of relations between the human and nonhuman. A certain valorisation of the psychological dimensions of pain was necessary. This facilitated the emergence of post-mechanistic (Cartesian) view of nonhuman animals, which awarded them a strategically placed degree of subjectivity. For instance, the Advisory Committee was reminded by witnesses that '... mental illness and neurosis are largely problems in modern civilisations, and their attention was drawn to the ... increasing interest in states of animal behaviour and psychological experiment.'[114] The Committee went on to state:

> ... We saw for ourselves, that animals exposed to environmental stimuli, such as loud noises or bright light exhibit physical signs of discomfort. These witnesses told us that manipulation of environment was likely to be much more widely used as an experimental technique in future, and urged that any procedure designed to produce the equivalent of stress in man should be subject to statutory control.[115]

Environmental conditions were considered to be stress-inducing in the animal, as well as creating physical discomfort. Scientific witnesses told the enquiry that 'acute fear, chronic anxiety or artificially produced conflict of motives or frustration could produce psychosomatic effects in animals ....'[116] This signified a move away from Cartesian Dualism, of viewing the animal as machine.

---

109 Foucault, "Omnes Et Singulatim: Toward a Critique of Political Reason." pp. 237–238.
110 Littlewood, "Report of the Departmental Committee on Experiments on Animals." p. 56.
111 Foucault, "Omnes Et Singulatim: Toward a Critique of Political Reason." p. 236.
112 Littlewood, "Report of the Departmental Committee on Experiments on Animals." p. 56.
113 Foucault, "Omnes Et Singulatim: Toward a Critique of Political Reason." p. 238.
114 Littlewood, "Report of the Departmental Committee on Experiments on Animals." p. 57.
115 Ibid.
116 Ibid.

In contra to Francione, who claims that it is the abolitionist movements alongside alternative medicine practitioners who are challenging this view in more recent times.[117] What we have here is a challenge to Cartesianism stemming from the scientific community itself in mid-twentieth century Britain.

It was the work of the UFAW that 'was the only body to offer serious criticism of the text of the [Pain] Condition.'[118] In their Handbooks (mentioned previously) from 1947 to the present, they discuss animal pain and acknowledge the psychological dimensions of the laboratory animal.[119] Professor T. Dalling, Director of the Veterinary Laboratory for the Ministry of Agriculture and Fisheries, wrote the *foreword* to the 1947 edition. In it, he clearly stated his desire to end Cartesianism thinking in animal-dependent laboratory science. He claimed the perspective of animal-as-machine was obsolete 'in view of what is now known of the biological relation between man and the lower animals.'[120] According to Dalling, 'this queer heirloom bequeathed by the great-grandfather of modern science is still lying about in intellectual lumber-rooms.' This indicated that the time was ripe for a change in the perception of nonhuman laboratory animals.[121] In other words, Dalling was sure that scientists were increasingly dismissing the advocacy of Cartesian ideas as erroneous. Yet, it continued to persist in some areas of scientific research.

This signifies the 'Pastoral turn'[122] in animal experimental science, as well as the connection of the practice to its legal regulation. The UFAW called for the recognition of animal subjectivity through recognising their wellbeing in the laboratory, by the observation of their expressed behaviour:

> There appears to be room for a good deal of research into the psychological conditions that make a happy and contented stock. Captive animals may suffer acutely from boredom, and they certainly need exercise, companionship and opportunity to play. Most rodents appear to be agoraphobic and appreciate a nestbox or hut into which they can retreat, and they like to store food. How far such wishes be gratified depends, no doubt, on experimental requirements ... but there is room for ingenuity and research in the matter.[123]

117 Francione, *Animals, Property and the Law*. pp. 174–176.
118 Littlewood, "Report of the Departmental Committee on Experiments on Animals." p. 58.
119 For example, Worden, *The UFAW Handbook on the Care and Management of Laboratory Animals*; Kirkwood, *The UFAW Handbook on the Care and Management of Laboratory and Other Research Animals*.
120 T. Dalling, "Foreword," in *The UFAW Handbook on the Care and Management of Laboratory Animals*, ed. Alastair N Worden (London: Bailliere, Tindall And Cox, 1947). p. 18.
121 Ibid.
122 Matthew Cole, "From "Animal Machines" to "Happy Meat"? Foucault's Ideas of Disciplinary and Pastoral Power Applied to 'Animal-Centred' Welfare Discourse," *Animals* 1 (2011). p. 83.
123 Dalling, "Foreword." p. 19.

It was imperative to research further the behaviour and psychology of experimental animals. Dalling acknowledged the psychological states of boredom and agoraphobia in rodents and signified to the reader ways to overcome this by changing their accommodation to make for 'happy and contented stock.' But, he recognised that this was dependent upon the requirements of the experiment which nonhuman animals would be used. As a result, nonhuman laboratory animals were co-opted in the process of lab science. This provoked an increase in knowledge about them as much as more control over them.

The UFAW's ideas on the psychological dimensions of pain became integral to the review of the 1876 Act. So much so that the Committee referred to them throughout the investigation.[124] As well as the UFAW, the Report consulted the Cruelty to Wild Animals Act of 1951.[125] Here reference was made to the 'mental suffering' of nonhuman animals, emphasising that 'animals suffer both mentally and physically.'[126] An analysis of the *behaviour* of the animals was integral to determining their anguish as '…animals squeal, struggle, and give other "behavioural" evidence which is generally regarded as the accompaniment of painful feelings.' This was coupled with the recognition of 'mental sufferings' in the form of experiencing fear and apprehension.[127] Taking note of this, and information gathered from the UFAW, the enquiry offered an expansion to the concept of pain as embodied by the current Act:

Within the concept of 'pain,' it is desirable to provide for at least three states of suffering:

a   Discomfort (such as may be characterised by such negative signs as poor condition, torpor or diminished appetite)
b   Stress (i.e. a condition of tension or anxiety predictable or readily explicable from environmental causes whether distinct from or including physical causes)
c   Pain (recognisable by more positive signs such as struggling, screaming or squealing, convulsions, severe palpitation)[128]

Contained within this definition is that nonhuman animals have sentience and an expressive self, particularly in the adjectives used to describe the three states of pain: anxiety, torpor, screaming, etc. Nonhuman animals 'tell' of their suffering, indicating their submission and self-mortification.[129]

---

124   See for example Littlewood, "Report of the Departmental Committee on Experiments on Animals." p. 18.
125   Ibid. pp. 254–255.
126   Ibid. p. 254.
127   Ibid.
128   Ibid. p. 57.
129   Foucault, "Omnes Et Singulatim: Toward a Critique of Political Reason.."; Cole, "From "Animal Machines" to "Happy Meat"? Foucault's Ideas of Disciplinary and Pastoral Power Applied to 'Animal-Centred' Welfare Discourse."

34 *Law, animal welfare and gender*

The new definition showed a depriviledging of the Cartesian mechanistic discourses associated with the experience of pain in the experimental animal. In effect, this *post*-Cartesian view enabled the ideology of domination to continue over nonhumans, giving it a more moral sense of righteousness and benevolence.

To convey this sense of benevolence, the Committee of Enquiry asked witnesses about the wording of the Pain Condition. It was stressed that most scientists found its phraseology 'verbose and confusing' and that some 'licensees found it less explicit than they would like.'[130] To remedy this, the UFAW proposed to the Committee a rewording of the Condition:

1 Each licensee shall take effective precautions to prevent, or reduce to a minimum, any pain or other distress or discomfort in the animals used
2 Every animal which is suffering discomfort which is likely to endure shall be painlessly killed as soon as the experiment has been completed
3 In no case shall any animal be subjected to severe pain which endures or is likely to endure[131]

This indicated that the licensee had to know the individual nonhuman animal and to kill them when they reached the pain limits stipulated by law. The new recommendation of the licensee taking responsibility was coupled with the new concept of pain. It was well received by the Committee who stipulated 'we, therefore, endorse the principles of the U.F.A.W. proposal and recommend that they should be embodied in the Act ....'[132] Laboratory and legal animal welfarism in this enquiry had shifted the relationship between the human and nonhuman, as well as extended further the notion of 'unnecessary suffering.' This was an ideological tactic that seemed to perpetuate the view that pain is removed, when in fact, it is just more deceptively controlled.

The discussion on 'Painless Killing' also evidenced this. Once again, drawing on the recommendations made from a UFAW pamphlet written in 1950 by the organisation's technical secretary Jean Vinter, entitled *Kind Killing*.[133] The Committee dedicated much space in the Report on humane killing, asserting:

We think that the killing of animals is an important feature in their general handling and protection, and recommend, therefore, that the destruction of animals used under the Act should be restricted by a requirement that this should be performed in a humane and painless manner by, or under direction of, the licensee.[134]

130 Littlewood, "Report of the Departmental Committee on Experiments on Animals." p. 58.
131 Ibid. pp. 58–59.
132 Ibid. p. 59.
133 Jean Vinter, "Kind Killing," ed. UFAW (London: UFAW, 1950).
134 Littlewood, "Report of the Departmental Committee on Experiments on Animals." p. 108.

For the Committee, the killing of animals was a necessary part of their care. To 'kill with kindness,' therefore encapsulated the promulgation in the report of responsibility.[135] The Shepherd must look after their flock, even in death. Nonhuman animals were still at the mercy (submission) of the human, but a benevolent one that would kindly kill them when it was their turn. This was coupled with the nonhumans' 'self-mortification,' the animals express their suffering,[136] and they are 'sacrificed' for the benefit of science.[137] This action of 'humane' killing forms part of the legal act of the pastoral approach to eliminating an animal in pain. It became a quasi-therapeutic technique that claimed to understand laboratory animals.[138] But, they were still viewed as 'stock,' indicating their property status:

> If animals are to be used at all, everyone will agree that they should be used efficiently and economically... our concern is more immediately to examine how far there is a risk that animals are wasted, and what can be done to prevent or minimise this. Taken in conjunction with the pain inflicted in the individual case, this is the most critical of all the problems in animal experiment.[139]

The concern, in concurrence with degrees of pain inflicted on nonhumans, was that the nonhuman animal might be wasted. In other words, no benefit to humans will be accrued if too much pain is inflicted on the animal, and consequently, this would obscure the result. Nonhuman experimental animals' bodies were discussed in light of their economic use-value *because* of their property status. They had to be used economically and efficiently. This indicates what Wadiwel terms a 'discourse of excess and waste'; one that only limits suffering when it does not contribute (exceeds) to the value of the experimental manipulation for human use.[140]

Conclusions of the Littlewood Report

In the end, the Littlewood Report made 83 recommendations for changes to the 1876 Cruelty to Animals Act, including the points raised above. Despite this in-depth and detailed enquiry, the Committee failed to make any

---

135 Foucault, "Omnes Et Singulatim: Toward a Critique of Political Reason."
136 See above discussion and also Cole, "From "Animal Machines" to "Happy Meat"? Foucault's Ideas of Disciplinary and Pastoral Power Applied to 'Animal-Centred' Welfare Discourse." p. 91.
137 Littlewood, "Report of the Departmental Committee on Experiments on Animals." p. 58.
138 For the idea of quasi-therapeutic see Cole, "From "Animal Machines" to "Happy Meat"? Foucault's Ideas of Disciplinary and Pastoral Power Applied to 'Animal-Centred' Welfare Discourse."
139 Littlewood, "Report of the Departmental Committee on Experiments on Animals." p. 82.
140 Wadiwel, *The War against Animals*.

36 *Law, animal welfare and gender*

significant legislative amendments at the time and instead reinforced the 1876 Act's administrative procedures. It was hoped that the general effect of their recommendations would:

> Extend protection to all animals in, or destined for laboratories; to apply more effective supervision over the granting of licences; to simplify and strengthen control over the use of animals for research purposes; to introduce provisions for regulations; to put the care of laboratory animals on a properly organised basis ....[141]

Animal welfare in this instance was to extend their use-value by regulating with a greater degree of precision the licensees. Importance was primarily placed on the 'introduction of [a] new system of control with its emphasis on increased technical guidance and supervision.'[142] Key to these recommendations was the increase in control and care. As has been discussed, these are not mutually exclusive categories; in fact, these two aspects of the Report are tightly woven together under the biopolitical rubric of pastoral power. As a result, a new discourse emerged about nonhuman experimental animals, as well as a redefinition of human-animal laboratory relations.

As we will see in the next part of this chapter, the effects of the Littlewood Enquiry only really came to pass in the 1980s. The then Conservative Government, under the direction of the CoE and the EU, made proposals to amend the 1876 Act fully.[143] In a memorandum from William Whitelaw, Secretary of State for the Home Office, to all governmental departments about the proposed change in legislation, reference was made to the Littlewood Report. Whitelaw stated no previous governments since the enquiry had implemented any of the recommendations. But, the Report demonstrated that 'British scientists have a tradition of humaneness which was endorsed by the Littlewood Committee of 1965.'[144] This signifies that welfare was firmly on the agenda in British scientific research at the time and that it was about to be integrated into a new statute. The result was the ASPA 1986, and this strongly reflected the Littlewood Report's recommendations on the Pain Condition.[145]

*

---

141 Littlewood, "Report of the Departmental Committee on Experiments on Animals." p. 198.
142 Ibid.
143 TNA, T489/69, Animal Experiments: Proposals to Amend the Cruelty to Animals Act 1876 and the European Convention Proposals on Animal Experiments. Letter from G. P. Pratt Home Office to J. B. Brown Department of Health and Social Security, Animal Experiments: Council of Europe Convention: "The Pain Condition", 11 August 1979.
144 TNA, T489/69, Animal Experiments: Proposals to Amend the Cruelty to Animals Act 1876 and the European Convention Proposals on Animal Experiments. Memorandum by Secretary of State for the Home Department, Animal Experiments. 11 August, 1981.
145 Lyons, *The Politics of Animal Experimentation*.

TIME FOR CHANGE: 'BRINGING ANIMALS INTO POLITICS,' 1979–1981

In an RDS' press release of 15 August 1979 the third Earl of Halsbury, John Anthony Hardinge Giffard, eminent scientist, President of the RDS and life peer in the House of Lords was quoted as saying:

> There is widespread recognition of the need to modernise the law on laboratory animals because, unfortunately, we will have to continue their use in science and medicine for a long time to come.[146]

Halsbury's recognition of the need for reformation of the law captured the zeitgeist of the time. Richard Ryder states that the 1970s was a decade of 'revival' for animal advocacy movements.[147] After the stagnation of such movements in the mid-twentieth century, it was a decade which helped to put animals on the political agenda (and of which Ryder played an integral role in fomenting).[148] Specifically, it was a decade which was to see an increase in public and political concern for the welfare of laboratory animals. This was for several reasons. First, the successful campaigns of animal welfare organisations such as the BUAV and RSPCA.[149] Related to this, and one of the most significant events to stimulate political discussion was the declaration that 1976 would be Animal Welfare Year. One of the campaigns during this time was the presentation to Labour Home Secretary Merlyn Rees, of a paper on animal experimentation.[150]

Second, the formation of the Animal Rights movement. This was signified by the publication of popular Animal Rights books, which included Ryder's *Victims of Science* and also Peter Singer's *Animal Liberation*.[151] Finally, another contributory factor to the increasing political recognition of the protection of laboratory animals was extraneous to Britain. This was in the guise of the CoE, as mentioned earlier. The CoE formed a Committee of Experts in 1977 on the use of animals in scientific procedures which led to the European Convention on the Protection of Animals in Experiments and Other Scientific Procedures.[152]

---

146 The Welcome Library [Forthwith Well]: PP/WDP/E/4: Box 60 Royal Society Committee on Animal Experiments, Research Defence Society Press Release. 15 August 1979. p. 1.
147 Richard Ryder, "Putting Animals into Politics," in *Animal Rights: The Changing Debate*, ed. Robert Garner (London & Basingstoke: Macmillan Press Ltd, 1996).
148 *Animal Revolution: Changing Attitudes Towards Speciesism*; "Putting Animals into Politics."
149 "Putting Animals into Politics.
150 Well: SA/PHY/G/1/62: Box 100, Animals (Scientific Procedures) Act: Liaison with MPs and Lords over final stages of Bill, FRAME publication: Animals (Scientific Procedures) Act 1986: The Animals Procedures Committee, ALTA (1986) 14, pp. 6–13. p. 6.
151 Ryder, *Victims of Science: The Use of Animals in Research*; Peter Singer, *Animal Liberation*, 3rd ed. (London: Pimlico, 1975); Ryder, "Putting Animals into Politics."
152 Well: PP/WDP/E/4/: Box 60: Royal Society Committee on Animal Experiments, untitled meeting. n.d. p. 1.

Within Britain, the use of animals in experiments was dominating the headlines of the *National Press* and this increased public concerns about animal experimentation quite significantly.[153] This was no coincidence. The early 1970s saw the formation of the first animal welfare lobby group to pressurise politicians to change the law relating to animal experiments.[154] This group comprised of Richard Ryder, Clive Hollands, scientists and the then former Cabinet Minister and Chairman of the Parliamentary Labour Party Lord Houghton.[155] Together they formed the RSPCA's animal experimentation committee in 1972, which by 1978 was to become the first animal welfare lobby group, entitled the Committee for the Reform of Animal Experiments (CRAE).[156] They helped to foment public concern as much as increasing political pressure.[157] CRAE was to play an integral role in the drafting of the ASPA, 1986. However, their main concern in this decade was to pressurise the government into reforming the 1876 Act.[158]

The Laboratory Animals Protection Bill, 1979

With thanks to the likes of CRAE, political parties across the spectrum had to recognise that animals mattered. CRAE initiated a campaign to get the main parties to include legislative reform in their General Election manifestos of 1979.[159] As Halsbury indicated in the quote above, the question on the political agenda was not complete abolition of vivisection, but rather comprehensive reform of the law to ensure its continuation.[160] Ryder and his compatriots managed to achieve this, and all parties pledged reform in their manifestos. The Conservative Government won the 1979 General Election under the leadership of Margaret Thatcher.[161] It was this government which promised new legislation to consider re-drafting the 1876 Act. The new legislation would address the concerns of the public and the CoE.[162]

In order to anticipate future legislative change under the new government, the pro-vivisection societies, represented by the RDS, introduced a Private Members Bill into the House of Lords via Lord Halsbury.[163]

---

153 Ryder, "Putting Animals into Politics."
154 Ibid.; Lyons, *The Politics of Animal Experimentation*.
155 Ryder, "Putting Animals into Politics." p. 170.
156 Ibid. p. 173.
157 Lyons, *The Politics of Animal Experimentation*.
158 Ryder, "Putting Animals into Politics."
159 Ibid.
160 Ibid. pp. 72–73.
161 Peter Clarke, *Hope and Glory: Britain 1900–2000*, 3rd ed. (London: Penguin Books, 2004).
162 The Welcome Library [Forthwith Well]: SA/PHY/G/1/62: Box 100, Animals (Scientific Procedures) Act: Liaison with MPs and Lords over final stages of Bill, FRAME publication: Animals (Scientific Procedures) Act 1986: The Animals Procedures Committee, ALTA (1986) 14, p. 8.
163 Lyons, *The Politics of Animal Experimentation*.

Halsbury did not like the idea of including animals in party politics to attract voters:

> [A]t the season of the party conferences, legislation was discussed based on the slogan of bringing animals into politics. I then decided in my own mind that if this meant bringing them into party politics I was against it. I could imagine no more unedifying spectacle than the parties bidding for the anti-vivisectionist vote in marginal constituencies ....[164]

However, despite Halsbury's misgivings about 'bringing them [animals] into politics,' in 1979 Halsbury introduced the RDS' 'Laboratory Animals Protection Bill.'[165] Halsbury aimed to implement the recommendations of the Littlewood Committee into legislation. One of his main reasons for introducing the Bill was because of his unease that:

> ... laboratories of men of science are being vandalised and men of science are being threatened over the telephone, though their only guilt is in doing experiments to try to benefit mankind. These threats, of course, come from what I call the protestational neurotics who infiltrate, soil and sully every reform movement, however worthy. They do not have the support of the genuine animal welfare societies.[166]

Halsbury was alarmed that more members of the public were turning their backs on animal experimentation and siding with the radical animal rights groups. By implementing the recommendations of the Littlewood Report, with its heavy emphasis on animal welfare, it was hoped that this would mollify the 'protestational neurotic' laypeople. Welfare in Halsbury's case, acted as an ideological tool as much as a material practice, in order to ensure the continuation of experiments on animals:

> The Bill is evolutionary, not revolutionary, in scope. It builds on the present Act, incorporates those recommendations of the Littlewood Report needing legislation – now, as I have said, over 15 years out of date – and seals off some grey areas which have inevitably developed since 1876, the date of the present Act. I should perhaps remind your Lordships that the whole – I repeat the whole – of immunology,

---

164 Hansard: Laboratory Animals Protection Bill House of Lords [HL] Deb 25 October 1979, vol 402, cc204–213.
165 Well: PP/WDP/E/4: Box 60 Royal Society Committee on Animal Experiments, Research Defence Society Press Release. 15 August 1979. p. 1.
166 Hansard: Laboratory Animals Protection Bill HL Deb 25 October 1979, vol 402, cc204–213.

hormone-based therapy, vitamin-based dietetics, chemotherapy, antibiotics, anthelmintics – modern medicine, in fact – has been developed since the present Act came into force ...[167]

The Laboratory Animals Protection Bill aimed at weakening regulation over animal experiments.[168] It had some success in the House of Lords, but it failed to deliver support in the House of Commons.[169] Instead, it was referred to a House of Lords Select Committee, which drew on the recommendations postulated in the Bill. They created their Report for the Government in 1980, which listed many deficiencies of the 1876 Act.[170] One such criticism was on the role of the Advisory Committee and its operation. The report argued that because of its non-statutory status, it did not operate stringent regulation over the use of animals. As a consequence, there was not a satisfactory channel of accountability to Parliament.[171] This failed to impress upon government due to lack of Parliamentary time.[172]

The Protection of Animals (Scientific Purposes) Bill, 1979

Another Bill which was introduced in Parliament (House of Commons) in 1979 was Peter Fry's Protection of Animals (Scientific Procedures) Bill. It was supported by 1.25 million members of the public who signed the National Petition for the Protection of Animals.[173] The petition aimed to pressurise the government into taking measures to address several concerns related to animal experiments, including the minimising of pain and suffering 'before, during and after experiment.'[174] Ryder's RSPCA drafted the Bill, and it had the support of many other animal welfare groups.[175] Again, the emphasis was on the revision of the 1876 Act, alongside more statutory measures of welfare, with Fry arguing:

---

167 Ibid.
168 Garner, *Political Animals: Animal Protection Politics in Britain and the United States.* pp. 180–181.
169 Well: SA/PHY/G/1/62: Box 100, Animals (Scientific Procedures) Act: Liaison with MPs and Lords over final stages of Bill, FRAME publication: Animals (Scientific Procedures) Act 1986: The Animals Procedures Committee, ALTA (1986) 14, p. 8.
170 Ibid.
171 Well: SA/PHY/G/1/62: Box 100, Animals (Scientific Procedures) Act: Liaison with MPs and Lords over final stages of Bill, FRAME publication: Animals (Scientific Procedures) Act 1986: The Animals Procedures Committee, ALTA (1986) 14, pp. 6–13. p. 8.
172 William Paton, "Animal Experiment: British and European Legislation and Practice," *Annals New York Academy of Sciences* 406 (1983); Garner, *Political Animals: Animal Protection Politics in Britain and the United States.*
173 Hansard: Protection of Animals House of Commons [HC] Deb 16 November 1979, vol 973, c1653.
174 Ibid.
175 Bioethics, "The Ethics of Research Involving Animals." p. 27.

... if it is passed and comes into force, it will be a decisive step in the direction of greater protection for animals used for scientific purposes. It is a moderate Bill. It recognises the need for essential medical research, whether in the interests of human beings or of animals, but it sets out to restrict the use of so many animals and to require cause to be shown when animals are to be used. Above all, it requires the use of alternatives where they are reasonably available.[176]

For the animal welfare lobbyists, the abolition of animal experimentation was not a priority. Instead, like the Halsbury Bill, reformation of the law was advocated. Fry himself stated that this was a 'moderate Bill,' highlighting the continual need for vivisection. Again, the human right to use animals was the prerogative. This use remained unquestioned. Welfare was the cornerstone to this Bill, with a call for increased surveillance over laboratory animals.[177] This had a second reading in the Commons, but the Government considered that the Bill was too restrictive. Fry withdrew it, and he ended up expressing support for the Halsbury Bill.[178]

We can conclude here that after the Littlewood review of the 1960s and the introduction of two Private Member's Bills in the 1970s, a legal 'Pastoral turn' was underway.[179] Both welfarists and animal experimental scientists wanted animal experimentation to continue, while simultaneously being seen to provide for the needs of nonhuman animals. This call for increased care of laboratory animals is a further pronouncement of human domination over nonhumans' right to life, namely, the right to use nonhumans in experiment in a sagacious manner.[180]

The two Bills drew heavily on the recommendations of the Littlewood Report. As we will see, this, in turn, influenced the outcomes of the ASPA, 1986. In concurrence with Wadiwel, this would suggest that pastoral power does not start from the idea of beneficence, but rather from a position of absolute power and human domination.[181] Care and welfare operated from a position of human dominion over nonhuman life. Laboratory animal welfare was to eventually become enfolded within institutional and epistemic

---

176 Hansard: Protection of Animals (Scientific Purposes) BILL HC Deb 16 November 1979, vol 973, cc1666–1740.
177 Well: SA/PHY/G/1/62: Box 100, Animals (Scientific Procedures) Act: Liaison with MPs and Lords over final stages of Bill, FRAME publication: Animals (Scientific Procedures) Act 1986: The Animals Procedures Committee, ALTA (1986) 14, pp. 6–13. p. 7.
178 TNA: T489/69: Animal experiments: proposals to amend the Cruelty to Animals Act 1876 and the European Convention proposals on animal experiments, Advisory Committee on Animal Experiments - Report to the Secretary of State on the Framework of Legislation to Replace the Cruelty to Animals Act 1976. p. 6.
179 Cole, "From 'Animal Machines' to 'Happy Meat'? Foucault's Ideas of Disciplinary and Pastoral Power Applied to 'Animal-Centred' Welfare Discourse."
180 Wadiwel, *The War against Animals*. p. 123.
181 Ibid. p. 116.

realms of legal life in order to render animal experimentation legitimate and ensure its continuation.

Conclusion

I have outlined how the emergence of a concern for the care and treatment of individual laboratory animals in jurisprudential discourse was contingent upon redefining how nonhuman animals experience laboratory life: in their pain, death and 'care.' For instance, the recommendation for broadening the definition of the Pain Condition to encompass the psychological aspects of stress and distress in the animal. This enabled a contradictory and powerful discourse to emerge that at once seemed to facilitate more degrees of 'freedom' for the lived experience of the experimental animal; while at the same time would allow for the continuation and intensification of vivisection.

Key to understanding this curious and contradictory discourse was to analyse the ruminations presented in the Report about animal pain and their husbandry. The UFAW led the way in influencing the Report on this aspect. It was this organisation which preached a 'humane' approach to laboratory animal welfare, they had established links to the RDS, and had prominent scientists and members of the House of Lords involved in the group. By deploying Foucault's ideas on pastoral power, I demonstrated how the UFAW's influential concerns about pain and their recommendations to improve animal welfare highlighted the conditional nature of this form of animal welfare. It was conditional on the fact that it allowed for the perpetuation of animal experimentation through an a priori assumption of human dominance over other living beings. This assumed domination stems from the nonhumans' status as being objects of property in law. The property status of nonhuman animals remained unquestioned; they were still objectified through the discourse of welfare in the report. This is evidenced on many levels, most notably through the recommendations to increase the workers' *responsibility* over nonhuman animals in the laboratory, coupled with a suggestion for the licensee to have better *individualised knowledge* over each animal in their 'care,' and to get to know the animal when it was 'out of sorts.' As I have shown, it was only in the context of the instrumental use of the nonhuman that these power relations of responsibility and individualised knowledge came about in the first place.

Less evident in the Report is Foucault's ideas of *Self-mortification* and *submission*. But, the section on humane (kind) killing demonstrates elements of this. Experimental animals always practice self-mortification through what Foucault deemed an 'everyday death,' they serve the interests of human use-value.[182] Despite the rhetoric in the Report about improving

---

182 See Cole, "From 'Animal Machines' to 'Happy Meat'? Foucault's Ideas of Disciplinary and Pastoral Power Applied to 'Animal-Centred' Welfare Discourse."

accommodation and husbandry, their natural lives would remain unfulfilled. For that reason, they continually experienced an 'everyday death.' For Foucault, *submission* was also about the flock accepting their shepherd and willingly baying to their every demand. Submission in this instance is closely bound up with responsibility and individualised knowledge. The suggestion that laboratory animals should be 'happy and contented stock,' signifies the essence of making sure laboratory animals are tame. To induce tameness in nonhuman animals is to facilitate their submission to humans, in the end making them more malleable and open to manipulation. Re-defining the humans' level of responsibility towards fostering an ethos of care over nonhuman experimental animals would enable this submission, as much as make for 'happier' and 'healthier' animals that would be more open to manipulation.

There were powerful vested interests for the scientific profession to align themselves with this particular episteme. By acknowledging that nonhuman animals have psychological lives, it would help them produce more docile and less fearful (submissive) beings. However, this would not have happened if nonhuman animals were not ascribed property status in law. The property status of nonhuman animals paved the way for the construction of welfare and accordingly, automatically qualified nonhuman animals to experience more suffering. The Report delineated suffering to such an extent that it granted laboratory-dependent science the continuing right to use and *enjoy* their objects of property. Pastoral power has helped to uncover this attempt at the reconfiguration of laboratory human-animal relations; it also demonstrates that welfare is a construction that modifies the means of exploitation of nonhuman animals, but does nothing to end it.

The next chapter demonstrates how this turn to welfare became incorporated into the law via the ASPA, 1986. We turn to Foucault's ideas on governmentality to demonstrate how the liberal optic enabled a greater degree of biopolitical control of animals of the laboratory.

Bibliography

"1876 Cruelty to Animals Act."
(BUAV), British Union for the Abolition of Vivisection. *Animals Defender Magazine*, 1948.
Animal-Law. "Brexit, Article 13, and the Debate on Recognising 'Animal Sentience' in Law." In A-Law Expert Legal Briefing Note, The UK Centre for Animal Law, 2017.
"Animals (Scientific Procedures) Act." 1986.
Bioethics, Nuffield Council on. *The Ethics of Research Involving Animals*. London: Nuffield, 2005.
Calley, Darren. "The Aggregation of Suffering in the Regulatory Context: Scientific Experimentation, Animals, and Intrinsic Value." *Journal of Animal Ethics* 7, no. 1 (2017): 1–30.
Clarke, Peter. *Hope and Glory: Britain 1900–2000*. 3rd ed. London: Penguin Books, 2004.

Cole, Matthew. "From 'Animal Machines' to 'Happy Meat'? Foucault's Ideas of Disciplinary and Pastoral Power Applied to 'Animal-Centred' Welfare Discourse." *Animals* 1 (2011): 83–101.

Dalling, T. "Foreword." In *The UFAW Handbook on the Care and Management of Laboratory Animals*, edited by Alastair N. Worden. London: Bailliere, Tindall and Cox, 1947.

Dror, Otniel E. "The Affect of Experiment: The Turn to Emotions in Anglo-American Physiology, 1900–1940." *Isis* 90, no. 2 (1999): 205–237.

Duxbury, Catherine. *Animals, Science and Gender: Animal Experimentation in Britain, 1947–1965*. PhD, University of Essex, 2017.

Edgerton, David. *Warfare State: Britain, 1920–1970*. Cambridge, UK: Cambridge University Press, 2006.

Foucault, Michel. "Governmentality." In *The Foucault Effect: Studies in Governmentality*, edited by Colin Gordon, Graham Burchell, Peter Miller, 87–104. Chicago: University of Chicago Press, 1991.

———. "Omnes Et Singulatim: Toward a Critique of Political Reason." In *Power*, edited by J.D. Faubion, 298–325. London: Penguin, 2002.

———. *Security, Territory, Population (Michel Foucault: Lectures at the Collège De France)*, edited by Arnold Davidson, Graham Burchell. 2nd ed. Basingstoke; New York: Palgrave Macmillan, 2009.

———. "The Subject and Power." In *Power: The Essential Works of Michel Foucault 1954–1984: Volume 3*, edited by James D. Faubion, Paul. Rabinow, Robert Hurley. London: Penguin Books, 2001.

Francione, Gary. *Animals as Persons: Essays on the Abolition of Animal Exploitation*. New York: Columbia University Press, 2008.

Francione, Gary L. *Animals, Property and the Law*. 2nd ed. Philadelphia: Temple University Press, 2007.

French, Richard D. *Antivivisection and Medical Science in Victorian Society*. Princeton, New Jersey: Princeton University Press, 1975.

Garner, Robert. *Political Animals: Animal Protection Politics in Britain and the United States*. Basingstoke: Macmillan Press Ltd, 1998.

Golder, Ben. "Foucault and the Genealogy of Pastoral Power." *Radical Philosophy Review* 10, no. 2 (2007): 157–176.

HM Government. "Animal Testing and Research" https://www.gov.uk/guidance/research-and-testing-using-animals#animals-scientific-procedures-act-1986

———. "The Animals (Scientific Procedures) Act 1986 Amendment Regulations 2012." 2012.

Javier Guillén, Jan-Bas Prins, Bryan Howard, Anne-Dominique Degryse, Marcel Gyger. "The European Framework on Research Animal Welfare Regulations and Guidelines." In *Laboratory Animals: Regulations and Recommendations for the Care and Use of Animlas in Research*, edited by Javier Guillén, 117–202. London: Elsevier, 2018.

Kean, Hilda. *Animal Rights: Political and Social Change in Britain since 1800*. London, UK: Reaktion Books Ltd, 1998.

———. "The 'Smooth Cool Men of Science': The Feminist and Socialist Response to Vivisection." *The History Workshop Journal* 40 (1995): 16–38.

Kirk, Robert G.W. "'Wanted-Standard Guinea Pigs': Standardisation and the Experimental Animal Market in Britain Ca. 1919–1947." *Studies in the History, Philosophy, Biology and Biomedical Science* 39, no. 3 (2008): 280–291.

Kirkwood, Robert, Hubrecht, James, ed. *The UFAW Handbook on the Care and Management of Laboratory and Other Research Animals*. 8th ed. Chichester: John Wiley & Sons, 2010.
Littlewood, Sydney. "Cruelty to Animals Act, 1876." *British Medical Journal* 2, no. 5351 (1963): 256.
———. "Report of the Departmental Committee on Experiments on Animals," edited by Home Office. London: Her Majesty's Stationery Office, 1965.
Lyons, Dan. *The Politics of Animal Experimentation*. Hampshire: Palgrave Macmillan, 2013.
Palmer, Clare. "'Taming the Wild Profusion of Existing Things?' A Study of Foucault, Power, and Human/Animal Relationships." *Environmental Ethics* 23, no. 4 (2001): 339–358.
Paton, William. "Animal Experiment: British and European Legislation and Practice." *Annals New York Academy of Sciences* 406 (1983): 201–214.
Peggs, Kay. "Nonhuman Animal Experiments in the European Community: Human Values and Rational Choice." *Society and Animals* 18, no. 1 (2010): 1–20.
Rattray, R.F. "RSPCA Campaign." *British Medical Journal* 1, no. 5282 (1962): 946.
Ritvo, Harriet. *The Animal Estate: English and Other Creatures in the Victorian Age*. London, UK: Penguin Books Ltd, 1990.
Robertson, Ian. *Animals, Welfare and the Law*. Abingdon & New York: Routledge, 2015.
Rupke, Nicolaas, ed. *Vivisection in Historical Perspective*. London: Routledge, 1990.
Ryder, Richard. *Animal Revolution: Changing Attitudes towards Speciesism*. 2nd ed. Oxford & New York: Berg, 2000.
———. "Putting Animals into Politics." In *Animal Rights: The Changing Debate*, edited by Robert Garner, 166–93. London & Basingstoke: Macmillan Press Ltd, 1996.
———. *Victims of Science: The Use of Animals in Research*. London, UK: National Anti-Vivisection Society, 1983.
Singer, Peter. *Animal Liberation*. 3rd ed. London: Pimlico, 1975.
Union, Council of the European. "Council Directive of 24 November 1986 on the Approximation of Laws, Regulations and Administrative Provisons of the Member States Regarding the Protection of Animals Used for Experimental and Other Scientific Purposes." 1986.
———. "Directive 2010/63/EU of the European Parliament and of the Council of 22 September 2010 on the Protection of Animals Used for Scientific Purposes." *Official Journal of the European Union* (2010).
Vinter, Jean. *Kind Killing*, edited by UFAW. London: UFAW, 1950.
Wadiwel, Dinesh Joseph. *The War against Animals*. Leiden & Boston: Brill Rodopi, 2015.
Worden, Alastair N, ed. *The UFAW Handbook on the Care and Management of Laboratory Animals*, edited by Alastair Worden. 1st ed. London: Bailliere, Tindall and Cox, 1947.

2 The march of Thatcherism

Neoliberal laboratory 'care' and the assent of the ASPA, 1981–1986

With the election of the Conservative Party under the leadership of Margaret Thatcher in 1979, came a new form of governance: neoliberalism. She believed that since 1945, there had been a suppression of the free market under the economic model of Keynesianism.[1] For the Conservatives, the containment of the free market had created a welfare state which intervened too heavily in people's lives.[2] The aim was to increase privatisation at a substantial rate, as well as encourage rampant individualism and competition.[3] This was as much an economic endeavour as it was a quest for a psychic [re-]formation of the human population.

Within 1980s Britain, economic liberalism may have been the ideological imperative, but for Thatcher, nineteenth century Victorian-style values underpinned much of her socio-economic framework.[4] Tory paternalism ensured that despite the cuts to the public sector, state intervention in the guise of welfare provision would continue. This ran alongside a firm belief in individualism, the free market and consumer capitalism.[5]

As we can see, there is a deep-set irony attached to the Thatcherite neoliberal agenda. The economic model used by Thatcher advocated deregulation but remained actively interventionist in certain areas of public life. As Foucault states, neoliberalism involves 'taking the formal principles of a market economy and referring and relating them to, projecting them on to, a general art of government.'[6] In turn, this shapes the nature of all

---

1 Michael Oliver, "The Retreat of the State in the 1980s and 1990s," in *20th Century Britain: Economic, Cultural and Social Change*, ed. Francesca Carnevali; Julie-Marie Strange (Harlow: Pearson Education Ltd., 2007).
2 Ibid.
3 Peter Clarke, *Hope and Glory: Britain 1900–2000*, 3rd ed. (London: Penguin Books, 2004).
4 Ibid.
5 Ibid.
6 Michel Foucault, *The Birth of Biopolitics*, ed. Michel Senellart, François Ewald, Allessandro Fontana, Arnold Davidson, Graham Burchell, 2nd ed. (Basingstoke, UK: Palgrave Macmillan, 2010). p. 131.

state activities and social relationships by orientating them towards the economic. The social policies of the 'Keynesian era' were slowly being transformed by Thatcher into economic ones.[7] This is very much reflective of the Conservative Party's neoliberal form of governance at the time, in the fact that it is interventionist to the extent that all laws accede to and are framed around an economic imperative.[8]

The drive towards individualism under a neoliberal agenda meant that not only human lives but nonhuman ones too would 'be shaped in a new form' and subjected to new kinds of intervention.[9] Pastoral power is then synonymous with neoliberal governance, and it forms the 'background' to neoliberal governmentality. As we will see, Foucault's biopolitical idea of governmentality is intrinsically tied to this neoliberal ideal of individualism, and animals-as-objects (property).

Governmentality

Governmentality is an 'art of governance' present in Western liberal societies since the sixteenth and seventeenth centuries. Population becomes the target, where apparatuses of security are its 'essential technical instruments' by which they are managed.[10] Consequently, these state-based governmentalities are to be found in the pre-Christian East, and later the Christian East as a form of pastoral power. They are then transformed into statist endeavours to maintain society's primary function, that of the economic imperative (see discussion above).[11] Hence, pastoral power acts as both the 'prelude' and 'background' to modern forms of governmentality.[12]

Governmentality then is when individuals are operated upon in myriad ways through an array of technologies. These technologies of power shape peoples' conduct so that their actions would reflect and contribute to a broader 'rationality' of government. During the period analysed here, the governmental rationality which obtained in Britain was a 'liberal' one. With the liberal mode of governmentality, freedom rather than representing the obverse of governance is instead a form of management. Governing through freedom rests upon the conditioning of individuals to practice a regulated form of freedom, in turn integrating them into the wider individual society.[13] Moulded through multiple disciplinary interventions, and scrutinised by numerous supervisory gazes, people would govern themselves according to

---

7   Ibid.
8   Ibid.
9   Ibid.
10 Foucault, *Security, Territory, Population* (Michel Foucault: Lectures at the Collège De France). p. 108.
11 Ibid.; Foucault, "Omnes Et Singulatim: Toward a Critique of Political Reason."
12 Golder, "Foucault and the Genealogy of Pastoral Power."
13 Foucault, "Governmentality."

certain sanctioned norms of conduct. In this way, individuals are fashioned as both the objects and the subjects of liberal governance.[14]

Even though Foucault was speaking in strictly human terms, as Matthew Chrulew and Dinesh Joseph Wadiwel stress, Foucault's ideas are 'extremely profitable for understanding our conflicted relationships with animals.'[15] Nonhuman laboratory animals are agentic beings[16] and are enmeshed in a whole array of material–semiotic relations, both in and outside the laboratory. Governmentality helps us to trace the historically contingent origins of contemporary experimental science. It allows us to reveal both the logic of rationality and material impact of power relations on nonhuman laboratory animals. First, in the way pastoral power operated in the review of the 1876 Act reveals the beginnings of the development of a rationality of animal welfare. Second, the transformation of this into an 'art of governance' in the formation of the ASPA 1986 helps to reveal its material impact and biopolitical nature. In this sense, I want to link this critique to the insights offered by Critical Animal Studies (CAS) scholars, such as Wadiwel,[17] and provide a historical account of the intermingling of law and animal experimental science. I do this by demonstrating how law-making practices were not just based on a logic of rationality but also had implications for the very practice of animal-dependent science.

The Advisory Committee Report, 1981

The new Conservative Government of 1979 issued a Ministerial Statement declaring their commitment to reform the 1876 Act.[18] In 1980, they also restructured the Advisory Committee (AC) (renamed the Advisory Committee on Animal Experiments) and asked the Committee to produce a report on the framework of legislation to replace the 1876 Act.[19] The AC report drew heavily on the recommendations of the Halsbury Bill,

---

14 Nikolas Rose, *Powers of Freedom: Reframing Political Thought* (Cambridge: Cambridge University Press, 1999).
15 Matthew Chrulew, Dinesh Joseph Wadiwel, "Introduction: Foucault and Animals," in *Foucault and Animals*, ed. Matthew Chrulew, Dinesh Joseph Wadiwel (Leiden & Boston: Brill, 2017). p. 1.
16 Joshua Specht, "Animal History after Its Triumph: Unexpected Animals, Evolutionary Approaches, and the Animal Lens," *History Compass* 14, no. 7 (2016).
17 Wadiwel, *The War against Animals*.
18 TNA: T489/69 Animal experiments: proposals to amend the Cruelty to Animals Act 1876 and the European Convention proposals on animal experiments. Advisory Committee on Animal Experiments – Report to the Secretary of State on the Framework of Legislation to Replace the Cruelty to Animals Act 1876. p. 1.
19 TNA: T489/69 Animal experiments: proposals to amend the Cruelty to Animals Act 1876 and the European Convention proposals on animal experiments. Advisory Committee on Animal Experiments – Report to the Secretary of State on the Framework of Legislation to Replace the Cruelty to Animals Act 1876. p. 1.

its modified version in the form of the Select Committee's Report and the Littlewood Report of 1965[20]:

> We felt bound to give due weight in our considerations, on the one hand, to the doubts expressed about the Protection of Animals (Scientific Purposes) Bill, and the original version of the Laboratory Animals Protection Bill, on the other hand, to the measure of agreement achieved by members of the Select Committee in their proposals. Accordingly, where we have considered it appropriate, we have modelled a number of our recommendations on the provisions of the Select Committee's Bill.[21]

The AC would use the Select Committee's Bill as a model for the construction of their report. It was also felt that an update of the 1876 Act was necessary in light of the Council of Europe (CoE)'s convention.[22] Several problems with the current law were listed. These deficiencies included: how the licensing system operated; the amount of scientific progress which the Act did not account for, and its paucity of regulation concerning animal welfare.[23] The AC in its report was hoping to neutralise these shortcomings of the current law and make recommendations that could help to form a new Bill to be debated in Parliament.[24]

The report was a comprehensive analysis of the present state of law relating to animal experimentation. It followed the path taken by the Littlewood Inquiry and examined every facet of contemporary legal regulation over vivisection. They made 25 recommendations for changes to the 1876 Act, including proposing an alternative license system consisting of two schemes of application. The scientists applying would have to justify their use of non-human animals in their work and also demonstrate their competence to carry out the research. They also recommended widening the scope of the definition of 'animal' to include all vertebrates of the phylum Chordata. This includes some species of fish and also protection to mammalian foetal, and embryonic or larval young of classes of species (including egg-laying animals).[25]

The government responded positively to the AC's report, and this helped to shape the writing of their first White Paper in 1983 on proposed revisions of the 1876 Act.[26] The AC report was one of the precursors to the complete revision of the 1876 Act. It helped to set a standard for the legal change to come later in the decade.

---

20 Ibid. pp. 8–9.
21 Ibid. p. 9.
22 Ibid. p. 4.
23 Ibid. pp. 5–6.
24 Ibid.
25 Ibid. pp. 11–12 and 34.
26 TNA: HO285/181 Government proposals for legislation to replace the Cruelty to Animals Act 1876: White Paper on Scientific Procedures on Living Animals, Jan 1983–Dec 1983. p. 5.

The 1983 and 1985 White Papers: Rationalising animal experimentation

As previously stated, modern forms of governance involve economic strategies.[27] This involves the rationalisation of management techniques which aim to intervene in the lives of populations and to give order to behaviour.[28] This 'governmentality' is a form of administrating societies in an economically efficient manner, while concomitantly intervening in the lives of its citizens. Where the Littlewood Inquiry demonstrated the ideological role of pastoral power in hoping to shape the lives of nonhuman laboratory animals, the ASPA 1986 demonstrates its material transmutation. Besides, it shows how the lives of nonhuman animals were to be governed by a biopolitical practice for experimentation to continue. Pastoral power and biopolitics converge to produce a governmental material-semiotic practice over nonhuman laboratory animals.

The assent of the ASPA exemplifies the implementation of this logic of governmentality. The creation of a new law facilitated further the regulation over nonhuman bodies, and also enabled the *production* of specific kinds of experimental nonhuman bodies (*al la* bodies reminiscent of the pastorate). Kristin Asdal and Tone Druglitrø argue that animal experimentation regulation is one example of the *techniques* of law.[29] For the ASPA, these techniques (or tactics) included the generation of a whole new experimental code of conduct that encapsulated animal care and welfare, as well as a change in the semantics of vivisection. The law in this instance came to act as a moral technology which shaped the values and beliefs of animal-dependent scientists. This, in turn, helped to buffer the impact of its economic rationalisation.[30]

The government White Papers of 1983 and 1985 epitomise the coalescence of law as a moral technology and as an economic art of governance. The 1983 Bill states:

> This will be the first legislation of its kind this century, it will repeal the Cruelty to Animals Act, 1876 and bring in completely new controls which will give better protection to animals used in scientific experiment...We are [also] very glad to see agreement in Europe on common minimum standards. Not only will this provide protection to animals

---

27 Graham Burchell, Colin Gordon, Peter Miller, ed., *The Foucault Effect: Studies in Governmentality: With Two Lectures by, and an Interview with, Michel Foucault* (Chicago: University of Chicago Press, 1991).
28 Dinesh Joseph Wadiwel, *The War against Animals* (Leiden & Boston: Brill Rodopi, 2015). p. 102.
29 Kristin Asdal; Tone Druglitrø, "Modifying the Biopolitical Collective: The Law as Moral Technology," in *Humans, Animals and Biopolitics: The More-Than-Human Condition*, ed. Kristin Asdal, Tone Druglitrø, Steve Hinchcliffe (Oxon: Routledge, 2017). p. 69.
30 Ibid.

throughout Europe, it will also help to ensure work we would not allow in this country is not simply undertaken abroad. The UK has a large pharmaceutical industry which makes a big contribution to our balance of payments.... In devising new controls it is very important not to put industry at risk unnecessarily.[31]

Here, the new Conservative Government maintained its commitment to the pharmaceutical industry's commercial interests. A monetary policy began in 1976 and was solidified further under the Conservatives.[32] There was a conflation of economics with laboratory animal 'protection.' This too was following the European Union's (EU) proposals for harmonisation of animal experimentation regulation across its member countries.

As well as stipulating the government's economic interests in maintaining the regulation of experimentation, the Bill expressed consideration of the rewording of the Pain Conditions. Following the CoE's preliminary draft framework, the 1983 White Paper stipulated the need for a 'radical tightening up of existing protection for animals.[33] It argued that under the new law, no animal would be 'subjected to a level of pain greater than is appropriate to the procedure in question.'[34] However, the report still insisted that to go further than is necessary, by prohibiting the use of animals entirely, if pain and suffering are more than 'trivial' would be to the detriment of 'man and animals.'[35]

The White Paper stipulated the needed to maintain the 1876 Pain Conditions. This stated 'if at any time an animal is found to be suffering severe pain which is likely to endure it shall be painlessly killed.'[36] It was argued that by preserving the 1876 Pain Conditions, this would go beyond the controls stipulated in Article 9 of the draft European Convention. Article 9 allowed scientists and establishments to circumvent pain controls if 'it is specifically authorised and is of exceptional importance.'[37]

The 1983 White Paper received quite some criticism from animal welfare bodies for its heavy reliance on the Halsbury Select Committee Bill of 1980 and its failure to stipulate clearly defined restrictions on the infliction of pain

---

31 TNA HO285/181, Government proposals for legislation to replace the Cruelty to Animals Act 1876: White Paper on Scientific Procedures on Living Animals. Scientific Procedures on Living Animals presented to Parliament by the Secretary of State for the Home Department by Command of Her Majesty. May 1983. p. 2.
32 Dan Lyons, *The Politics of Animal Experimentation* (Hampshire: Palgrave Macmillan, 2013). pp. 226–227.
33 TNA HO285/181, Government proposals for legislation to replace the Cruelty to Animals Act 1876: White Paper on Scientific Procedures on Living Animals. Scientific Procedures on Living Animals presented to Parliament by the Secretary of State for the Home Department by Command of Her Majesty. May 1983. p. 5.
34 Ibid.
35 Ibid.
36 Ibid. p. 9.
37 Ibid.

and suffering.[38] Consequently, the 1983 White Paper ideologically divided the animal welfare lobby into three main factions. The RSPCA, which adopted an ambiguous stance towards the reformation of the 1876 Act, the anti-vivisection lobby who disagreed with all proposals. The anti-vivisection societies included the BUAV, National Antivivisection Society, Animal Aid and the Scottish Antivivisection Society, which established a coalition called the 'Mobilisation Against the Government White Paper.' It was the third faction in the guise of the continuing CRAE alliance with FRAME and the BVA, which was to be most successful at gaining government support. The CRAE alliance helped to influence some of the redrafting of the 1983 White Paper for the government's 1985 Supplementary White Paper.[39] The main protagonists of this alliance who came under the Chairpersonship of Lord Houghton, were Clive Hollands of the RSPCA, John Seamer of the BVA and Michael Balls of FRAME.[40]

The government felt it was essential to maintain 'considerable consensus' with the 'moderate' animal welfare lobby groups. This was to allay the high level of public and political scrutiny animal experimentation which was increasing. The Conservative Party feared that if they neglected the views of the welfare lobby, the opposition parties 'may be compelled to draft a more extreme position.' Having the CRAE alliance on board would help to dull the criticism currently being meted out by the press, public and other political parties.[41]

That did not mean that the Tories were abandoning their support of private industry and animal-dependent scientists. On the contrary, Secretary of State, William Whitelaw vociferously argued:

> We badly need to concentrate the minds of many people in biomedical science and industry on the need to come up from behind the parapet and stand up and be counted in support of our proposals. They must stop lying low and start lobbying properly.[42]

The Conservatives were concerned about the threat to British industry, particularly the pharmaceutical firms which were 'one of [Britain's] biggest

---

38 J. E. Hampson, "Law Relating to Animal Experimentation," in *Laboratory Animals: An Introduction for New Experiments*, ed. A. A. Tuffery (New York; Chichester: Wiley, 1987); Lyons, *The Politics of Animal Experimentation*.
39 Hampson, "Law Relating to Animal Experimentation."; Lyons, *The Politics of Animal Experimentation*.
40 TNA HO285/189 Government proposals for legislation to replace the Cruelty to Animals Act 1876: White Paper on Scientific Procedures on Living Animals; Home Secretary's briefing. Letter to John Seamer (BVA) from Home Office N. M. Johnson. p. 1.
41 TNA HO 285/189, Government proposals for legislation to replace the Cruelty to Animals Act 1876: White Paper on Scientific Procedures on Living Animals; Home Secretary's briefing. Memo from William Whitelaw Home Secretary to Various Departments, 12 June 1984. pp 2–3.
42 Ibid. p. 2.

success stories.'⁴³ They were seemingly pleading with industry to play a role in drafting the new legislation to protect Britain's economic interests. For the government, the economic imperative was a strong case *a fortori* in drafting new legislation. It was also a demonstration in '[living] up to international expectations' by complying with EU policy and ratifying the CoE Convention.

One significant change in the 1985 White Paper was the government's position on pain. Whereas the 1983 Paper outlined the government's intention of maintaining the 1876 Status Quo with regards to pain, the 1985 White Paper proposed a radical new departure.[44] Following the CoE recommendation and the Universities Federation for Animal Welfare (UFAW)'s definition in the Littlewood Report, pain was to be broadened to include 'pain, suffering, distress and or lasting harm.'[45] According to the Secretary of State Mr Mellor, broadening the Pain Conditions would help to 'keep [the] support of the moderate animal welfare groups on this issue….' This would also help prevent dissension in the welfare ranks. As Mellor argued 'if we enter the parliamentary debate having alienated the moderate groups on pain, they would have the influence to drive the Government off its chosen path.'[46]

Having ignored the CRAE alliance's proposals on pain in the drafting of the 1983 White Paper, the government chose this time to try and publicly display their active involvement in the writing of the 1985 Paper. Clive Hollands of CRAE argued that there should be provision on the 'face of the Bill' for the correlation of the maximum permitted degree of pain or distress which may be inflicted on an animal with the purpose of the procedure. Hollands proposed that there should be two statutory Pain Conditions. One that granted a complete restriction on pain for all general procedures, with permitted exemptions only in exceptional circumstances. Second, Hollands advised on providing a termination condition. This would apply if an animal was found to be suffering from severe pain or distress, which was likely to continue.[47]

The government argued that 'Mr Hollands' proposals [were] unacceptable' as it would lend itself to causing quite some confusion in a court of

---

43 Ibid. p. 3.
44 Judith Hampson, "Legislation: A Practical Solution to the Vivisection Dilemma?," in *Vivisection in Historical Perspective*, ed. Nicolaas Rupke (London; New York; Sydney: Croom Helm, 1987). p. 318.
45 TNA HO285/202 Animal Experiments Bill: first print. p. 2.
46 TNA HO285/189 Government proposals for legislation to replace the Cruelty to Animals Act 1876: White Paper on Scientific Procedures on Living Animals; Home Secretary's briefing. Note of a meeting held on 27 July 1984. Legislation to replace the Cruelty to Animals Act 1876: Pain. p. 1.
47 TNA HO285/189 Government proposals for legislation to replace the Cruelty to Animals Act 1876: White Paper on Scientific Procedures on Living Animals; Home Secretary's briefing. Note to Replace Cruelty to Animals Act 1876. From M. E. Head to Mr Sutton, Mr Heald, Mr Johnson, Miss Edwards and Mr Richards. p. 2.

law.[48] The government wanted neither a statutory correlation between pain and purpose of an experiment nor a statutory Pain Conditions. Instead a new licencing system, covering personal and project licences 'should achieve the same degree of control over pain as Mr Hollands [CRAE] requires – but in a more realistic fashion.'[49]

> Although we can't give in to him, we must keep talking to Mr Hollands. We see him anyway every six months or so and we can use these occasions to continue explaining how personal and project licences will in practice provide the control he seeks. If we can keep Mr Hollands not only personally convinced of our good faith in wanting to tighten up controls but armed with some useful 'inside' evidence of the steps we're taking he may be able to keep his house in order while we get on with devising our new system.[50]

Hollands was causing quite some consternation with the government. Mellor and his compatriots wanted to demonstrate visible solidarity with the animal welfare lobbyists, by persuading Hollands that they were strengthening pain controls for the new legislation. In reality, Hollands and his CRAE alliance were seemingly acting as the government's diversionary tactic in order to pass the controls they ultimately wanted. Instead, the government proposed an inclusion of a Pain Conditions in the granting of personal and project licences to scientists. This was akin to the UFAW's definition in the Littlewood Report.[51] Rather than pain being a statutory inviolable condition which could be contested in a court of law, it would become an exercise in administration.

Licences were to be the administrative apparatuses which would encapsulate the non-statutory application of the Pain Conditions and make sure scientists and research organisations were carrying out regulated procedures. Regulated procedures were 'experimental or other scientific processes applied to a protected animal,' for example, injections and killing of the animal.[52] The 1985 White Paper proposed three licencing schemes:

---

48 TNA HO285/189 Government proposals for legislation to replace the Cruelty to Animals Act 1876: White Paper on Scientific Procedures on Living Animals; Home Secretary's briefing. Note of a meeting held on 27 July 1984. Legislation to replace the Cruelty to Animals Act 1876: Pain. p. 1; 4.
49 TNA HO285/189 Government proposals for legislation to replace the Cruelty to Animals Act 1876: White Paper on Scientific Procedures on Living Animals; Home Secretary's briefing. Note to Replace Cruelty to Animals Act 1876. From M. E. Head to Mr Sutton, Mr Heald, Mr Johnson, Miss Edwards and Mr Richards. p. 3.
50 Ibid. pp. 5–6.
51 Sydney Littlewood, "Report of the Departmental Committee on Experiments on Animals," ed. Home Office (London: Her Majesty's Stationary Office, 1965). pp. 58–59.
52 TNA HO 285/202, Animal Experiments Bill: first print. 1 September 1985. pp. 2–3.

personal and project licences, and registration certificates.[53] The Secretary of State would authorise all licences. Registration certificates would include breeding, supply and user establishments. Each establishment had a designated person responsible for the care and welfare of the experimental animals. A veterinary surgeon also had to be on hand to provide advice and record the health and welfare of each animal.[54] A personal licence granted the person authorisation to carry out a regulated procedure and the holder:

> Shall take appropriate precautions to prevent or reduce to a minimum consistent with the purposes of the authorised procedures any pain, distress or discomfort to the animals to which those procedures may be applied.[55]

The emphasis on individual responsibility for experimental animals is encouraged. Personal licence holders need to have individualised knowledge over the experimental animals in their procedure in order to keep pain, distress and discomfort to minimum. An 'art of governance' over experimental animals was being encouraged, coupled with the neoliberal ideology of individual obligation. In this case, the individual scientist was to be held responsible and accountable for their actions.[56] The personal licence made it a mandatory obligation for the licensee to demonstrate an assessment of the likelihood of pain and suffering. The project licence would be awarded for a specified programme of work[57]:

> In determining whether to grant a project licence and what conditions to include in it the Secretary of State shall weigh the effect on the animals concerned against the benefit likely to accrue as a result of the programme specified in the licence.[58]

Applicants for project licences would be required to describe the background, aims and procedures involved in their work and to assess the severity of the research. The Home Secretary would then balance the predicted severity of the effects on the animals against the potential benefit of the experiment.[59]

---

53 Ibid. pp. 3–7.
54 Ibid. p. 5.
55 Ibid. p. 3.
56 David Harvey, *A Brief History of Neoliberalism*, 2nd ed. (Oxford: Oxford University Press, 2007). p. 65.
57 Ibid. p. 4.
58 Ibid. p. 5.
59 Well SA/PHY/G/1/62: Box 100, Animals (Scientific Procedures) Act: Liaison with MPs and Lords over final stages of Bill. Home Office Guidance Notes. Draft of the Advisory Committee. 5 June 1986.

Assessment of severity was an exercise in biopolitical governmentality. It included a detailed breakdown in the application for licence of the number of animals used, their age, sex and health status. Physical and psychological pain, suffering and distress had to be weighed against the purpose of the experiment in a utilitarian fashion. Morbidity and mortality predicted if there could be a 'reversibility of physical/mental/behavioural handicaps' in animals after the experiment. Suitability of the applicant had to be demonstrated as well as the design of the experiment. Other factors which had to be considered were: the provision of suitable accommodation, environment and husbandry, use of anaesthesia and analgesia, and a demonstration of the consideration of the three 'Rs': Reduction, Replacement and Refinement.[60] Pain and distress were measured by a classificatory schema. This 'severity banding' was in line with the proposals stipulated by the CoE.[61] It was also thought that 'in working up our proposals on this basis we think we have developed them closer to Mr Hollands' thinking than we had previously thought possible or acceptable.'[62] Thus, placating the outcries from the welfare lobby, especially its most vocal supporter and the government's seeming ostensive nemesis, Clive Hollands of CRAE.

Permitted and protected degrees of pain: The Animals (Scientific Procedures) Act, 1986 and the institutionalisation of welfare

The 1985 supplementary White Paper formed the basis of the passage of the Act in 1986. It was quickly passed through both Houses of Parliament: The Lords and Commons, completing its passage in May 1986.[63] In concurrence with Judith Hampson, the Act facilitated the furtherance of vivisection rather than restricted it.[64] It helped to maintain the 'vivisection-industrial-complex'[65] by broadening its scope to include the regulation of everything from experiments to vaccines. While, on the other hand and quite contrarily, being seen to show that much stricter controls over scientists use of nonhumans, via the new licensing system had been imposed. Held within this licensing system

---

60 TNA HO 285/189 TNA HO285/189 Government proposals for legislation to replace the Cruelty to Animals Act 1876: White Paper on Scientific Procedures on Living Animals; Home Secretary's briefing. Note from MR N.M. Johnson. 5 November 1984. p. 1.
61 Council of Europe, "European Convention for the Protection of Vertebrate Animals Used for Experimental and Other Scientific Purposes," *European Treaty Series* 123 (1986): 4.
62 TNA HO 285/189 Government proposals for legislation to replace the Cruelty to Animals Act 1876: White Paper on Scientific Procedures on Living Animals; Home Secretary's briefing. Memo from N.M. Johnson E4 Division to Mr Head and Mr Davidson. p. 1.
63 Hampson, "Law Relating to Animal Experimentation." p. 26.
64 Ibid.
65 Núria Almiron; Natalie Khazaal, "Lobbying against Compassion: Speciesist Discourse in the Vivisection Industrial Complex," *American Behavioural Scientist* 60, no. 3 (2015): 256–275.

was the Pain Conditions, which did not make it onto the legislation as a separate statutory requirement, despite protestations from the likes of CRAE. Instead, the licensing system constructed the assessment of pain in utilitarian terms. It became an exercise in administration rather than an explicit legal requirement. How that administration was to work was laid out in a document issued by the Home Office: *Guidance on the Operation of the New Legislation to Replace the Cruelty to Animals Act 1876*.[66]

The *Guidance* offered by the Home Office was written jointly by the Royal Society and the UFAW.[67] It was very similar to the proposals offered by the UFAW in the Littlewood Report of 1965. It involved details of the responsibilities licence holders had to have, the nature of the care, welfare and accommodation of experimental animals, as well as the aspects relating to the assessment of severity.[68] This guidance was completed a few years later with the publication of a Code of Practice, shifted the *idea* of the relationship between research worker and animal to a different mode of existence. This new relationship was one which was still held under the auspices of a human dominance hierarchy. However, it was reconstructed as one which was framed around care, welfare and duties of responsibility.[69]

The consequence of this new law, which is still in operation today, is that humans are allowed to inflict harm and kill nonhuman laboratory animals more *responsibly*.[70] Hence, the ASPA was an 'art of governance' which operated on nonhuman bodies in a particular manner. Laboratory animals were re-formed around a biopolitical order of 'things' which reshaped their very existence. However, their existence was primarily to serve human ends, securing a moral hierarchy of worth which differentiated between necessary suffering, and the benefit the research would serve to humans.[71] Achieving this was only possible with the introduction of the notion of animal 'welfare.' This modern form of pastoral power enfolded animals within an ethical framework. This framework worked in a twofold manner. First, it acted as a direct form of governance over nonhuman laboratory animals and second, as an indirect form of governance over humans. Here, the law acted upon individuals and organisations requiring them to make specific moral judgements.

66 Home Office, "Guidance on the Operation of the New Legislation to Replace the Cruelty to Animals Act 1876," HMSO, https://webarchive.nationalarchives.gov.uk/19970429190800/http://www.open.gov.uk:80/home_off/aspag.htm.
67 TNA HO 285/189 Government proposals for legislation to replace the Cruelty to Animals Act 1876: White Paper on Scientific Procedures on Living Animals; Home Secretary's briefing. Memo from N. M. Johnson E4 Division to Mr Head and Mr Davidson. 16 November 1984. p. 1.
68 Home Office, "Guidance on the Operation of the New Legislation to Replace the Cruelty to Animals Act 1876."
69 Ibid.
70 Wadiwel, *The War against Animals*. p. 215.
71 Druglitrø, "Modifying the Biopolitical Collective: The Law as Moral Technology." p. 73.

58 *Law, animal welfare and gender*

The governmental apparatus of 'security' fits neatly with this understanding of the ASPA's requirement of severity assessment. Foucault conceptualised the apparatuses of security as 'those institutions and practices concerned to defend, maintain and secure a national population and those that secure the economic, demographic and social processes that are found to exist within that population.'[72] He ascribed three features to security. First, it deals with a series of possible events; second, it evaluates through calculations of cost and benefit and third, security outlines conditions of what is to be permitted and prevented by 'the specification of an optimal mean within a tolerable bandwidth of variation.'[73]

Security operates in the ASPA's severity assessment in several ways. The management of risk (harm) serves as a governmental tactic of security as it represents ways to deal with probable pain and suffering felt by the nonhuman animal before, during and after the procedure. The *Guidance* issued operates as an educative programme and is used to manage risks both in the laboratory and animal house. This includes risks that occur before, during and after an experiment. Recommendations about animal care, welfare and accommodation are given in this supplementary document, to help manage the threat of negative physiological and psychological consequences the research has on nonhuman animals.[74] The new licencing system legitimates these guidelines. For instance, in the calculation of the benefits of the research against the amount of nonhuman pain and suffering.[75] The optimal mean in terms of pain and suffering is about keeping it to a minimum. However, any form of pain, suffering, distress and lasting harm is permitted within this bandwidth, but carries with them specific sets of management practices and conditions:

> It is not possible to lay down hard and fast rules about how potential severity should be assessed. The taking of small or infrequent blood samples; skin irritation tests with substances expected to be only mildly irritant; conventional minor surgical procedures under anaesthesia such as laparoscopy, small superficial tissue biopsies or cannulation of peripheral blood vessels; are likely to be regarded as mild unless there is significant combination or repetition of procedures using the same animal. Many procedures are likely to be assessed as moderate. This could include much of the screening and development of potential

---

72 Mitchell Dean, *Governmentality: Power and Rule in Modern Society* (London: Sage, 1999). p. 20.
73 Colin Gordon, "Governmental Rationality: An Introduction," in *The Foucault Effect: Studies in Governmentality*, ed. Graham Burchell, Colin Gordon, Peter Miller (Chicago: University if Chicago Press, 1991). p. 20.
74 Home Office, "Guidance on the Operation of the New Legislation to Replace the Cruelty to Animals Act 1876."
75 "Animals (Scientific Procedures) Act 1986," ed. HM Government (1986).

pharmaceutical agents; toxicity tests avoiding lethal endpoints; and most surgical procedures, *provided that suffering can be controlled by reliable post-operative analgesia and care.* Procedures will be regarded as being of substantial severity if they result in a major departure from the animal's usual state of health or well-being. If it were expected that a single animal would suffer substantial effects, the procedure would warrant a severity limit of 'substantial.'[76]

These features of security developed in the ASPA combined in various ways with pastoral, disciplinary and biopower relations in the government of the lives of nonhuman experimental animals.

*

EUROPE AND BREXIT: EUROPEAN GOVERNMENTALITIES AND THE BRITISH REGRESSION TO NATIONALISM, 1986–PRESENT

As stated in the introduction to this section of the book, at the time of writing, the EU Directive 2010/63 frames the contemporary legal obligations that animal-dependent scientists and research organisations in Britain have to abide by. What I have shown thus far is that pressure to renew the 1876 Act that came from a variety of forces, both internal and external to the UK. Internally, from the likes of animal welfare bodies such as CRAE and the RSPCA; externally via the CoE and the EU. Britain has been a member of the EU since 1993 with the ratification of the Maastricht Treaty. Before that, a member of the European Communities (EC) since a referendum in 1973.[77]

The EU is made up of 28 Member States (including Britain); it is a union based on political and economic cooperation, which functions primarily under a neoliberal agenda.[78] Its political bodies include the European Court of Justice, Council of the European Union and the European Parliament. The EU has enabled freedom of movement of goods, services and people via their internal single market, in order to promote trade and economic affluence amongst its Member States.[79] On the other hand, the CoE is a separate organisation from the EU and was founded in 1949 to help rebuild Europe after the atrocities of the Second World War. It created the European Convention on Human Rights and helped to create the European

---

76 Home Office, "Guidance on the Operation of the New Legislation to Replace the Cruelty to Animals Act 1876." My italics.
77 Steven McCulloch, "Brexit and Animal Protection: Legal and Political Context and a Framework to Assess Impacts on Animal Welfare," *Animals* 8, no. 11 (2018).
78 Dermot Hodson, John Peterson, ed., *Institutions of the European Union*, 4th ed. (Oxford: Oxford University Press, 2017).
79 Ibid.

Economic Community (EEC) in 1957. Former British Prime Minister Winston Churchill was one of a group of six men who created the Council. Countries who join the EU usually become a member of the CoE first.[80]

In 1986, the CoE's Treaty Series 123 was transposed with very few additions into Directive EEC 86/609.[81] With the bringing into operation of the ASPA in 1986, this enabled Britain to ratify the CoE's 'Convention for the Protection of Vertebrate Animals Used for Experimental and Other Scientific Purposes,' as well as implement the legally binding EEC Directive.[82] The main aim of the Directive was to:

> Ensure that where animals are used for experimental or other scientific purposes the provisions laid down by law regulation or administrative provisions of Member States for their protection are approximated so as to avoid affecting the establishment and functioning of the common market, in particular by distortions of competition or barriers to trade.[83]

The impetus behind the Directive was economic, with an emphasis on the harmonisation of legislation concerning animal experiments across the Member States. This is no surprise, as the founding of the EEC in 1957 under the Treaty of Rome was premised on the dissolution of monetary barriers between member countries in order to allow for free trade.[84]

As we saw in the ASPA, the government wanted to protect British industry, especially the pharmaceutical companies. Consequently, in order to allow for the continuation of animal experimentation, scientists had to be seen to be concerned about their welfare. Economics, animals as objects of property and their welfare are intrinsically linked. For instance, in *Annex II: Guidelines for Accommodation and Care of Animals* nonhuman animals' freedom of movement comes second to the human entitlement to use:

> ...The great majority of animals used in experiments must for practical reasons be kept under some sort of physical control in facilities ranging

---

80 Council of Europe, "Council of Europe: Our History," https://www.coe.int/en/web/about-us/founding-fathers.
81 House of Lords, "The Revision of the Eu Directive on the Protection of Animals Used for Scientific Purposes," https://publications.parliament.uk/pa/ld200809/ldselect/ldeucom/164/16402.htm.
82 Well: SA/PHY/G/1/62: Box 100, Animals (Scientific Procedures) Act: Liaison with MPs and Lords over final stages of Bill. Home Office News Release: Animals (Scientific Procedures) Bill Published. 15 November 1985. p. 2.
83 Council of the European Council of the European Union, "Council Directive of 24 November 1986 on the Approximation of Laws, Regulations and Administrative Provisons of the Member States Regarding the Protection of Animals Used for Experimental and Other Scientific Purposes" (1986). p. 1.
84 Mike Radford, *Animal Welfare Law in Britain: Regulation and Responsibility* (Oxford: Oxford University Press, 2001). pp. 141–142.

from outdoor corrals to cages for small animals in a laboratory animal house. This is a situation where there are highly conflicting interests. On the one hand, the animal whose needs in respect of movement, social relations and other manifestations of life must be restricted, on the other hand, the experimenter and his assistants who demand full control of the animal and its environment. *In this confrontation of interests the animal may sometimes be given secondary consideration.*[85]

The language used to describe this particular human–animal relation is one of human 'control' over the nonhuman animal and their ability to express their subjective state. Although the wording depicts a contradiction between animal wellbeing and the confines of laboratory life, the human still prevails. With an indication that '*sometimes*' the animal will be given secondary consideration, in reality, there is a restriction on laboratory animals' entire lives. Consequently, human domination is *a priori* to any notion of 'freedom' permitted for nonhumans by the Directive:

> Care is a word which, when used in connection with animals intended for use in experiments covers all aspects of the relationship between animals and man. Its substance is the sum of material and non-material resources mobilized by man *to obtain and maintain an animal in a physical and mental state where it suffers least and performs best in experiments.* It starts from the moment the animal is destined to be used in experiments and continues until it is killed by a humane method or otherwise disposed of by the establishment... after the close of the experiment.[86]

The idea of care is to enable the laboratory animal to be physically and mentally well enough to promote more valid experiments. That is until they are killed or 'disposed of' when they have fulfilled the objectives of the research. Care is a way to control nonhuman animals, while simultaneously producing research that would benefit human health, and help in the development and manufacture of goods and substances.[87] Thus, welfare renders visible the economic aims and goals of the Directive. It also demonstrates how nonhuman governmentalities exist to mediate between animals' status as objects of property and their economic use-value. Nonhuman animals are still objects of property by the very fact they are at the behest of the laboratory worker. By law, the research organisation *owns* the animals; *animals*

---

85 Council of the European Union, "Council Directive of 24 November 1986 on the Approximation of Laws, Regulations and Administrative Provisons of the Member States Regarding the Protection of Animals Used for Experimental and Other Scientific Purposes." Annex II, Introduction No. 2. p. 7. (My italics.)
86 Ibid. No. 5. p. 7. (My italics.)
87 Ibid. Article 3. p. 2.

do not own themselves.[88] Nonhuman animals are commodities to be bought, sold (supplied and bred) on the market; hence, they are objects of property. Directive 86/609 hoped that this kind of animal experimentation regulation could be synchronised throughout the EU in order to enhance its economic competitiveness in a globalised world.

Twenty-two years later in November 2008, with labour in power, under the leadership of Prime Minister Tony Blair,[89] the European Commission published a proposal outlining necessary changes to EEC Directive 86/609.[90] It highlighted the following objectives: First, to strengthen the protection of animals used in scientific procedures. Second, to promote the 3R's. Third, to ensure practices are implemented consistently across member states.[91] The main concern of the European Commission was the considered failure of its attempt to consistently apply the 1986 Directive across all Member States. It was hoped that a review of the existing law would 'bring about a level playing field across the EU for companies and institutions carrying out research.'[92]

The main changes agreed upon are numerous but included extending the scope of 'protected animals' in the Directive to include certain classes of live invertebrates and a ban on the use of the Great Apes in research. In terms of the practice of experiments, a mandatory pre-authorisation of individuals, projects and places is required (similar to ASPA's licensing system). The implementation of a robust inspection system across the EU, and a requirement that each establishment promotes the 3Rs and establishes a permanent Ethical Review Body (ERB) to advice on animal welfare is also required.[93] In the new Directive and subsequent ASPA amendments, explicit reference is made to the 3Rs (see Chapters 4 and 5 for further information about the 3Rs), thus making it a statutory requirement. The definition of a 'regulated procedure' was also extended:

> Subject to the provision of this section, 'a regulated procedure' for the purposes of this Act means any procedure applied to a protected animal for a qualifying purpose which may have the effect of causing the animal a level of pain, suffering, distress or lasting harm equivalent to, or higher than, that caused by the introduction of a needle in accordance with good veterinary practice.[94]

---

88 Kimberly Smith, *Governing Animals: Animal Welfare and the Liberal State* (Oxford; New York: Oxford University Press, 2012). pp. 70–73.
89 Clarke, *Hope and Glory: Britain 1900–2000*.
90 House of Lords, "The Revision of the Eu Directive on the Protection of Animals Used for Scientific Purposes."
91 Ibid.
92 Ibid. p. 5.
93 Ibid. pp. 8–9.
94 HM Government, "Changes over Time For: Animals (Scientific Procedures) Act 1986," https://www.legislation.gov.uk/ukpga/1986/14/2013-01-01.

Supplementing this expansion of a 'regulated procedure' was the new severity classification. The European Commission's working group submitted the new classificatory schema. It now ranged from 'non-recovery' to 'mild,' 'moderate' and 'severe' classifications of pain, distress and lasting harm.[95] These new classifications are analogous to the ones detailed in the *Guidelines* accompanying ASPA.[96] Other considerations added to the ASPA included: specified minimum requirements for the care and accommodation of laboratory animals, humane killing techniques (although already present in Schedule 1 of ASPA[97]) and provision for the research with and care of genetically modified animals.[98] For Britain, the 1986 Act already encapsulated most of these changes suggested by the European Commission.[99] Instead, the Brits wanted to push for greater harmonisation across EU Member States.[100] All-in-all, the British government were supportive of the amendments to Directive 86/609, and the revised 1986 Act came into force on 1 January 2013.[101]

The revised Act still encapsulated the Pain Conditions in the statutory requirements for licensing, rather than making it a legal requirement *per se*. For instance, when deciding on granting a licence, Section 2C (2) of the ASPA states 'The Secretary of State may grant a licence under this section only if satisfied that the person who is to be the holder and the place that is to be specified are in compliance with the requirements of the Animals Directive [Directive 2010/63].'[102] Reference is made to the updated Directive. This stipulates the need for the applicant to abide by the conditions relating to animal care and welfare. They have to demonstrate that they have used the severity classifications to pre-assess the likelihood of the animal/s being used to experience pain, suffering distress and lasting harm. Then the Secretary of State is required to evaluate the programme of work concerning the applicants' qualifications, experience and 'expertise in animal husbandry and care...' (Section 5B (4) (d)).[103]

---

95 Lords, "The Revision of the Eu Directive on the Protection of Animals Used for Scientific Purposes." pp. 12–13.
96 Home Office, "Guidance on the Operation of the New Legislation to Replace the Cruelty to Animals Act 1876."
97 "Animals (Scientific Procedures) Act 1986."
98 Government, "Changes over Time For: Animals (Scientific Procedures) Act 1986."
99 Lords, "The Revision of the Eu Directive on the Protection of Animals Used for Scientific Purposes." p. 9.
100 House of Commons, "Sixth Delegated Legislation Committee: Draft Animals (Scientific Procedures) Act 1986 Amendment Regulations 2012," (London: House of Commons, 2012). p. 4.
101 HM Government, "Changes over Time For: Animals (Scientific Procedures) Act 1986." [accessed 13/08/19].
102 Ibid.
103 Ibid.

It could be argued that this increase in moral concern and ethical extension afforded to nonhuman animals in experiment means that EU regulation and UK law have advanced beyond human egotism and utilitarian considerations of nonhumans' use-value,[104] as well as going beyond the definition of property and legal welfarism espoused by Francione at the beginning of this section. However, what this new moral position signifies is not animal equality but rather one still of human dominance. Domination which is based on hierarchy and difference, and continues to render nonhuman laboratory animals as objects of property.[105] As noted earlier, 'protected' animals, and consequently, those who are considered sentient and have some 'moral worth,' only include vertebrates and *some* invertebrates. This produces what sociologist Kay Peggs calls a 'hierarchy of moral worth,' which delimits those considered to be morally protected and those who are not.[106]

This hierarchy of 'moral worth' is fundamentally human-centric and centred around language and discourse. Wadiwel identifies the link between language, human domination and nonhumans' property status.[107] He claims that language is inherently political as it establishes a separation between humans and animals in order to 'immunise' (protect) the *idea* of the human from the threat of the 'Other'(animal).[108] This 'immunity' offered by human domination[109] emerges through hierarchical differentiation.[110] It is through this naturalisation of hierarchy between the species that ties animal–human relations to notions of property. Nonhuman lab animals are decreed as sentient (living and feeling beings), but are still conceptualised through their use-value and economic worth. Hence, they are still objects to be owned and manipulated:

> While it is desirable to replace the use of live animals in procedures by other methods not entailing the use of live animals, *the use of live animals continues to be necessary to protect human and animal health and the environment.*[111]

---

104 Kay Peggs, "Nonhuman Animal Experiments in the European Community: Human Values and Rational Choice," *Society and Animals* 18, no. 1 (2010): 2.
105 Ibid. p. 7; Wadiwel, *The War against Animals*.
106 Peggs, "Nonhuman Animal Experiments in the European Community: Human Values and Rational Choice." p. 7.
107 Wadiwel, *The War against Animals*.
108 Ibid. p. 131.
109 Wadiwel's use of Foucault also extends to him using a range of Foucauldian inspired scholars to address the issue of human sovereignty of nonhuman animals. This includes the work of Roberto Esposito (2008) in terms of the notion of 'immunity.'
110 Wadiwel, *The War against Animals*. pp. 132, 134.
111 Council of the European Council of the European Union, "Directive 2010/63/EU of the European Parliament and of the Council of 22 September 2010 on the Protection of Animals Used for Scientific Purposes," *Official Journal of the European Union* (2010): 34. Emphasis added by author.

While Directive 2010/63 states that it would be good to replace animals in experiment with alternatives, it claims that there is still a strong need for the use of animals. This necessity for animal use in scientific procedures is deemed essential in order to protect human, animal and environmental health. Human health is placed first on the list, indicating hierarchised differentiation and human exceptionalism. Nonhumans' use-value overrides their acknowledged sentience.

With nonhuman animals' use-value taking priority over their self-worth, it is clear that the economic imperative of animal experiments takes precedence. In Directive 2010/63, the main aim is not to protect nonhuman laboratory animals but to harmonise regulations across the EU. Otherwise, the disparities in laws and regulations would be:

> Liable to constitute barriers to trade in products and substances the development of which involves experiments on animals. Accordingly, this Directive should provide for more detailed rules in order to reduce such disparities by approximating the rules applicable in that area and *to ensure a proper functioning of the internal market.*[112]

Economic priorities outweigh the consideration of the use of nonhuman animals. The hope of Directive 2010/63 is to achieve a 'level playing field' across Member States, in order to make the trading of goods and services more accessible. These economic imperatives undermine the sentience of nonhuman animals, as Recital 7 states:

> Attitudes towards animals also depend on national perceptions, and there is a demand in certain Member States to maintain more extensive animal-welfare rules than those agreed upon at the level of the Union. In the interests of the animals, *and provided it does not affect the functioning of the internal market,* it is appropriate to allow the Member States certain flexibility to maintain national rules aimed at more extensive protection of animals...[113]

Member States can apply stricter rules to the protection of laboratory animals, but only if this does not disrupt the functioning of the internal market. If the welfare of nonhuman laboratory animals is emphasised over and above that of the economic benefits, then this would be detrimental to the EU's aim of strengthening the single market.[114] Welfare is secondary but intrinsically tied to the neoliberal economic system and animals' use-value.

---

112 Council of the European ibid. Recital 1, p. 33. My emphasis.
113 Ibid. My emphasis.
114 Peggs, "Nonhuman Animal Experiments in the European Community: Human Values and Rational Choice." p. 12.

Nonhuman laboratory animals may have been granted the status of sentience and their entitlement to care increased under contemporary law. However, they are still objectified via this inclusion into the legal realms of the living. What we have here is exclusion *within* this legal attribution of inclusion.[115] This is characterised by species-specific hierarchical distinctions embedded in the Directives' conceptualisation of 'protected animal.' This in turn, links to the argument of continued use that places nonhuman use-value above their sentience.

Then, Brexit happened...

On 23 June 2016, a referendum was held under the instruction of Conservative Prime Minister David Cameron. The British people were asked to decide whether or not they wanted to remain in the EU. Due to pressures from within his party and with the rise in popularity of the nationalistic political party the UK Independence Party (UKIP), Cameron decided to implement his in/out referendum. The vote was a close one, with the electorate voting having a 51.9 per cent majority to leave the EU.[116]

The success of the Leave campaign to secure a victory is a testimony to a growing nationalistic discourse currently permeating a lot of the Western world. Brexit was framed as a defence of 'British' identity. This nationalist rhetoric mobilised people to vote Leave and was due to a combination of coincidental factors: the support of the right-wing press, discontent with austerity measures imposed by government, a mass refugee crisis in Europe and the power of social media, such as Facebook, in shaping peoples' views.[117] However, what implications are there of leaving the EU on the current legal regulation of animal experiments? How does the rise in British Nationalism extend to the protection (or not) of nonhuman animals? These questions may be too broad and have too many unknown answers at the moment. However, debates in Parliament have already occurred concerning the EU's denotation of animals as sentient beings and how Brexit will impact the law in this respect.

As we have seen, EU regulation, alongside the CoE, has had a significant influence on shaping British animal experimentation law, in particular, the ASPA. Similarly, Britain has played a major role in shaping the aims and goals of European legislation concerning animal welfare and

---

115 Mark Rowlands, *Animals Like Us* (London: Verso, 2002).p. 27. Rowlands aptly describes the welfare of nonhuman animals as being viewed as having some moral worth but only as 'second class members of the moral club.'
116 Edward Best; Thomas Christiansen, "Regionalism in International Affairs," in *The Globalisation of World Politics: An Introduction to International Relations*, ed. John Baylis, Steve Smith, Patricia Owens (Oxford: Oxford University Press, 2017). p. 377.
117 John Breuilly, "Nationalism, National Self-Determination, and International Relations," ibid. p. 446.

experimentation.[118] Directive 2010/63 evidences this. Very few amendments had to be made to the ASPA, as they were already embodied in the law. Incidentally, Britain was a significant force in lobbying the EU to recognise that animals are sentient beings. This recognition of sentience became effective in 2009, in the guise of Article 13 of the Lisbon Treaty, which is part of the Treaty on the Functioning of the EU (TFEU).[119] It states:

> In formulating and implementing the Union's agriculture, fisheries, transport, internal market, research and technological development and space policies, the Union and the Member States shall, since animals are sentient beings, pay full regard to the welfare requirements of animals, while respecting the legislative or administrative provisions and customs of the EU countries relating in particular to religious rites, cultural traditions and regional heritage.[120]

This decrees Member States to recognise animals as sentient beings and to fully incorporate welfare measures when formulating and implementing new policies and legislations.[121] EU law means that welfare is seen as being central to the use of nonhuman animals in practices such as farming, transport, research and food. However, the use of animals is still permissible. They are still seen as 'goods' to be traded on the internal market, as well as being used for experiments whereby they can suffer physical and psychological pain.

In November 2017, questions of animal sentience caused a furore amongst the public, press and politicians.[122] The controversy was centred around the European Union (Withdrawal) Bill's failure to incorporate Article 13. In 2018, the Bill was passed through both Houses of Parliament to become an Act. It stipulates that after Britain's official exit day on 31 October 2019, all EU legislation will immediately be 'part of domestic law on and after Brexit day.'[123] Thus, Article 13's absence was immediately noticed by The Green Party's only MP, Caroline Lucas. She tabled a notion to ensure that Article 13 was carried through into British law after Brexit. Lucas was subsequently voted down by the Conservative Government, but their position on animal sentience was reported widely in the media.[124]

---

118 McCulloch, "Brexit and Animal Protection: Legal and Political Context and a Framework to Assess Impacts on Animal Welfare." p. 2.
119 Animal-Law, "Brexit, Article 13, and the Debate on Recognising "Animal Sentience" in Law," in *A-Law expert legal briefing note* (The UK Centre for Animal Law, 2017). p. 3.
120 European Commission, "Animal Welfare," https://ec.europa.eu/food/animals/welfare_en.
121 Donald Broom, "Animal Welfare in the European Union," (Brussels: European Parliament, 2017).
122 Alasdair Cochrane, *Sentientist Politics: A Theory of Global Inter-Species Justice* (Oxford: Oxford University Press, 2018).
123 HM Government, "European Union (Withdrawal) Act 2018," ed. UK Parliament (London: HMSO, 2018).
124 McCulloch, "Brexit and Animal Protection: Legal and Political Context and a Framework to Assess Impacts on Animal Welfare."

In response, Michael Gove, Brexiteer and then Secretary of State for Environment, Food and Rural Affairs released a Ministerial statement on the issue. He argued 'this Government is committed to the very highest standards of animal welfare. As the Prime Minister has set out, we will make the United Kingdom a world leader in the care and protection of animals,' adding 'voting against the amendment was not a vote against the idea that animals are sentient and feel pain - that is a misconception.'[125] Gove claimed that Article 13 does not go far enough to protect the welfare and animals. By leaving the EU, Gove argued that Britain would be in a better position to apply more stringent regulations concerning the interests of animals.[126] Despite several attempts at amendments to the EU Withdrawal Bill, animal sentience was voted down at every committee stage in Parliament.[127] Instead, the government responded by producing a new Bill in 2018, the *Animal Welfare (Sentencing and Recognition of Sentience) Draft Bill*.[128] This Bill aims to strengthen the Animal Welfare Act, 2006, which enforces strict anti-cruelty penalties. It came under severe criticism including from government bodies such as the Environment, Food and Rural Affairs Select Committee. Critics claimed that the notion of sentience in the Bill had been substantially watered down. In 2018, the government responded and advised that it is continuing to consult with stakeholders on its approach to sentience.[129]

However, the proposed new Bill on animal welfare would not apply to experimental animals used in scientific research. It would only apply to those instances of cruelty carried out by members of the public, not by research or other such business organisations. We can see here a stark difference between sanctioned institutional forms of violence against nonhuman animals and condemned forms of violence against animals by individual members of society. Interestingly, the types of violence affecting nonhuman animals carried out by individuals are analogous to those carried out by organisations such as research establishments. The kinds of violence used in research establishments are seen as normative practices and are protected by law.[130]

With regards to Brexit, we may have no specific answers as yet. However, we do know that EU Directive 2010/63 will still be applicable in the guise of

---

125 Michael Gove, "Environment Secretary Confirms Sentience of Animals Will Continue to Be Recognised and Protections Strengthened When We Leave the Eu," https://www.gov.uk/government/news/environment-secretary-confirms-sentience-of-animals-will-continue-to-be-recognised-and-protections-strengthened-when-we-leave-the-eu.
126 Ibid.
127 Elena Ares, "Animal Sentience and Brexit," ed. House of Commons Library (London, 2019).
128 HM Government, "Animal Welfare (Sentencing) Bill," (London, 2019). https://commonslibrary.parliament.uk/research-briefings/cbp-8612/.
129 Ares, "Animal Sentience and Brexit."
130 Gary Francione, "Animals, Property, and Personhood," in *People, Property, or Pets?*, ed. Marc Hauser, Fiery Cushman, Matthew Kamen (West Lafayette, Indiana: Purdue University Press, 2006). p. 83.

the ASPA. As previously stated, ASPA and Directive 2010/63 are mutually reinforcing and have shaped each other throughout their reviews and subsequent implementations.[131] With the Conservative Party still in power after the resignation of Theresa May and the instalment of anti-EU right-wing populist Boris Johnson as Prime Minister, one thing we can be sure about is it that neoliberalism will continue.[132] As a result, the lives of nonhuman laboratory animals may become even more precarious.

Conclusion: Nonhuman governmentalities and the link between property and sentience

This chapter has outlined the emergence of a concern for the care and treatment of individual laboratory animals in jurisprudential discourse. I have shown that this advent of 'legal welfarism' was contingent upon re-defining how nonhuman animals experience laboratory life: in their care, pain and death. The historical emergence of such legal regulation enabled contradictory and powerful discourses to emerge that at once seemed to facilitate more degrees of freedom for the lived experience of the experimental animal, while at the same time would allow for the continuation of their use in scientific research.

Key to understanding these curious and paradoxical discourses in the mid-late twentieth century was to focus on the legal discussions on animal pain carried out by intra/inter-governmental, non-governmental organisations and welfare groups in the post-World War II era. As Chapter 1 demonstrated the first indication that the welfare of laboratory animals was central to the regulation of animal experimentation came in the post-1945 review of the 1876 Cruelty to Animals Act in the guise of the Littlewood Report. This then paved the way for the legal implementation of welfare in the Animals (Scientific Procedures) Act, 1986 (ASPA).

By deploying Foucault's ideas on pastoral power and governmentality,[133] this analysis has demonstrated the evolution of contemporary animal experimentation governmentalities. The Littlewood Report's views on welfare operated as an ideological device, a precursor to the mandated welfare practices present in the ASPA. Pastoral Power in the Littlewood Report was

---

131 McCulloch, "Brexit and Animal Protection: Legal and Political Context and a Framework to Assess Impacts on Animal Welfare."
132 David Cameron resigned as Prime Minister on 24 June 2016, one day after the EU referendum. Theresa May took over as Prime Minister and promptly called a General Election. May only won the election due to her political alliance with the Northern Ireland Democratic Unionist Party (A pro-British, right-wing political party). After a tumultuous Premiership, May stood down on 7 June 2019. Boris Johnson is now Prime Minister of Britain.
133 Michel Foucault, "Omnes Et Singulatim: Toward a Critique of Political Reason," in *Power*, ed. J. D. Faubion (London: Penguin, 2002); "Governmentality," in *The Foucault Effect: Studies in Governmentality*, ed. Colin Gordon Graham Burchell, Peter Miller (Chicago: University of Chicago Press, 1991).

promulgated as a powerful *idea* in order to justify the continued exploitation of nonhuman bodies. Pastoral Power then operated as both a precursor and background to the formation and assent of the ASPA, whereby several forces coalesced to produce an 'art of governance' over nonhuman laboratory life. These forces were biopolitical, disciplinary and pastoral they 'worked' on the reproduction and confinement of nonhuman bodies.

In the context of the formation of the ASPA, pastoral power acted as the back-drop to its creation and eventually, implementation. Pastoral power became a very real material practice after the assent of the new law. However, it only functioned as one aspect of a myriad of ways of human domination of nonhuman laboratory life.

The ASPA did not merely control the operation of welfare regulation. Instead, it remade it as *the* object of its scrutiny. The system presupposed and was organised around particular conceptions of the animal as a manipulable being. The passage of the Act and the subsequent institutionalisation of a system requiring scientists to provide animal welfare precipitated a transformation in the practices of the laboratory which had existed in rhetorical form during the Littlewood Inquiry in 1965. The inauguration of the ASPA, established in 1986, served to reinscribe the historic practice of vivisection, rendering the practice a normative endeavour.

The 'project' of the ASPA was formulated within a new form of governance in the 1980s: neoliberalism. Hence, I have argued that nonhuman governmentalities are framed around one particular objective: the economic. The idea that liberal governance should not govern too much made way for the animal to become even more of an economic object to be used and disposed of at will. The variegation of animal experimentation in the era of neoliberalism is prevented via the European Union Directives 86/609 and 2010/63. These EU regulations hoped to harmonise practices across the Member States and thus promote the economical functionality of animal experimentation. As I have shown, the inscription of the word 'sentience' in Directive 2010/63 helps to facilitate the economic exploitation of animal bodies even further, rather than impede it in any way.

Sentience acts as another ideological device which serves to desubjectify nonhumans more by engendering them to more degrees of permitted suffering. Thus, making them ripe for further economic exploitation. In British law, animals are seen as objects of property rather than living beings with rights and/or moral worth.[134] In this sense, nonhuman governmentalities (welfare) mediate between nonhumans as sentient beings and as objects of property.

The next chapter will demonstrate how this idea of property and welfare is reflected in legal discourses framed around women's rights and moral worth. Nonhuman governmentalities also help to demonstrate the

---

134 Animal-Law, "Brexit, Article 13, and the Debate on Recognising 'Animal Sentience' in Law."

historical parallels between the treatment of nonhuman beings and marginalised groups of human beings who are discriminated against because of their sex, race and/or class.

Bibliography

Animal-Law. "Brexit, Article 13, and the Debate on Recognising "Animal Sentience" in Law." In *A-Law Expert Legal Briefing Note*. The UK Centre for Animal Law, 2017.
"Animals (Scientific Procedures) Act 1986." edited by HM Government, 1986.
Ares, Elena. "Animal Sentience and Brexit." edited by House of Commons Library. London, 2019.
Breuilly, John. "Nationalism, National Self-Determination, and International Relations." In *The Globalisation of World Politics: An Introduction to International Relations*, edited by John Baylis; Steve Smith, Patricia Owens. Oxford: Oxford University Press, 2017.
Broom, Donald. "Animal Welfare in the European Union." Brussels: European Parliament, 2017.
Christiansen, Edward, Best Thomas. "Regionalism in International Affairs." In *The Globalisation of World Politics: An Introduction to International Relations*, edited by John Baylis; Steve Smith; Patricia Owens. Oxford: Oxford University Press, 2017.
Clarke, Peter. *Hope and Glory: Britain 1900–2000*. 3rd ed. London: Penguin Books, 2004.
Cochrane, Alasdair. *Sentientist Politics: A Theory of Global Inter-Species Justice*. Oxford: Oxford University Press, 2018.
Cole, Matthew. "From "Animal Machines" to "Happy Meat"? Foucault's Ideas of Disciplinary and Pastoral Power Applied to 'Animal-Centred' Welfare Discourse." *Animals* 1 (2011): 83–101.
Commission, European. "Animal Welfare." https://ec.europa.eu/food/animals/welfare_en
Commons, House of. "Sixth Delegated Legislation Committee: Draft Animals (Scientific Procedures) Act 1986 Amendment Regulations 2012." London: House of Commons, 2012.
Dean, Mitchell. *Governmentality: Power and Rule in Modern Society*. London: SAGE, 1999.
Druglitrø, Tone, Kristin Asdal. "Modifying the Biopolitical Collective: The Law as Moral Technology." In *Humans, Animals and Biopolitics: The More-Than-Human Condition*, edited by Kristin Asdal, Tone Druglitrø, Steve Hinchcliffe, 66–84. Oxon: Routledge, 2017.
Europe, Council of. "Council of Europe: Our History." https://www.coe.int/en/web/about-us/founding-fathers
———. "European Convention for the Protection of Vertebrate Animals Used for Experimental and Other Scientific Purposes." In *European Treaty Series* 123, 1986.
Foucault, Michel. *The Birth of Biopolitics*. Edited by Michel Senellart, François Ewald, Allessandro Fontana, Arnold Davidson, Graham Burchell. 2nd ed. Basingstoke, UK: Palgrave Macmillan, 2010.
———. "Governmentality." In *The Foucault Effect: Studies in Governmentality*, edited by Colin Gordon Graham Burchell, Peter Miller, 87–104. Chicago: University of Chicago Press, 1991.

———. "Omnes Et Singulatim: Toward a Critique of Political Reason." In *Power*, edited by J. D. Faubion, 298–325. London: Penguin, 2002.

Francione, Gary. "Animals, Property, and Personhood." In *People, Property, or Pets?*, edited by Marc Hauser, Fiery Cushman, Matthew Kamen, 77–102. West Lafayette, Indiana: Purdue University Press, 2006.

Gordon, Colin. "Governmental Rationality: An Introduction." In *The Foucault Effect: Studies in Governmentality*, edited by Graham Burchell, Colin Gordon, Peter Miller, 1–51. Chicago: University of Chicago Press, 1991.

Gove, Michael. "Environment Secretary Confirms Sentience of Animals Will Continue to Be Recognised and Protections Strengthened When We Leave the Eu." https://www.gov.uk/government/news/environment-secretary-confirms-sentience-of-animals-will-continue-to-be-recognised-and-protections-strengthened-when-we-leave-the-eu

HM Government. "Animal Welfare (Sentencing) Bill." London, 2019.

———. "Changes over Time For: Animals (Scientific Procedures) Act 1986." https://www.legislation.gov.uk/ukpga/1986/14/2013-01-01

———. "European Union (Withdrawal) Act 2018." edited by UK Parliament. London: HMSO, 2018.

Hampson, J. E. "Law Relating to Animal Experimentation." In *Laboratory Animals: An Introduction for New Experiments*, edited by A. A. Tuffery, 21–52. New York: Chichester: Wiley, 1987

Hampson, Judith. "Legislation: A Practical Solution to the Vivisection Dilemma?" Chap. 13, In *Vivisection in Historical Perspective*, edited by Nicolaas Rupke, 314–39. London; New York; Sydney: Croom Helm, 1987.

Harvey, David. *A Brief History of Neoliberalism*. 2nd ed. Oxford: Oxford University Press, 2007.

Khazaal, Natalie; Núria Almiron. "Lobbying against Compassion: Speciesist Discourse in the Vivisection Industrial Complex." *American Behavioural Scientist* 60, no. 3 (2015): 256–75.

Littlewood, Sydney. "Report of the Departmental Committee on Experiments on Animals." edited by Home Office. London: Her Majesty's Stationary Office, 1965.

Lords, House of. "The Revision of the Eu Directive on the Protection of Animals Used for Scientific Purposes." https://publications.parliament.uk/pa/ld200809/ldselect/ldeucom/164/16402.htm

Lyons, Dan. *The Politics of Animal Experimentation*. Hampshire: Palgrave Macmillan, 2013.

McCulloch, Steven. "Brexit and Animal Protection: Legal and Political Context and a Framework to Assess Impacts on Animal Welfare." *Animals* 8, no. 11: 213 (2018).

Miller, Peter, Graham Burchell, Colin Gordon, ed. *The Foucault Effect: Studies in Governmentality: With Two Lectures by, and an Interview with, Michel Foucault*. Chicago: University of Chicago Press, 1991.

Office, Home. "Guidance on the Operation of the New Legislation to Replace the Cruelty to Animals Act 1876." HMSO, https://webarchive.nationalarchives.gov.uk/19970429190800/http://www.open.gov.uk:80/home_off/aspag.htm

Oliver, Michael. "The Retreat of the State in the 1980s and 1990s." In *20th Century Britain: Economic, Cultural and Social Change*, edited by Francesca Carnevali, Julie-Marie Strange. Harlow: Pearson Education Ltd., 2007.

Peggs, Kay. "Nonhuman Animal Experiments in the European Community: Human Values and Rational Choice." *Society and Animals* 18, no. 1 (2010): 1–20.

Peterson, John, Dermot Hodson, ed. *Institutions of the European Union*. 4th ed. Oxford: Oxford University Press, 2017.

Radford, Mike. *Animal Welfare Law in Britain: Regulation and Responsibility*. Oxford: Oxford University Press, 2001.

Rowlands, Mark. *Animals Like Us*. London: Verso, 2002.

Smith, Kimberly. *Governing Animals: Animal Welfare and the Liberal State*. Oxford; New York: Oxford University Press, 2012.

Union, Council of the European. "Council Directive of 24 November 1986 on the Approximation of Laws, Regulations and Administrative Provisons of the Member States Regarding the Protection of Animals Used for Experimental and Other Scientific Purposes." 1986.

———. "Directive 2010/63/EU of the European Parliament and of the Council of 22 September 2010 on the Protection of Animals Used for Scientific Purposes." *Official Journal of the European Union* (2010).

Wadiwel, Dinesh Joseph. *The War against Animals*. Leiden & Boston: Brill Rodopi, 2015.

3 The power–pain nexus

How women's subjugation subtends speciesism in the legal system

In 1948, the Universal Declaration of Human Rights defined what it meant to be human, stating that 'recognition of the inherent dignity and of the equal and inalienable rights of all members of the human family is the foundation of freedom, justice and peace in the world.'[1] Yet, for many feminist scholars, the main grounds for contention regarding this definition is the fact that the notion of personhood excludes women.[2] This international legalisation of women's rights also includes the Convention on the Elimination of All Forms of Discrimination Against Women of 1979 (CEDAW), a comprehensive piece of international law ratified by 75 countries during the World Conference of the U.N. Decade for Women in Copenhagen, 14–31 July 1980.[3] With this Convention, the preamble affirms the notion of personhood stated in the U.N. Declaration of Human Rights (UNDHR). Still, it adds that 'extensive discrimination against women continues to exist,' and emphasises that 'such discrimination violates the principles of equality of rights and respect for human dignity.'[4]

Yet, as I write this chapter, we are amidst the worst global pandemic since the Spanish Flu of the early twentieth century. Governments worldwide have implemented national lockdowns, restricted our movements locally, nationally and globally, and implemented new bio-surveillance measures beyond anything we could have imagined in previous years. The virus causing such international tumult is COVID-19, zoonotic in origin and a variant of the SARS virus. It's a disease that engulfs the human body and places it

---

1 United Nations, "A Universal Declaration of Human Rights General Assembly Resolution 217 A," https://www.un.org/en/ga/search/view_doc.asp?symbol=A/RES/217(III).
2 Roberto Guerrini, Marysia Zalewski, "Negotiating Difference/Negotiating Rights: The Challenges and Opportunities of Women's Human Rights," *Review of International Studies* 33 (2007): 5–10; Catharine MacKinnon, *Are Women Human? And Other International Dialogues* (Cambridge, Massachusetts & London, England: Harvard University Press, 2006).
3 Catherine Tinker, "Human Rights for Women: The U.N. Convention on the Elimination of All Forms of Discrimination against Women," *Human Rights Quarterly* 3, no. 2 (1981): 32.
4 United Nations Women, "Convention on the Elimination of All Forms of Discrimination against Women," https://www.un.org/womenwatch/daw/cedaw/text/econvention.htm#intro.

DOI: 10.4324/9780429461644-4

in a state of shock, causing it to experience flu-like symptoms that restrict breathing and can lead to death.[5] As a result of the national lockdowns, women are suffering from the worst of this plague of pestilence. This is not in terms of infection, but, instead, in terms of the pain experienced at their partners' hands.[6] In Britain, phone calls to the National Domestic Abuse helpline have skyrocketed during the first lockdown instigated in March 2020,[7] and in response, the government's parliamentary select committee published a report on domestic abuse and risk of harm to women and girls since the advent of COVID-19.[8] This begs the question, then, why women are still treated as less than human? This is despite the UNDHR of which Britain became a signatory in 1950, which boldly declares 'everyone is entitled to all the rights and freedoms outlined in this Declaration, without distinction of any kind, such as race, colour, sex, language, religion, political or other opinion, national or social origin, property, birth or other status,' confirming in Article 5 that 'No one shall be subjected to torture or to cruel, inhuman or degrading treatment or punishment.'[9] So why is this happening to women?

Now here is the shocker: women are still *not* human in law. Sexism and violence towards women subtend speciesism, which becomes most evident when we analyse the discourses of law concerning the notion of Rights, personhood and property status. As we have seen, the historical formation of the law relating to animal experiments is decidedly politically motivated rather than ethical and moral praxis. The central debates surrounding the relevance of the law for contemporary scientific practice revolves around the idea of animal pain and suffering. Enshrined in law is the notion that nonhuman animals are objects, bound by property ownership's legalities. This final chapter of the section advances the idea of nonhumans in law as parallel to discourses about women as represented in British jurisprudence's legal structures. I will be arguing in this section that both animals and women are

---

5 Steve Matthewman; Kate Huppatz, "A Sociology of Covid-19." *Journal of Sociology* 56, no. 4 (2020): 675–683.
6 I am aware that I am situating women in this regard as being in heterosexual relationships, with men being the main domestic abuse perpetrators. However, gender-based violence across all sexes is on the increase; the violence committed is still predominantly by men's hands towards women in heterosexual partnerships. See: Gwen Hunnicutt, *Gender Violence in Ecofeminist Perspective: Intersections of Animal Oppression, Patriarchy and Domination of the Earth* (Abingdon & New York: Routledge, 2020).
7 Refuge, "Refuge Responds to Reports of Potential Increase in Domestic Abuse During Covid-19," https://www.refuge.org.uk/refuge-responds-to-reports-of-potential-increase-in-domestic-abuse-during-covid-19/.
8 U.K. Parliamentary Select Committee Publications, "Home Office Preparedness for Covid-19 (Coronavirus): Domestic Abuse and Risks of Harm within the Home," https://publications.parliament.uk/pa/cm5801/cmselect/cmhaff/321/32105.htm.
9 United Nations, "A Universal Declaration of Human Rights General Assembly Resolution 217 A."

entangled in what Kimberlé Crenshaw calls 'intersectional oppression[s].'[10] This means the binding together of several systems of subjection,[11] in this case, the structural interrelationship between animals and women through the confines of legal discourses, and policies that are not directly associated with either agent. Crenshaw asserts that 'what distinguishes this intersectional problem [from others] is that the policy in question is not in any way targeted toward women... it simply intersects with other structures to create a subordinating effect.'[12] In this sense, we can argue that the legal systems in place are very much organised and based on principles of hierarchy that subordinate some groups to others, namely, animals over humans. In this instance, we can return to my earlier refrain and confidently say that *women are not human in the eyes of the law.*

One of the contradictions in the UNDHR is the idea of the right to non-interference in the private sphere. Article 12 states, 'no one shall be subjected to arbitrary interference with his privacy, family, home or correspondence, nor to attacks upon his honour and reputation...'[13] As many feminists have documented over the decades, it is the private sphere that remains firmly within the feminine realm.[14] Women's legal dehumanisation also extends beyond the private sphere to their position in public life, in employment and reproductive rights. In other words, I am arguing that nonhuman bodies share their legal position with that of the female bodies in contemporary society, and this is historically contingent. As Catharine MacKinnon, a prominent feminist legal scholar, argues, 'the legal system's response to animals is gendered, highlighting its response to women's inequality to men as well.'[15] This is because of the socially structured binaries that manifest as hierarchies in particular societies at particular points in time. MacKinnon explains these social hierarchies as divided into the binaries of animate–inanimate, human–animal and male–female divisions.[16] Where, you guessed it, women and animals are firmly entrenched on the underside of this binary. This too echoes the discussions in the forthcoming chapters regarding the philosophies and methodologies of science: is the problem then, not necessarily men *per se*, but rather the ubiquity of an

---

10 Kimberlé Crenshaw, "The Structural and Political Dimensions of Intersectional Oppression," ed. Patrick R Grzanka (Colorado: Westview Press, 2014). pp. 16–22.
11 Ibid. p. 17.
12 Ibid. p. 21.
13 United Nations, "A Universal Declaration of Human Rights General Assembly Resolution 217 A."
14 Adrienne Rich, *Of Woman Born - Motherhood as Experience and Institution*, Reissue ed. (London & New York: W.W.Norton & Company, 1996); Betty Friedan, *The Feminine Mystique*, 2nd ed. (London: Penguin, 2010).
15 Catharine MacKinnon, "Of Mice and Men: A Feminist Fragment on Animal Rights," in *Women's Lives, Men's Laws*, ed. Catharine MacKinnon (Boston MA: Harvard University Press, 2007). p. 163.
16 Ibid.

ideology that stems from paternalistic thinking and socially constructed gender hierarchies?

Women, animals and legal rights

It is no coincidence that women historically dominated the antivivisection movement. It emerged at the same time as the suffragette movement in the nineteenth century.[17] As Mary Ann Elston has demonstrated, the nineteenth century also saw a conflation of women's bodies with images and representations of nature and animals in medical and popular cultural narratives.[18] The idea of what is seen as 'natural' shapes a particular society's views on who is deemed a subject in their own right, and who is not.[19] This then links to the law and legal rights: the person in law who is deemed 'rights-bearing' rests upon a historically contingent *liberal* theory (private property ownership) of legal philosophy still present in the practice of law in the Western world today. It creates a distinction between the objects of knowledge (non-rights bearers) and the inquirers or subjects (rights bearers).[20] This kind of legal doctrine holds that animals have no inherent rights or interests or none that supersede human ones.[21] Therefore, nonhumans have become classified as property and as having object status.

This too parallels the objectification of women as represented in law.[22] Historically, women were seen as ownable property and non-rights bearers.[23] In 1929, by the Privy Council order, a select group of senior political advisors to the Monarch enacted a law to allow women to become persons in their own right.[24] However, despite women's personhood status, there is a

---

17 Hilda Kean, *Animal Rights: Political and Social Change in Britain since 1800* (London, UK: Reaktion Books Ltd, 1998); Harriet Ritvo, *The Animal Estate: English and Other Creatures in the Victorian Age* (London, UK: Penguin Books Ltd, 1990); Joanna Bourke, *What It Means to Be Human: Reflections from 1791 to Present* (London, UK: Virago Press, 2011); Diana Donald, *Women against Cruelty: Protection of Animals in Nineteenth-Century Britain* (Manchester: Manchester University Press, 2020).
18 Mary Ann Elston, "Women and Anti-Vivisection in Victorian England, 1870–1900," in *Vivisection in Historical Perspective*, ed. Nicolaas Rupke (London and New York: Routledge, 1990). pp. 259–294. See also: Ludmilla Jordanova, *Sexual Visions: Images of Gender in Science and Medicine between the Eighteenth and Twentieth Centuries* (Wisconsin: The University of Wisconsin Press, 1989). Londa Schiebinger, *Nature's Body: Gender in the Making of Modern Science* (Boston, MA: Beacon Press Books, 1993).
19 Judith E. Grbich, "The Body in Legal Theory," in *At the Boundaries of Law: Feminism and Legal Theory*, ed. Martha Albertson Fineman, Nancy Sweet Thomadsen (London and New York: Routledge, 1991). p. 62.
20 Ibid. p. 63.
21 Gary L. Francione, *Animals, Property and the Law*, 2nd ed. (Philadelphia: Temple University Press, 2007). p. 46.
22 Grbich, "The Body in Legal Theory." p. 69.
23 Lisa Johnson, *Power, Knowledge, Animals* (Basingstoke: Palgrave Macmillan, 2012). p. 131.
24 http://www.mmu.ac.uk/equality-and-diversity/doc/gender-equality-timeline.pdf, "The Women's Timeline." https://www.mmu.ac.uk/business-school/research/research-centres/vote100/history/ [accessed: 01/05/16].

host of complex and often contradictory (legal) doctrines which affect women's lives and parallelly those of nonhuman animals in scientific research.[25] This begs the question: are women seen as not fully human, but rather as active objects? MacKinnon noted: 'Women's suffering, particularly in sexual forms, has not delivered us full human status. It has gotten us more suffering.' This suffering or pain women bear is stigmatised and historically been attributed to the underside of the dualistic divide of mind and body.[26]

Feminist socio-legal scholar Wendy Brown concurs (to some extent) with MacKinnon and argues that late modernity and its political organisations keep people suspended in a permanent state of injury. Under the guise of the terms 'freedom,' 'rights' and 'equality' that women have 'acquired' in the modern era, Brown argues that this extension of civil liberties legitimises further exploitation of those lower in the social hierarchy.[27] For Brown, it provides 'mirror reversals of suffering without transforming the organisation of the activity through which suffering is produced and without addressing the subject constitution that domination effects,'[28] with the constitution being the social differentials of women, people of colour and, I would add, animals. Consequently, this notion of 'liberal freedom' prescribed by the legal system fits an economic order suited to creating polarised opposites: property ownership and personhood status for a few and abject marginalisation for others.[29]

So, what is pain? Pain is said to be a physical, psychological and sensory experience. It is a powerful phenomenological state that is heavily emotional.[30] Experiences of pain are always subjective and difficult to objectively assess. Yet, in the case of laboratory animal scientists, pain suffered in nonhuman animals is primarily attributed to the physical and any emotional state is directly attributed to this physiological component.[31] For women, the government has only recently acknowledged that abuse (and therefore the experience of pain and suffering) could take on an affective element. With the introduction of the Domestic Abuse Bill in 2020 (of which it is soon to become law), the British government has altered its statutory definition of gender-based violence. This includes the psychological aspects of pain: 'domestic abuse is not just physical violence, but can also be emotional, coercive or controlling, and economic abuse.'[32]

---

25 Elizabeth Wilson, *Only Halfway to Paradise Women in Postwar Britain: 1945–1968* (London: Tavistock Publications Ltd, 1980). p. 3.
26 MacKinnon, "Of Mice and Men: A Feminist Fragment on Animal Rights." p. 171.
27 Wendy Brown, *States of Injury: Power and Freedom in Late Modernity* (Princeton, NJ: Princeton University Press, 1995). p. 20.
28 Ibid. P. 7.
29 Ibid.
30 Lori Gruen, *Ethics and Animals: An Introduction* (Cambridge, UK: Cambridge University Press, 2018). p. 114.
31 Ibid.
32 Home Office, "Domestic Abuse Bill 2020: Overarching Factsheet," https://www.gov.uk/government/publications/domestic-abuse-bill-2020-factsheets/domestic-abuse-bill-2020-overarching-factsheet.

Capitalism in late modernity profits from suffering, no more so than the suffering of women and animals. Animals, women and people of colour assume the state of exception posited by Agamben. We become part of the juridical order of law and society. Thus, our status becomes accepted as the norm – 'the norm becomes indistinguishable from the exception' – and yet, we are still being beaten, harassed, sexually abused and killed by men.[33] The U.K.'s leading organisation, The Femicide Census illustrates this irreducible state of exception with their latest research on women being killed by men in the U.K. (2009–2018). Over the last ten years, women killed by men have not decreased but instead kept at a steady state, with between 124 and 168 femicides occurring each year.[34]

This normative state of exception for women results in the law being cast as an arbiter of truth, and it is projected as being neutral, objective and well-meaning. Thus, the effort to legislate against gender-based violence at the same time legitimises a system that codifies women as being in a perpetual state of suffering and needing protection.[35] While providing little funding to specialist services in the women's sector, inadequate charging of men for their crimes by the Crown Prosecution Service, the inconsistency of sentencing with perpetrators being sentenced is from as little as 23–44 months and an inadequate probation service resulting in offenders killing again.[36] Additionally, this castigates individual violence but does nothing to address the dominating tendencies of the liberal state, it seeks 'not power or emancipation for the injured or the subordinated, but the revenge of punishment, making the perpetrator hurt as the sufferer does.'[37]

I am not saying that any forms of anti-discrimination law and legal resolutions to tackle gender-based violence are worthless. Instead, they can act as a distraction from deeply rooted structural levels of violence in a given society, rendering women and animals suffering as interpersonal, individual and reduced to atomised punishments. We are still talking about women's rights, and legal standing signifies the 'Otherness' of being designated female. When the Domestic Abuse Bill 2020 becomes law next year, gender-based violence will be prohibited.[38] Yet, how can domestic abuse have escaped legislation after all these years? Granted, legislation has been implemented to tackle sex discrimination in Britain over the last 100 years[39];

---

33 Giorgio Agamben, *Homo Sacer: Sovereign Power and Bare Life* (Stanford: Stanford University Press, 1998). p. 170.
34 Dr Julia Long, Emily Wertans, Keshia Harper, Deirdre Brennan, Heather Harvey, Rosie Allen, Katie Elliott, "'If I'm Not in Friday, I Might Be Dead' Uk Femicides 2009–2018," femicidecensus.org
35 Brown, *States of Injury: Power and Freedom in Late Modernity*. p. 27.
36 Elliott, "'If I'm Not in Friday, I Might Be Dead' Uk Femicides 2009-2018."
37 Brown, *States of Injury: Power and Freedom in Late Modernity*. p. 27.
38 Office, "Domestic Abuse Bill 2020: Overarching Factsheet."
39 Rosemary Auchmuty, Erika Rackley, "The Women's Legal Landmarks Project: Celebrating 100 Years of Women in the Law in the Uk and Ireland," *Legal Information Management* 16, no. 1 (2016): 31.

80 *Law, animal welfare and gender*

however, in the social sphere, abuse towards women continues. No law has writ large the definition of personhood and what entitlements that decrees – injurious or otherwise.[40]

As we have seen, many laws prohibit cruelty to experimental animals, and there are a few that prevent cruelty to women. As will be recalled, the government expanded the objectification of pain in the nonhuman in the Animals (Scientific Procedures) Act, 1986 to include signs of stress and distress. I argued that with its objectification through these criteria, the very experience of pain is demolished by its discursive formation as espoused by legal and scientific representatives. This too echoes the law concerning women. For instance, the Equality Act 2010 defines sex as the male/female binary. A person's legal sex is this what they were assigned at birth. The Equality Act 2010 protects a person from discrimination according to their sex or gender identity.[41] Although these prohibit behaviours are thought to be discriminatory and cause suffering, such as domestic abuse, the law is not well enforced; same for nonhuman animals who continue to suffer in laboratories worldwide.[42] This, then, supports the notion of intersectional objectification through the philosophies of law and their material implications on animals and women. As MacKinnon observes, the way women have suffered at the hands of the legal system has meant that their pain and suffering has been 'denigrated, and denied and when recognised, more often used to see us as damaged goods than as humans harmed.'[43] Considering the above, does this sound familiar with a view to the conceptualisation of the nonhumans' pain and suffering?

The key to understanding these intersectional oppressions is by addressing the philosophies of science and law, and how they buttress, embellish and support each other by claiming to demonstrate ways of knowing and understanding nonhuman and human others through this discourse of 'Rights' and a growing discourse of animal welfare. These discourses of rights and welfare affect definitions of pain, which also are gendered.

Theorising 'Othered' bodies: The power–pain nexus

Pain, women and animals are conjoined in a legal epistemology grounded in positivism. What springs to mind here are several questions relating to this jurisprudential parallel between women and animals. Fundamentally, it centres on the measurement of pain in animals under experiment and recognising suffering in women. As I have argued, sexism underpins

---

40 MacKinnon, *Are Women Human? And Other International Dialogues*. p. 42.
41 Equality and Human Rights Commission, "Our Statement on Sex and Gender Reassignment: Legal Protections and Language," https://www.equalityhumanrights.com/en/our-work/news/our-statement-sex-and-gender-reassignment-legal-protections-and-language.
42 MacKinnon, "Of Mice and Men: A Feminist Fragment on Animal Rights." p. 269.
43 Ibid. p. 171.

speciesism, and this is most evident in law and its conceptualisation of pain in nonhuman animals. Ultimately, pain is gendered. The infliction of pain on 'Othered' bodies is a way to desubjectify them as much as it contributes towards codifying them as having sentient status.[44] The pain experience and nonhuman animals are regulated by a legal system that claims to acknowledge their subjectivity and presence in the world. This classification of their experience is an exercise of power. It is manifested through the institutions that sanction the infliction of that pain in the first place.

From the previous two chapters, what has become apparent is that to maintain animal experimentation in Britain, scientists had to acknowledge that nonhuman animals could suffer pain and psychological distress. It is evident of this chapter and the preceding ones that pain forms the basis of the nonhuman animal's experience in the laboratory and its relationship to humans. So too, does it apply to women's experiences of the social world? From my initial analyses, this pain experience echoes the comment made by feminist philosophy Wendy Lynne Lee: that it is rooted in Cartesian dualism.[45] This dualism is implicit in the construction of power–knowledge relations mentioned previously concerning women and the very experience of pain itself. This infliction of pain is a form of violence. Violence on the micro-scale acts as a veil to the violence perpetrated on the macro-scale. As Lee asserts, violence 'is so deeply woven into our social institutions (law, medicine, marriage, family and so on)'[46] that it inevitably goes unnoticed and even becomes normalised.

It is here that we might turn to the work of Bibi Bakare-Yusuf, Elaine Scarry, and the aforementioned Wendy Lee to address this question.[47] Scarry claims that pain (in the human) lacks referentiality, and hence precedes language. In other words, it desubjectifies the person and rests in the material realm of the body.[48] In a sense, Scarry is right; the human in pain becomes a person disassociated from language, culture, meaning and understanding.[49] But on the other hand, this too reinforces the human/animal divide by perceiving the human in pain as returning to a prelinguistic state that *animalises* the person, which is a form of speciesism. Scarry postulates a

---

44 By subjectifying them, I mean to attribute status to them as living beings, but not as sentient ones; in other words, their status as active objects (see Chapter 4).
45 Wendy Lee, "On the (I'm)Materiality of Violence: Subjects, Bodies, and the Experience of Pain." *Feminist Theory* 6, no. 3 (2005): 277.
46 Ibid. p. 280.
47 Bibi Bakare-Yusuf, "The Economy of Violence: Black Bodies and the Unspeakable Terror," in *Feminist Theory and the Body: A Reader*, ed. Janet Price, Margrit Shildrick (Edinburgh: Edinburgh University Press, 1999). Elaine Scarry, *The Body in Pain: The Making and Unmaking of the World* (Oxford: Oxford University Press, 1985); Lee, "On the (I'm)Materiality of Violence: Subjects, Bodies, and the Experience of Pain."
48 Scarry, *The Body in Pain: The Making and Unmaking of the World.*
49 Lee, "On the (I'm)Materiality of Violence: Subjects, Bodies, and the Experience of Pain." p. 280.

form of dualism that ignores nonhuman experience. It presupposes that it is only human beings with the gift of language, culture, and experience and reiterates the discourses of the animal/human dualism circulating in Britain to this day. While I am sympathetic to this account, and its usefulness to this aspect of law, Scarry ultimately reinforces the very logic that supports the institutions that inflict pain.[50] She assumes nonhuman animals lack cognitive/emotional capacities and inadvertently turns the experience of pain into a process of 'Othering.' Consequently, simultaneously excluding and including women in the process of her analysis.

Nevertheless, the lawmakers and scientists conceptualise and normalise the experience of pain by their very acknowledgement and objectification of that pain. To draw on Scarry's notion of the indescribability of pain is essential, yet it needs to be extended to include nonhuman bodies. A body that is seen as always a part of culture and language *is inscribed* by culture and experienced *through* culture. The black feminist scholar Bakare-Yusuf discusses this process about slavery. The situation of the body outside of culture was 'not the case for slaves' as from the moment of enslavement, a slave had 'no claim to her person, no right to citizenship; she [was] the property of her master or mistress.'[51] This is not to compare the experience of slaves with that of laboratory animals. Still, Bakare-Yusuf's point is relevant, as the body of nonhumans, from the moment of their use in the laboratory to the discussions which abounded in the 1960s–1980s about their legal standing, had no claim to rights but rather was seen in law as having the status of property.[52]

Nonhumans' property status allows for the continuation of vivisection, which removes any chance of acknowledgement that animals are living sentient beings *in their own right*. In other words, nonhuman animals are – despite the admission from scientists of the capacity for animals to suffer physically and psychologically – desubjectified. This new definition of pain further entrenches this desubjectification, making the laboratory animal *more* vulnerable to objectification.[53] This further ingrains the subject–object dualism, which produces the circumstances within which the experience of pain in nonhumans has a purpose. This being that animal experimentation is both expedient and right, science is the best way to develop a civilisation and defend one, thus 'licensing any pain necessary to secure it.'[54] This includes the military and medical laboratory that produces a biopolitics of

---

50 Bakare-Yusuf, "The Economy of Violence: Black Bodies and the Unspeakable Terror."
51 Ibid. p. 319.
52 Johnson, *Power, Knowledge, Animals*; Francione, *Animals, Property and the Law*.
53 Bakare-Yusuf, "The Economy of Violence: Black Bodies and the Unspeakable Terror." p. 318. Lee, "On the (I'm)Materiality of Violence: Subjects, Bodies, and the Experience of Pain." pp. 281–282.
54 "On the (I'm)Materiality of Violence: Subjects, Bodies, and the Experience of Pain." Ibid. p. 284.

care, which has disciplinary techniques that make nonhumans docile, and under its control.

Likewise, women are bodies in a perpetual state of pain – believe me, daily life can be a struggle! This conflation of pain and animality is partly through our bodies' codification as being a part of nature (thus, nonhuman). As Mackinnon observes, animality is part of the identity of being a woman.[55] As Carol J. Adams identifies, violent insults to women often include the absent referent – 'Bitch,' 'cow,' 'dog' and 'bird' being the most obvious.[56] All this renders women and animals as beings that are tortured via the very systems in place designed to protect us. Wendy Lynn Lee observes:

> The tortured body speaks through the subject's attempts to protect herself, through her compliance, and through the physical space, she occupies... Her very comportment signifies the institutions and practices reinforced in the violence acted out against her. Even in death, her body signifies her an individuated thing whose identity is past or spent, and whose treatment in death is as much prescribed by law as her actions in life... Dualism functions as a justificatory instrument in law in that, while it is not the truth about the law's foundation in the positing of materiality through language, it does provide the conceptual ontological framework within which devaluation, and the violence necessary to enforce it can be codified and preserved.[57]

Pain then is fundamental to all aspects of *legalised* laboratory life. The power–pain nexus can be defined as the (historical) *conceptualisation* of a body experiencing pain, forged by various powerful institutions in society (medical, military and legal institutions). Institutions that exercise this power–knowledge collude in *regulating* bodies, subjectifying some bodies (male) whilst desubjectifying others (nonhuman and women). This creates relations and hierarchies of power between groups of living beings.

Conclusion

This chapter is by no means a comprehensive theoretical exploration into the legal conflation of women, animals and their suffering. Instead, take this chapter as a starting point for discussion and reflection. I will be exploring this aspect more thoroughly at a later date. For now, I would like it to be seen as a much larger conclusion to this section on law and animal experimentation by highlighting how jurisprudence is saturated with patriarchal

---

55 MacKinnon, "Of Mice and Men: A Feminist Fragment on Animal Rights."
56 Carol Adams, *The Sexual Politics of Meat* (Oxford, U.K.: Polity Press, 1990).
57 Lee, "On the (I'm)Materiality of Violence: Subjects, Bodies, and the Experience of Pain." p. 288.

and dominant tendencies that conflate women and animals at a philosophical level.

I have discussed relevant intersections of legal jurisprudence, such as how gender-based violence avoids the strategies put in place by the UNHRC when it comes to protecting people from harm and demonstrating how statutory definitions of pain for experimental animals run parallel to this. In an attempt to theorise this, my concept of the power–pain nexus (admittedly, largely underdeveloped) helps to encapsulate the logic of violence perpetrated by a legal system that claims to protect women's lives and animals. Power and pain are intrinsically linked by elite networks that uphold a dominance hierarchy and help to maintain (neo)liberalism's tight grip over marginalised living beings.

Bibliography

Adams, Carol. *The Sexual Politics of Meat*. Oxford, U.K.: Polity Press, 1990.

Agamben, Giorgio. *Homo Sacer: Sovereign Power and Bare Life*. Stanford: Stanford University Press, 1998.

Bakare-Yusuf, Bibi. "The Economy of Violence: Black Bodies and the Unspeakable Terror." In *Feminist Theory and the Body: A Reader*, edited by Janet Price and Margrit Shildrick, 311–323. Edinburgh: Edinburgh University Press, 1999.

Bourke, Joanna. *What It Means to Be Human: Reflections from 1791 to Present*. London, UK: Virago Press, 2011.

Brown, Wendy. *States of Injury: Power and Freedom in Late Modernity*. Princeton, NJ: Princeton University Press, 1995.

Commission, Equality and Human Rights. "Our Statement on Sex and Gender Reassignment: Legal Protections and Language." https://www.equalityhumanrights.com/en/our-work/news/our-statement-sex-and-gender-reassignment-legal-protections-and-language.

Crenshaw, Kimberlé. *The Structural and Political Dimensions of Intersectional Oppression*. edited by Patrick R Grzanka. Colorado: Westview Press, 2014.

Donald, Diana. *Women against Cruelty: Protection of Animals in Nineteenth-Century Britain*. Manchester: Manchester University Press, 2020.

Elliott, Katie; Julia Long; Emily Wertans; Keshia Harper; Deirdre Brennan; Heather Harvey; Rosie Allen. ""If I'm Not in Friday, I Might Be Dead" UK Femicides 2009–2018." femicidecensus.org

Elston, Mary Ann. "Women and Anti-Vivisection in Victorian England, 1870–1900." In *Vivisection in Historical Perspective*, edited by Nicolaas Rupke. London and New York: Routledge, 1990.

Francione, Gary L. *Animals, Property and the Law*. 2nd ed. Philadelphia: Temple University Press, 2007.

Friedan, Betty. *The Feminine Mystique*. 2nd ed. London: Penguin 2010.

Grbich, Judith E. "The Body in Legal Theory." In *At the Boundaries of Law: Feminism and Legal Theory*, edited by Martha Albertson Fineman and Nancy Sweet Thomadsen. London and New York: Routledge, 1991.

Gruen, Lori. *Ethics and Animals: An Introduction*. Cambridge, UK: Cambridge University Press, 2018.

https://www.mmu.ac.uk/business-school/research/research-centres/vote100/history/. "The Women's Timeline."

Hunnicutt, Gwen. *Gender Violence in Ecofeminist Perspective: Intersections of Animal Oppression, Patriarchy and Domination of the Earth*. Abingdon & New York: Routledge, 2020.

Huppatz, Kate; Steve Matthewman. "A Sociology of Covid-19." *Journal of Sociology* 56, no. 4 (2020): 1–9.

Johnson, Lisa. *Power, Knowledge, Animals*. Basingstoke: Palgrave Macmillan, 2012.

Jordanova, Ludmilla. *Sexual Visions: Images of Gender in Science and Medicine between the Eighteenth and Twentieth Centuries*. Wisconsin: The University of Wisconsin Press, 1989.

Kean, Hilda. *Animal Rights: Political and Social Change in Britain since 1800*. London, UK: Reaktion Books Ltd, 1998.

Lee, Wendy. "On the (I'm)Materiality of Violence: Subjects, Bodies, and the Experience of Pain." *Feminist Theory*. 6, no. 3 (2005): 277–295.

MacKinnon, Catharine. *Are Women Human? And Other International Dialogues*. Cambridge, Massachusetts & London, England: Harvard University Press, 2006.

———. "Of Mice and Men: A Feminist Fragment on Animal Rights." In *Women's Lives, Men's Laws*, edited by Catharine MacKinnon. Boston MA: Harvard University Press, 2007.

Nations, United. "A Universal Declaration of Human Rights General Assembly Resolution 217 A." https://www.un.org/en/ga/search/view_doc.asp?symbol=A/RES/217(III)

Office, Home. "Domestic Abuse Bill 2020: Overarching Factsheet." https://www.gov.uk/government/publications/domestic-abuse-bill-2020-factsheets/domestic-abuse-bill-2020-overarching-factsheet.

Publications, U.K. Parliamentary Select Committee. "Home Office Preparedness for Covid-19 (Coronavirus): Domestic Abuse and Risks of Harm within the Home." https://publications.parliament.uk/pa/cm5801/cmselect/cmhaff/321/32105.htm.

Rackley, Erika; Rosemary Auchmuty. "The Women's Legal Landmarks Project: Celebrating 100 Years of Women in the Law in the UK and Ireland." *Legal Information Management* 16, no. 1 (2016): 30–34.

Refuge. "Refuge Responds to Reports of Potential Increase in Domestic Abuse During Covid-19." https://www.refuge.org.uk/refuge-responds-to-reports-of-potential-increase-in-domestic-abuse-during-covid-19/.

Rich, Adrienne. *Of Woman Born - Motherhood as Experience and Institution*. Reissue ed. London & New York: W.W. Norton & Company, 1996.

Ritvo, Harriet. *The Animal Estate: English and Other Creatures in the Victorian Age*. London, UK: Penguin Books Ltd, 1990.

Scarry, Elaine. *The Body in Pain: The Making and Unmaking of the World*. Oxford: Oxford University Press, 1985.

Schiebinger, Londa. *Nature's Body: Gender in the Making of Modern Science*. Boston, MA: Beacon Press Books, 1993.

Tinker, Catherine. "Human Rights for Women: The U.N. Convention on the Elimination of All Forms of Discrimination against Women." *Human Rights Quarterly* 3, no. 2 (1981): 32–43.

Wilson, Elizabeth. *Only Halfway to Paradise Women in Postwar Britain: 1945–1968*. London: Tavistock Publications Ltd, 1980.

Women, United Nations. "Convention on the Elimination of All Forms of Discrimination against Women." https://www.un.org/womenwatch/daw/cedaw/text/econvention.htm#intro

Zalewski, Marysia; Roberta Guerrini. "Negotiating Difference/Negotiating Rights: The Challenges and Opportunities of Women's Human Rights." *Review of International Studies* 33 (2007): 5–10.

Section II
Scientific intersections
The practice of animal experimentation and its gendered dimensions

4 Animal experimentation at Porton Down

Britain's Military-Animal-Industrial Complex, 1948–1955

The funniest thing, according to J.D Morton, the scientific trials officer at Porton Down Chemical and Biological Defence Research Establishment (CBDE) in 1952, was the fact that monkeys could possibly have rights. In his narration over a grainy 1952 film about a secret experiment conducted off the coast of Scotland, Morten joked about the experimental monkeys. He highlighted the behaviour of one particular monkey in the film who was seen to be moving frantically about in his cage, and wryly exclaimed: 'He's obviously a political agitator, haranguing the rest about the rights of monkeys, though they're only paying casual attention to him!'[1] This passing comment, made with a sense of humour, may seem odd to the contemporary reader. Where is the humour in expressing that monkeys *may* possible have rights? As the noted cultural historian Robert Darnton claims, '[w]hen we cannot get a proverb, or a joke, or a ritual, or a poem, we know we are on to something.'[2] The perception of this event from a distance might serve as a starting point in understanding the culture of military animal experimentation in Britain at this point in time.

Situated on the Salisbury Plain in Southern England, nestled between an Area of Outstanding Natural Beauty and the picturesque New Forest, lies Britain's most top-secret military establishment, Porton Down CBDE. Created in 1916 as a response to the German use of chemical weapons (mustard gas) during World War I,[3] CBDE remains Britain's most secretive and controversial military research establishment. Its agenda, having changed over the years as much as its name, is to investigate and compile research on modern day warfare technologies which enable the British army to be advantageous against those they deem its enemies. The official government line taken states that this 'ensure[s] that the UK's military and wider public benefit from the latest technical and scientific developments' and therefore

---

1 http://www.youtube.com/watch?v=CPA_yce0Swg [accessed 12/05/14].
2 Robert Darnton, *The Great Cat Massacre and Other Episodes in French Cultural History* (New York: Basic Books, 1984). pp. 75–104.
3 (Carter 1992).

DOI: 10.4324/9780429461644-5

inevitably 'in the interests of national security much of this work is secret.'[4] Because of its top-secret nature, Porton Down has seen over the years many conflicting and contradictory narratives about its practices circulating in the public milieu. Moreover, the use of nonhuman animals in its scientific experiments was, and remains, integral to its *modus operandi*. Still to this day, newspapers occasionally run articles raising concerns about the experimental practices undertaken at the establishment, but still, these practices persist.

This first chapter of the section, on the material practices of laboratory animal experimentation, aims to 'set the scene' with regards to the landscape of British experimental science after the Second World War. The chapter sets the context for what is to follow in this section, by contextualising the creation of Britain's animal-industrial-complex, while the next two chapters outline its maintenance via the discourses of animal welfare.

For this chapter, I investigate this seemingly trivial and humour-filled relationship between the human and nonhuman, by focusing on the use of nonhuman animals in British biological warfare trials in mid-twentieth century Britain. My argument is twofold: first, I argue that the use of thousands upon thousands of nonhuman bodies (living and dead) helped to create Britain's military-animal-industrial complex (MAIC). At this time, not only was Britain creating an immense military-industrial complex in this era in order to compensate for its loss of Empire and steady economic decline since the Second World War, but, with the use of thousands of animals in the creation of weapons of mass destruction, was also creating an MAIC.[5] Second, to enable this creation of the British MAIC, it was necessary to examine in precise detail and expediency, the pathological state of the dead animal body who was subject to these novel biological weapons. My argument here follows the work of many Foucauldian inspired Critical Animal Studies (CAS) scholars when discussing the biopolitical role of nonhuman animals in human social and political life.

Previous historical analyses of Britain's chemical and biological warfare practices have focused on the human and ethical dimensions, as well as the policy and politics of Porton Down, with Ulf Schmidt and Brian Balmer being the foremost scholars in this area.[6] The problem with this is that the

---

4 Gov.co.uk.
5 Salter, 2014.
6 Brian Balmer, "The Drift of Biological Weapons Policy in the UK, 1945–1965," *The Journal of Strategic Studies* 20, no. 4 (1997): 115–145. "Killing 'without the Distressing Preliminaries': Scientists' Defence of the British Biological Warfare Programme," *Minerva* 40, no. 1, Special Issue: Ethics and Reason in Chemical and Biological Weapons Research (2002); *Secrecy and Science: A Historical Sociology of Biological and Chemical Warfare* (Surrey: Ashgate Publishing Ltd, 2012); "The Uk Biological Weapons Programme," in

focus is very much placed on the human experiments that took place there, with the very significant use of animals in the development of weapons of mass destruction mentioned only occasionally. For instance, Ulf Schmidt, although discusses the use of nonhuman animals in the creation of biological and chemical weapons at Porton Down, still tends to downplay the integral role they played in the creation of WMD, as well as their structural impact in shaping and contributing to the economy.⁷ Rather I argue that the nonhuman animal should be seen as integral to the writing of military history, especially with regards to establishments such as Porton Down. Animals themselves are a force of social and economic change and this needs to be narrated and systematically analysed. If we take J.D. Morten's unruly monkey at the start of this piece, we can actively see their agency. The monkey is resisting, they are stressed, and clearly demonstrating their dislike of the situation. Despite this resistance, their own lowly position in the human hierarchy of existence sealed their fate and deemed them suitable for experiment, and ultimately this monkey was euthanised for the purposes of British warfare capabilities. Their body was central to Britain's postwar military goals and subsequent modern economic agenda. This shows how their death as much as their life, was productive for the biopolitics of Britain's emerging MAIC at this time. Without them, would Porton Down been able to develop such potent weapons of war?

The military historian David Edgerton has argued that in order to understand the effects of modernity on the arms production and military technological processes, we need to examine the peculiar implications of modernity's relationship to warfare. To do this, he claims that we must make sense of '…the most important yet neglected aspects of economic life of the twentieth century.'⁸ One of these 'important yet neglected' aspects of economic and, consequently, military life of the twentieth century in Britain is the role that nonhuman animals have played in the construction of weapons of mass destruction. To do this, I am extending the concept of the military–industrial complex, and following the work of Critical Animal

---

Deadly Cultures: Biological Weapons since 1945, ed. Lajos Rózsa Mark Wheelis, Malcolm Dando (Cambridge M.A. & London UK: Harvard University Press, 2006). pp. 47–83. Ulf Schmidt, "Cold War at Porton Down: Informed Consent in Britain's Biological and Chemical Warfare Experiments," *Cambridge Quarterly of Healthcare Ethic* 15, no. 4 (2006); Ulf Schmidt, Andreas Frewer, ed. *History and Theory of Human Experimentation: The Declaration of Helsinki and Modern Medical Ethics* (Stuttgart: Franz Steiner Verlag Wiesbaden GmbH, 2007); Ulf Schmidt, "Medical Ethics and Human Experiments at Porton Down: Informed Consent in Britain's Biological and Chemical Warfare Experiments," in *History and Theory of Human Experimentation: The Declaration of Helsinki and Modern Medical Ethics*, ed. Ulf Schmidt, Andreas Frewer (Stutgart: Franz Steiner Verlag Wiesbaden GmbH, 2007); *Secret Science* (Oxford: Oxford University Press, 2015).

7 *Secret Science*. pp. 48–52.
8 David Edgerton, "The British Military-Industrial Complex in History: The Importance of Political Economy," *The Economics of Peace and Security Journal*, 3 no. 1 (2008): 9.

Scholars Anthony Nocella, Colin Salter and Judy Bentley, and argue that Britain in the immediate post-World War II era created an MAIC.[9] With the military–industrial complex being that which comprises a partially impervious set of networks between the economic sector (industrial bases that support the military), governments and scientific domains in a given society.[10] This relationship includes political contributions and approval for military spending.[11] The term originated as a reference to the US military system, but as we shall see is equally applicable to Britain.

With regards to this, Edgerton's account of the British warfare state, 1920–1970, is relevant. According to Edgerton, the historiography of the development of state militarism in Britain remains sparse. Furthermore, 'in all the vast commentary on the British state, there is hardly even an allusion to the 'military-industrial complex.'[12] I posit, alongside Edgerton, that Britain in this period developed a vast military–industrial complex, albeit one that involved the use of nonhuman animals for the development of biological warfare. With that in mind, the extension of the military–industrial complex to one that includes nonhuman animals draws initially on the work of Barbara Noske. Noske claimed that the relations of capitalism deem 'exploitation of nonhuman animals [as being] natural, ethical and appropriate'[13] and is central to the 'total commodification of the natural world' in the modern industrial system.[14] Noske identifies the roots of this complex in the 'hyper-reductionism'[15] of the modern (capitalist) agricultural labour force alongside 'the mechanized and routinized slaughter of nonhuman animals, and the nonhuman animals themselves.'[16] As a result of Noske's analysis of the agricultural labour force, Nocella *et al* postulate the foundations of a theory in the guise of the MAIC.[17] This includes the mass production of various weapons of war not favourable to human and animal wellbeing, but

---

9 Anthony J. Nocella, Colin Salter, Judy, K. C. Bentley, *Animals and War: Confronting the Military-Animal-Industrial Complex* (London: Lexington Books, 2015).
10 Richard Twine, "Revealing the 'Animal-Industrial Complex' – a Concept & Method for Critical Animal Studies?," *Journal for Critical Animal Studies* 10, no. 1 (2012): 8.
11 Jon Agar, *Science in the Twentieth Century and Beyond* (Cambridge, UK and Malden, MA: Polity Press, 2012). p. 339.
12 David Edgerton, *Warfare State, Britain, 1920–1970* (Cambridge: Cambridge University Press, 2006). p. 9.
13 Barbara Noske, *Beyond Boundaries: Humans and Animals* (London, New York and Montréal: Black Rose Books, 1997). pp. 22–39.
14 Ibid. p. 36.
15 Ibid. p. 37.
16 Colin Salter, "Introducing the Military-Industrial Complex," in *Animals and War: Confronting the Military-Animal Industrial Complex*, ed. Anthony J. Nocella II, Judy K. C. Bentley, Colin Salter (Lexington Books, 2014). In Anthony J. Nocella, Colin Salter, Judy, K. C. Bentley, *Animals and War: Confronting the Military-Animal-Industrial Complex* (London: Lexington Books, 2015). p. 5.
17 Anthony J. Nocella II, Judy K. C. Bentley, Colin Salter, ed. *Animals and War: Confronting the Military-Animal Industrial Complex* (Lexington Books, 2014). pp. 1–17

are nevertheless pursued and exploited in order to persist with economic interests in this area.[18]

On that note, this focus on the use of the living and dead animal body in the creation of biological weapons and their contribution to Britain's political economy at the time, shifts the historical analysis away from the distinctly human dimension and into the terrain of the concept of the animal body and its socio-economic functions. What this book reveals is how the notion of the 'caring' for nonhuman animals of laboratory developed since the immediate post-war period; and further, how this notion of lab animal welfare is *gendered* in a direct relationship with the exponential increase of the use of animals in experiments since this time.

Gender, warfare and nonhuman animals

As the title of this book indicates, I am analysing this historical relationship between animal welfare, the use of nonhuman bodies and its gendered inflections. At first glance, one may ask, but where is the gender? At times, it is both explicit and on the surface (see Chapter 6). At other times, it remains hidden and unconscious but seeps out like oil on the surface of water. Animal oppression comes in many guises and cross-cuts race, gender and class[19]; for me, it is ultimate in patriarchal oppression.

So how do we go about revealing the intersections of sexism, speciesism and the 'Othering' of bodies that do not fit the white, masculine ideal? One way to do this is to pay attention to language and text – how we speak and the words we use sometimes betray our implicit meanings.[20] Also, it is important to analyse the representations and perspectives presented to specialist and lay audiences, whether that be in scientific books and journals or newspapers and government documents. What these reveal is a gaze, a male gaze, that sweeps over bodies and constructs a representation of the world which is believed to be a fact.[21]

The gaze of the scientist over nonhuman bodies in any experimental research is essential in order to ascertain the efficacy pathogens have under experimental conditions and the effect diseases have on the body. Furthermore, it's the very *method* itself that determines the outcomes of these experiments. The experimental approach used by any branch of experimental science which uses nonhuman animals is rooted in a philosophy

---

18 Twine, "Revealing the 'Animal-Industrial Complex' – A Concept & Method for Critical Animal Studies?," *Journal for Critical Animal Studies* 10 no. 1 (2012): p. 8.
19 Gwen Hunnicutt, *Gender Violence in Ecofeminist Perspective: Intersections of Animal Oppression, Patriarchy and Domination of the Earth* (Abingdon & New York: Routledge, 2020).
20 Eward Said, *Orientalism*, 5th ed (London: Penguin Books, 2003).
21 Carol J Adams, *Neither Man nor Beast: Feminism and the Defense of Animals* (New York: The Continuum Publishing Company, 1995); Laura. Mulvey, "Visual Pleasure and Narrative Cinema.," in *Film Theory and Criticism : Introductory Readings.*, ed. Leo Braudy, Marshall Cohen (New York and Oxford: Oxford University Press, 1999).

that presents a particular way of understanding and seeing the world. It is grounded in an epistemology that dates back to the seventeenth century scientists, Rene Descartes and Francis Bacon.[22] The 'way to knowledge' is labelled, in this sense, as 'objective,' the observers (scientists) are distinct from the known (the body of the nonhuman that has to be dissected in order to produce facts). This scientific approach is historically dependent upon binary categories that separate nature from culture, animal from human and male from female.[23] These binary categories leave traces of gender labels that produce a powerful hierarchal structure linked to a specific set of gendered social relations, as well as seemingly aiding in our construction of contemporary understandings of human–animal relationships.

Scientific research (in general) has been said to be identified as 'masculine,' with emotional and embodied ways of knowing about the world, labelled 'subjective' and 'feminine'[24]; and 'because the Western world-view values objectivity over subjectivity and men's knowledge over women's, 'feminine' ways to know are by their nature [seen as] inferior.'[25] In historical terms, the biological warfare trials conducted by Porton Down scientists could arguably been seen as firmly entrenched within the domain of the masculine, because of their adherence to the strict rules governing scientific methodological techniques.

Consequently, the series of B.W. trials were at once a product of culture and politics as they were a product of the very domain of knowledge that underpinned the research. Incidentally, as we will see, none of the major experiments conducted by the Porton scientists explicitly raised any issues of gender. However, the omnipresent influence of gender played out in these experiments on a number of levels. First, in terms of the socio-political relations of the trials: the world of B.W. research at the time was an entirely male world, no female staff were present. This reflected contemporary gender relations occurring in broader society, for instance, the desire to get women to return to the role of being a housewife and mother following the mobilisation of British women during the Second World War, and the contemporary biological reductionist arguments regarding the limitations which women's biology imposed upon their ability to be in education and work.[26]

---

22 Carolyn Merchant, *The Death of Nature: Women, Ecology and the Scientific Revolution* (New York: Harper & Row Publishers Inc., 1983). p. xi.
23 Evelyn Fox-Keller, *Secrets of Life, Secrets of Death: Essays on Language, Gender and Science* (London: Routledge, 1992). p. 18.
24 Sandra Harding, *The Science Question in Feminism* (Ithaca: Cornell University Press, 1986).
25 Ruth Hubbard, *The Politcs of Women's Biology* (New Jersey: Rutgers University Press, 1992). p. 8.
26 Elizabeth Wilson, *Only Halfway to Paradise Women in Postwar Britain: 1945–1968* (London: Tavistock Publications Ltd, 1980). p. 58. Lynda Birke, *Feminism, Animals and Science: The Naming of the Shrew* (Buckingham, UK: Open University Press, 1994). p. 104.

Second, the language and format of the reports employed the scientific philosophy of 'positivism,' an ontological standpoint which stipulates that reality is 'out there' to be observed, captured and understood. This, *a priori*, is what directed the gaze of the observer and determined the totality of experience within biological weapons research, i.e. what counted as 'valid' knowledge and which facilitated the formation of a discourse of 'things' that could be recognised as true.[27] This was in part evident in the analysis of the results: the nonhuman animals were transformed into quantitative data. Guinea-pigs were noted for their 'important contribution to the quantitative value of the work.'[28] It was also observed that in the past they had been wasted due to their health, which incidentally made 'calculations of infectivity practically valueless.'[29] The animals who were less susceptible to infectivity were constructed in terms of their ability to generate mathematical data.

This depersonalised authority can be used here to draw on parallels with constructions of women at the time. During the 1950s, a proliferation of scientific studies about women and their capabilities in terms of their 'biological nature' was widely circulated in popular culture. In these, women were often seen as objects, and descriptions permeated the public milieu about the science behind women's 'natural' disposition to motherhood, housework and marriage (to the opposite sex of course).[30] Consequently, scientists also had an important role to play in defining what it means to be a woman, and hence, 'feminine.' This was in terms of defining what is 'normal' and 'natural' for women to do, and how this related to their 'innate biological propensities.'[31] It was also around this time that women were taking up part-time work, as well as remaining at home to look after their husband and children. This dual-role also facilitated an increase in women attending higher education institutions. However, government researchers still depended on moral and eugenicist arguments to assert women's propensity for motherhood despite their desire to work.[32] For instance, the Standing Joint Committee of Working Women's Organisations, which incidentally argued for women to be able to work outside the home, was actually still morally conservative

---

27 Michel Foucault, *The Order of Things*, 11th ed. (Oxon and New York: Routledge, 2008). p. 172.
28 TNA, WO 195/12213: Chiefs of Staff Committee: Biological Warfare Sub-Committee, Ministry of Supply, B.R.A.B., Operation Cauldron 1952, Scientific Report by the Microbiological Research Department, Porton and Naval Report by the Naval Commander, p. 7.
29 Ibid. p. 7.
30 Wilson, *Only Halfway to Paradise Women in Postwar Britain: 1945–1968*. pp. 26–29 & p. 58 And see Hubbard, *The Poltics of Women's Biology*. pp. 17–18.
31 *The Poltics of Women's Biology*. p. 18.
32 Wilson, *Only Halfway to Paradise Women in Postwar Britain: 1945–1968*. p. 26.

96 *Scientific intersections*

in approach. The group publicly expressed the idea that women attending institutions of education ran the risk of it affecting their biology, as it would lead to a 'weakening of the biological urge and the desire for children.'[33] Accordingly, there was no increase of women being recruited onto science, technology and medicine courses in the late 1940s and 1950s: the notoriously masculinised subject of science was firmly entrenched to the exclusion of women.[34]

Science in post-war Britain remained firmly located within the domain of the masculine and the warfare state wanted to attract male science graduates into the post-war scientific officer classes of government.[35] Britain was becoming a society that developed a strong scientific culture; it became, 'the direct generator of economic, political, and social accumulation and control,[36] through the state's appointment of scientific experts in the field of warfare and welfare.[37] No longer was the scientist seen as marginal to the shaping of society – instead they became a workforce trained in the art of objectivity and value-neutrality.[38] Government laboratories were male dominated and included Porton Down Microbiological Research Department. Although funding tapered off for B.W. research from the mid-1950s onwards, and instead went into nuclear investigations; as we will see, the Porton scientists and their experiments were still essential to the generation of Britain's MAIC.

Biological warfare and the state

It was not until the 1930s that scientific concern about the dangers of biological warfare (B.W.) became a focus of attention in the corridors of Whitehall.[39] It was in this period that the government created a sub-committee on Bacteriological Warfare of the Committee of Imperial Defence to discuss policy formulations and military strategies of a biological warfare nature.[40] In October 1940, a British research programme was launched at Porton Down led by Dr Paul Fildes, a bacteriologist from the Medical Research Council (MRC).[41] Fildes was given orders to develop a biological bomb

---

33 Ibid. pp. 27–28.
34 David Edgerton, *Warfare State: Britain, 1920–1970* (Cambridge, UK: Cambridge University Press, 2006). pp. 176–177.
35 Ibid. p. 179.
36 Harding, *The Science Question in Feminism*. p. 16.
37 Edgerton, *Warfare State: Britain, 1920–1970*. p. 177.
38 Harding, *The Science Question in Feminism*. p. 16.
39 Peter Hammond and Gradon Carter, *From Biological Warfare to Healthcare: Porton Down 1940–2000* (Basingstoke: Palgrave Macmillan, 2002).
40 Ibid. p. 60.
41 G. B Carter, *Porton Down: 75 Years of Chemical and Biological Research* (London: HMSO Publications, 1992).

that could be used instantaneously if and when the country was attacked.[42] During the war, scientists at Porton Down designed and produced two key biological weapons: an anti-personnel anthrax bomb[43] and five million cattle cakes laced with anthrax to drop on livestock in Germany.[44] After the war, the B.W. programme was expanded and the B.W. department at Porton Down was re-named as the Microbiological Research Department (MRD).

In the post-war period, state approval ensured the continuation of research into B.W. in peacetime, and more formalised advisory committees were established to supervise B.W. research and policy. One of these was the Biological Research Advisory Board (BRAB) of the Ministry of Supply (MoS), which provided scientific advice on researchable biological problems in relation to weapons development. BRAB were accountable to the Advisory Council on Scientific Research and Technical Development of the MoS, and provided technical advice to the Chiefs of Staff Biological Weapons Subcommittee. This board consisted of a variety of experts from various government departments including people from the MoS, the Home Office and Ministry of Health, as well as independent scientists, the Admiralty, War Office and Air Ministry staff.[45] This sub-committee worked with the Defence Research Policy Committee (DRPC) on the strategy and technical aspects of biological warfare research.[46] B.W. policy became a top priority and the DRPC soon came up with a set of objectives for R&D in this area including research into defensive aspects of war, how to store and produce B.W., and defensive measures to protect the population at large.[47]

In 1946, Dr David Henderson replaced Fildes as superintendent.[48] And as a consequence, the research broadened considerably and ranged from basic experiments in laboratories, to open air trials of dangerous pathogens on land and at sea.[49] The experiments conducted by Porton Down scientists included the use of thousands of animals and they even had their own farm,

---

42 Balmer, "Killing 'without the Distressing Preliminaries': Scientists' Defence of the British Biological Warfare Programme."
43 Ibid.
44 Balmer, "Killing 'without the Distressing Preliminaries': Scientists' Defence of the British Biological Warfare Programme." Piers Millet, "Antianimal Biological Weapons Programs," in *Deadly Cultures: Biological Weapons since 1945*, ed. Lajos Rozsa, Mark Wheelis, Malcolm Dando (Cambridge MA: Harvard University Press, 2006).
45 "Antianimal Biological Weapons Programs."
46 Balmer, "The UK Biological Weapons Programme."
47 Ibid. p. 51.
48 Hammond and Carter, *From Biological Warfare to Healthcare: Porton Down 1940–2000*. p. vii.
49 Millet, "Antianimal Biological Weapons Programs"; Brian Balmer, *Britain and Biological Warfare: Expert Advice and Science Policy, 1930–65*, (Basingstoke: Palgrave Macmillan., 2001); "Killing 'without the Distressing Preliminaries': Scientists' Defence of the British Biological Warfare Programme."

98 *Scientific intersections*

Allington Farm, which bred and provided experimental animals for the scientists for their B.W. trials.[50] Most often these were guinea pigs, mice, rats, cats and monkeys.[51] In terms of the B.W. trials, dangerous viruses would be released in order to purposely infect the animals and test their immune response to such pathogenic organisms as the plague virus and anthrax. These experiments were an indicator not only towards the thinking that surrounded biological weapons and its position in the development of policies[52] but also, as we shall see, in the development of the MAIC.

Secret science and the mysterious case of 'Operation X'

The testing of dangerous pathogens for potential military use had to be kept top secret. Only key government advisors and military personnel could know about them. The very first post-war biological weapons trial was conducted from December 1948 to February 1949 and codenamed 'Operation Harness.'[53] The experiments were to be carried out in the Caribbean, and dangerous pathogens, such as the anthrax and *Brucella* viruses, were to be tested on sheep, guinea pigs and monkeys.[54] Despite the MoS and Porton scientists being sworn to secrecy, the British press soon became aware of this top-secret operation, and speculation about the secret experiments permeated the newspapers. Incidentally, the press did not suspect the testing of biological weapons at all, but rather, the focus, and concern was of atomic weapon testing. Even though the British press may have been wrong about the prospect of nuclear trials, they still developed dramatic narratives about animal testing. The weekly illustrated newspaper the *Daily Graphic* ran an article about 'Operation X, the Royal Navy's first big exercise to discover the effect of atomic weapons.'[55] Other newspapers were also misconceived in their notion that the Royal Navy was testing atomic weaponry; 'Two warships are being fitted out as floating laboratories for Britain's first atomic weapon experiments'[56] exclaimed the *Daily Express*, 'The tests are to be held before the end of this year.'[57]

---

50 Schmidt, *Secret Science*. p. 49.
51 Balmer, "The UK Biological Weapons Programme." p. 52.
52 Ibid.
53 Balmer, *Secrecy and Science: A Historical Sociology of Biological and Chemical Warfare*. p. 40.
54 The National Archives [TNA]: Department of the Ministry of Defence (DEFE5/15): DEFE5/15/267, B.W. Trials at Sea - Operation Harness: Report by the Biological Warfare Sub-Committee, 18 August, 1949.
55 TNA: Home Office Registered Papers (HO45): HO45/25867: 'Two Navy Ships Will Test Atom Ray Effect: Rabbits on Board,' *The Daily Graphic*, 14 October 1948.
56 TNA, HO45/25867:W. A Crumley, Navy fits out atom-ray ships, *Daily Express*, Monday, September 27, 1948, p. 1.
57 Ibid. p. 1.

Despite the journalists' conjecture about atomic weaponry, they were accurate about one thing – the use of animals for scientific experimentation on board the Royal Navy vessels. As reported by *The Daily Graphic*, '[P]ens have been fitted for rabbits, pigs and goats to be used for tests of the extent of radiation danger after atomic explosions.'[58] Consequently, as a result of the press coverage about the forthcoming animal experiments, the National Antivivisection Society, The British Anti-Vivisection Society and The National Canine Defence League wrote to senior government officials in the hope of preventing these tests being carried out. The British Antivivisection Society sent a letter addressed to the First Lord of the Admiralty that referred to the press coverage of the impending trials and the 'animal complement'[59] that would be used during the course of them. The letter condemned the use of animals in atomic experiments and compared the forthcoming experiments to those conducted by the U.S. during the Bikini Atoll trials on the Marshall Islands in 1946 and expressed the hope that '[Y]our department will seek, by every possible means to find a method by which the use of animals can be dispensed with.'[60] Mr Tyldesley, the head of the British Antivivisection Society, concluded the letter to the Secretary of State (SoS) by referring to the experiments as a precursor to 'this new kind of warfare' in which he and his society hoped for some assurance that the 'animals used… will not be used in such a way as to involve suffering.'[61] Following this, another letter was soon sent to the Secretary of State from R. Fielding-Ould of the National Antivivisection Society about the reports in the press of the proposed sea trials. Fielding-Ould made several points about the law and vivisection, requested a response from the SoS asking if the experiments were bound by law under the Cruelty to Animals Act 1876 and asked that, if the trials were to go ahead, to ensure that the experimenters would uphold the 'pain condition.'[62] The 'pain condition' formed a crucial part of the 1876 Act and guaranteed that animals that were used in experiments would not suffer unnecessary pain. The Act[63] was a vital piece of legal regulation that would guarantee that the experiments could be carried out lawfully despite protests by the public.

As a result of the press coverage and the public becoming increasingly aware of the forthcoming trials, the issue of law and the military's commitment to the Act was raised in Parliament, asking Mr Dugdale MP, then the Parliamentary Secretary 'whether he will give an assurance that any

---

58 TNA, HO 45/25867, Alan Gardner, Two Navy Ships Will Test Atom Ray Effect: Rabbits on Board, *The Daily Graphic*, 14 October 1948.
59 TNA, HO 45/25867, V. Tyldesley to First Lord of the Admiralty, 30 September 1948.
60 Ibid.
61 Ibid.
62 TNA, HO 45/25867, R. Fielding-Ould to Sectretary of State for the Home Office, 12 October 1948.
63 See chapter 1 for explanation of Cruelty to Animals Act, 1876.

animals used for this purpose will have to suffer no cruelty.'[64] The kind of animals to be used and the number involved in the experiments were also questioned several times by separate Members of Parliament.[65] Yet, his reply was somewhat oblique as he argued that it was 'not in the public interest to give details of experimental work which may be carried out to meet defence requirements' and further claiming that all animals taking part in the 'work' will be bound by law under the 1876 Act.[66] However, behind the public display of lawful obedience lay a sea of confusion regarding the 1876 Cruelty to Animals Act and the obligations of Porton Down scientists when it came to animal experiments and the law. Did the Crown bind Porton scientists, or could they flout the law when it came research in the military domain?

Power, knowledge and crown immunity

Clearly, the press had been mistaken in their atomic assumptions, but correct in their prediction of animal experimentation. The 'expedition' was indeed Operation Harness, and this was made clear in a letter to L.J.H. Naylor Esq. of the Ministry of Supply, from R.A. McCarthy of the Home Office. McCarthy stressed that Naylor should have been 'well aware of the implications of Operation Harness' because of the 'press statements and the questions raised in the House of Commons about the 'putting out of certain landing craft as laboratories and the use of animals therewith.'[67] The main concern of the Home Office was not the inferences of the press, but rather the concern that they were 'not yet in possession of legal confirmation that the Act [1876] covers any activities outside of the United Kingdom.'[68] Despite this doubt, replies to the anti-vivisection bodies assured them that these experiments were indeed governed by the Cruelty to Animals Act 1876 and 'that the animals shall not be subjugated to unnecessary suffering' as 'all experiments carried out by my Department for Defence research purposes the safeguards of the Cruelty to Animals Act, 1876 are applied.'[69]

So, as it was, the Home Office was unclear about the legal position but still persisted in telling the public that this law would govern any experiments conducted by the state. It was behind the scenes that officials corresponded with legal representatives about the forthcoming experiments and their right to test on animals. In a series of memorandums directed to and from the government's solicitors, an in-depth discussion ensued about

---

64 Historic Hansard, Experimental work (animals), HC debate, 10 November 1948, Vo 457 CC 19-1W.
65 Historic Hansard, Experimental work (animals), HC debate, 10 November 1948, Vo 457 CC 19-1W & HC Debate, 24 November 1948, 458, CC115–6W.
66 Ibid.
67 TNA, HO 45/25867, R. A. McCarthy to L. G. H. Naylor Esq, 19th November 1948.
68 Ibid.
69 TNA, HO 45/25867, G. R. Strauss to Anthony Nutting, 6 December 1948.

the Cruelty to Animals Act and its applicability to these forthcoming B.W. trials. Broadly speaking, the memos discussed the experiments in light of prospective publicity. And it was due to this anticipated public pressure that government bureaucrats asserted that 'there would now seem to be a case for seeking the opinion of Legal Advisors.'[70] This was so the experiments could be lawfully conducted. The general line taken was that 'the provisions of the Cruelty to Animals Act, 1876, should be applied to the experiments.'[71] Yet, what was actually the case was far more complex and convoluted.

The point at issue was discussed in light of the Act applying to ships in both British and foreign waters, as well as 'on the high seas.'[72] Whether or not ships that were the property of 'the Crown' or outside of territorial waters, the Act still created an opportunity for the government to carry out biological warfare testing on animals. Not only that, because these experiments were state implemented, ministers began to question whether the 'Crown is bound.'[73] With the general view from lawyers being that the Crown is not bound by the Cruelty to Animals Act, but stating that 'it is however, often inexpedient to claim Crown immunity: in practice immunity has not been claimed in the past case of the Act, and it is administratively agreed – in which I concur – that it would be a mistake to claim it.'[74]

It was asserted that it was not practicable to claim immunity under the aegis of the Monarch. This could have been for a number of reasons. Most obvious though, would be the fear of public retribution if it was to become known that animals were tested on because of a loophole in the law. Hence, it was asserted in the memorandums that, the Home Office 'would be embarrassed to bring to light the fact that the Crown is not bound by this statute,'[75] and of course this would trigger public outcry. One way the experiments could go ahead would be through the licencing of individual scientists conducting the experiments, as they would be bound by the Act.[76] This would help generate a more positive public image about the trials in their responses to the anti-vivisection societies.

Not only that, in anticipation of the resultant press furore concerning the experiments, it seemed expedient for the Ministers of the Home Office to point out to the Porton Down scientists 'that any work carried out... should be performed under the provisions of the Cruelty to Animals Act.'[77] So the responsibility of following the letter of the law was very much placed upon

---

70 TNA, HO 45/25867, Memorandum, October, 1948.
71 TNA, HO 45/25867, K. P. W. to Cooper November 1948.
72 TNA Home Office Registered Files [HO 45]: HO 45/25867, Memorandum, (October, 1948.)
73 TNA Home Office Registered Files [HO 45]: HO 45/25867, Memorandum by G. B. T. Barr, (5 November 1948).
74 TNA, HO 45/25867, Memorandum, October, 1948.
75 TNA, HO 45/25867, Memorandum by G. B. T. Barr, 21 July 1950.
76 TNA, HO 45/25867, K. P. W. to Cooper November 1948.
77 TNA, HO 45/25867, R. A McCarthy to L. J. H Talyor Esq. 19 November 1948.

the individual scientists. Not only that, further down the line, it came to light that the Act:

> [E]xtends to British ships, at any rate for some purposes, and Royal Navy ships would appear to be a case *a fortiori* (pace the Crown immunity questions). ... Accordingly though the whole subject is somewhat obscure and very lacking in authority, it would appear that the Act, again pace Crown immunity, applies to acts done on board His Majesty's Ships whether on the high sea or in territorial waters.[78]

It became apparent that it was important to emphasise that the Royal Navy was a 'strong case' (case *a fortiori*) for having permission from the Crown ('*pace*' by permission of the Crown) not to be immune from the legalities of the Act. However, the case was complex and demonstrated that the discourse of law in respect of the forthcoming biological weapons trials was obscure and unreliable in this respect. Yet, it was essential for the Home Office to be seen to have their scientists licenced and noteworthy to suggest that the law should be followed despite any suggestion of Crown Immunity.

It is here that we can see that the discourses about the Cruelty to Animals Act, 1876, created a permissive reality about animals and their use in experimentation.[79] What I mean by this is that the law was a legitimising apparatus for the biological warfare trials. It seems that Whitehall did everything it could to make sure these trials went ahead, but at the same time, made sure the politicians and scientists involved, upheld their public image in terms of being seen to be morally committed to the Act.

Despite the complexities of the law, the law still enabled Operation Harness to go ahead. This was because the knowledge conveyed by law was deemed as 'true,' and because the Act originated from people who held 'an office of authority to speak.'[80] These people who made the law held positions of power, had the status of someone who can make truth claims about animals and their right to be experimented on. This is even so despite the original 1876 Act being initially brought into being through early nineteenth century social movements such as the Anti-vivisection groups, led by people such as the feminist Francis Power Cobb.[81] Animals under the statute were deemed objects. The words that emanated from the Act held the mantle of power–knowledge. Thus, the Act contained 'paradoxical truths'[82] that protected animals from 'unnecessary suffering' but at the same time conceptualised them as objects.

---

78 TNA, HO 45/25867, Memorandum by G. B. T. Barr, 5 November 1948.
79 It was not until 1965 that the Act was reviewed, see Chapter 1.
80 Lisa Johnson, *Power, Knowledge, Animals* (Basingstoke: Palgrave Macmillan, 2012). p. 42.
81 Hilda Kean, *Animal Rights: Political and Social Change in Britain since 1800* (London, UK: Reaktion Books Ltd, 1998).
82 Johnson, *Power, Knowledge, Animals*. p. 42.

No peace for animals: The search for a biological weapon

For Operation Harness to go ahead as it did, a set of inwardly directed narratives circulated within the chambers of government in defence of B.W. research and the use of animals in such experiments. These appeasing narratives empowered the scientists and permitted the use of nonhuman animals in experiments under the aegis of law. But what were these experiments? What did they involve? Who did they involve? Beginning in 1948 with Harness and through to 1955, Britain alongside Canada and the U.S (The 'tripartite nations') colluded in a series of sea trials aimed at developing biological weapons for offensive measures. Despite the circulation of narratives about the role of the experiments in the creation of suitable *defensive* operations, what becomes clear is that these experiments were part of a strategic plan to build biological weapons of mass destruction in the Cold War era.[83] Nonhuman animals played a huge part in this and became constructed by scientists as living objects to be used in assessing the effect dangerous pathogens had on a living body. These nonhumans were not living *beings*, but living *matter* that could provide 'suitable' physiological comparisons when it came to measuring decline of living tissue once affected by biological agents.

Operation harness

A biological bomb that could reap wanton destruction became the central goal of the tripartite nations in a post-Second World War world.[84] It became the rhetoric of B.W. scientists that outdoor trials were of the upmost importance in supplementing 'data obtained in the laboratory' of the testing of B.W. agents and to 'augment the scanty evidence obtained during the war concerning the effectiveness of certain biological warfare agents under field conditions.'[85] Therefore, a suitable testing site was located in the Caribbean, off Antigua between December 1948 and February 1949.[86] 'Operation Harness' became the first of a series of trials to test dangerous pathogens on nonhuman animals in order to assess their effectiveness in creating a biological bomb.

The technique was simple; two landing ship tanks (L.S.T's) were to be fitted out with a series of sampling points 'each consisting of a rubber dinghy carrying an animal and sampling apparatus.'[87] The sampling points

---

83   See, TNA, DEFE 5/15, DEFE 5/47/310, AVIA 54/2251, DEFE 55/261 and DEFE 55/256.
84   Balmer, *Secrecy and Science: A Historical Sociology of Biological and Chemical Warfare.* p. 40.
85   TNA, Department of the Ministry of Defence (DEFE 5/15): DEFE 5/15/267, B.W. trials at Sea-Operation Harness: report by the Biological Warfare Sub-Committee, 18 August, 1949].
86   Ibid. p. 2.
87   Ibid. p. 1.

104 *Scientific intersections*

were placed on the surface of the water in an arc formation and clouds of biological agents would be released from a bomb or spray device upwind of the nonhumans.[88] The scientists would watch the release of the pathogens from H.M.S. Ben Lomond – designated as the laboratory ship for the exercise. Once the animals became infected, they would be transferred to one of the L.S.T's… removed to storage space… and the dinghy's and gear sterilized'[89]. The animals used in the trials consisted of sheep, guinea-pigs and monkeys, who were systematically exposed to a range of pathogens including anthrax, brucellosis, and tularemia.[90] Once infected with the pathogenic organisms, the animals were transported and sent to an onshore 'isolation farm where [the] infected animals could be kept under observation.'[91] The corpses of the infected animals were then cast away into the sea.[92]

In all, 22 trials were conducted on nonhuman animals, and not all were successful. Seven of the trials were either a 'complete failure' or only 'partially successful.'[93] Despite the lack of viable evidence produced by the elaborate scheme, and the hundreds of animals used in the trials, scientists from Porton Down did justify their work and claimed that the trials;

> (i) Confirm and augment the wartime findings in respect of two agents, (ii) Show that a third agent can infect animals in the field, (iii) Confirm the toxicity of those three agents is many times greater than that of any chemical agent, (iv) Support previous laboratory work which had shown improvement between ten and twenty fold in the effectiveness of one agent as the result of a modification.[94]

In general, notwithstanding the lack of positive results the Harness team supplemented this lack with the necessity of continuing B.W. trials in the open. Proposals were made for future trials as 'it was the opinion… that field trials are an essential complement to research in the laboratory.'[95] During a conference between the tripartite nations, there was' unanimous agreement that the ultimate objective should be full-scale field trials of toxic

---

88 Ibid. p. 1.
89 Ibid. p. 1.
90 Balmer, *Secrecy and Science: A Historical Sociology of Biological and Chemical Warfare.* p. 40.
91 TNA, DEFE 5/15/267, B.W. trials at Sea-Operation Harness: Report by the Biological Warfare Sub-Committee, 18 August 1949. p. 2.
92 Robert Harris & Jeremy Paxman, *A Higher Form of Killing: The Secret History of Chemical and Biological Warfare* (London: The Random House Group Ltd, 2002). p. 158.
93 TNA, DEFE 5/15/267, B.W. trials at Sea-Operation Harness: Report by the Biological Warfare Sub-Committee, 18 August 1949. p. 3.
94 Ibid. p. 3.
95 TNA, War Office (WO 195): WO 195/10483, Biological Research Advisory Board: Operation Harness Opinions and Recommendations of the Conference of Technical Representatives of the US, Canada and the UK, 12 July 1949. p. 1.

agents and weapons.'⁹⁶ However, it was subsequently thought that only a couple of species of animals were up to the task of being experimental 'subjects' and that Harness:

> Has provided information regarding the behaviour of new types of bacterial suspensions which contain experimental animals, and brought out the value of monkeys in this type of research. It will be unnecessary, in future, to rely on such clumsy animals as sheep in trials with bacterial clouds.⁹⁷

Only certain kinds of nonhuman animal were considered to be appropriate for subsequent operations. With the sheep being labelled as 'clumsy,' signifying their awkwardness when it came to their use for B.W. trials. Nevertheless, implicit in this account of Harness is the idea that nonhuman animals are essential in the creation of Britain and allied nations' military capabilities. It was towards the end of Harness that plans by Porton Down scientists were being made to follow up these trials with further experiments at sea in the next operation, Operation Cauldron.

Hubble bubble, toil and trouble: From Operation Cauldron to Operation Negation, 1952–1955

With the conduct and responsibility of sea trials firmly placed in the hands of the British scientists of Porton,⁹⁸ the Conservative governments of the 1950s (1951–1964) gave their approval and financial backing for further B.W. trials. A suitable site for the next two operations was found off the coast of Scotland near the Isle of Lewis. Similar to Operation Harness, these trials involved the testing of pathogens, the highly gendered *Brucella suis* virus (which causes 'abortion' in pigs and flu-like symptoms in humans) and *Pasteurella Pestis* (a variant of the plague virus), for offensive reasons. The technique of the trials differed slightly from Harness as it was thought that the previous operation had 'certain disadvantages; it required a large number of men and a great deal of equipment, and accurate control of trial conditions could not be exercised.'⁹⁹ Rather, the aim for Cauldron was to reduce the number of men and amount of equipment used and this was done

---

96 Ibid.
97 TNA, WO 195/10485, Biological Research Advisory Board: Technical Opinion on Operation Harness, 12 July 1949, p. 1.
98 TNA, WO 195/9765, Biological Research Advisory Board: Operation Harness, Minutes of Meeting of "Harness" Advanced Base Reconnaissance Group, Held at the Pentagon, Washington DC 29 January 1948, Enclosure A, p. 2.
99 TNA, Department of Defence (DEFE 5/47) DEFE 5/47/310, Ministry of Defence Chiefs of Staff Committee, Memorandum – Operation Cauldron, 1952, Summary of Scientific Report by the Biological Warfare Sub-Committee, 7 July 1953, p. 1.

106 *Scientific intersections*

through a variety of ways. First, the floating pontoon containing the experimental animals remained anchored at sea rather than having to be towed away by dinghy after each trial. These provided such advantages that 'the animals and sampling devices could be brought to the layout and taken away after a trial.'[100] The infected animals were then transferred to the 'dirty' hold of H.M.S. Ben Lomond.

In Operation Cauldron and in the subsequent trials after Harness, Ben Lomond acted as both the laboratory ship complete with 'clean' hold (for holding uninfected animals) and the 'dirty' hold (for holding infected animals).[101] Second, the pontoon for holding the animals during testing measured 200 ft by 60 ft in an arc of 25 yards radius. This had been modified since Operation Harness, so that no tow dinghy was necessary as the 'use of compartments below deck meant that several trials could be done in succession and men and animals could remain there during the trials.'[102] The pontoon was 'little more than a floating box with 24 compartments, 9 of which had to be converted to house diesel generators, pumps, 'clean' and 'dirty' animal stowage, change rooms etc.'[103]

The third difference between Harness and Cauldron was the number of staff involved; 'our determination to reduce to an absolute minimum the number of men directly involved, meant that each individual was charged with a fairly complex series of jobs that had to interlock with the other men's duties.'[104] The officer in charge of the operation was Commander Cowgill of the Admiralty who accordingly made an 'invaluable contribution as 'stage director' with infinite patience and an exact eye for detail.'[105] With the reduction in the number of staff, J.D. Morton made it perfectly clear in the report that these trials were not grounded in welfarist doctrines of rights of the working man, and this meant that 'there was no place for a strict "Trades Union" attitude.' There were seven men on the pontoon during trials; the officer joined the three vets in the ship for stowing of exposed animals – a total of only 12 men in full protective rig.[106] Modern military science clearly did not have time for left-wing labour sentiments when it came to fulfilling British hopes of achieving the construction of a powerful weapon of mass destruction.

With the techniques for the trials in place, the scientists, vets from the Royal Air Force Veterinary Core (R.A.V.C.) and Admiralty staff sailed from

---

100 TNA, WO 195/12213, Chiefs of Staff Committee: Biological Warfare Sub-Committee, Ministry of Supply, B.R.A.B., Operation Cauldron 1952, Scientific Report by the Microbiological Research Department, Porton and Naval Report by the Naval Commander.
101 Ibid. p. 4.
102 Ibid. p. 4.
103 Ibid. p. 5.
104 Ibid. p. 6.
105 Ibid. p. 6.
106 Ibid. p. 6.

Chatham docks on the 5 May 1952 and arrived on site on the 8 May 1952 to conduct the Cauldron trials. The first trials using the pathogens were not done until six weeks after arrival due to terrible weather conditions. The trials used Br. suis on guinea-pigs and monkeys. They gave the scientists 'reasonably good answers about the efficacy' of the diseases on such nonhuman animals.[107] The experiments of course were in the name of offense and testing of potential weapons to be used against opponents. With Br. suis[108] proving successful because 'data supporting this were provided by sampling devices used in the trials and it is satisfactory to note that of a large number of guinea-pigs exposed, a small bomb filling was capable of infecting nearly every one.'[109] *P. Pestis* (or virulent plague) was not as great a success with the experimenters, with the B.W. Sub-Committee remarking that the evidence obtained signified 'that it is not an agent of striking potentialities.' Having said this, the percentage infected with plague was 12% (guinea-pigs) and 38% (monkeys), with Br. suis, 85% of guinea-pigs were infected and 59% of monkeys.[110] All in all, 36 toxic trials were done using 3,500 guinea-pigs and 84 monkeys, all of whom were exposed to plague and Br. suis.

Operation Hesperus in 1953 continued in the same vein as Cauldron and in the same location. The same techniques, methods and species of animals were used. However, Hesperus not only tested Br. suis on hundreds of non-human animals but also Bacterium tularense.[111] Yet, it was clear that despite the claims coming from the Conservative government about B.W. research for defensive purposes, it is obvious that the Porton scientists in these trials were testing bombs, and the viability of bacterium in certain types of bomb, with the scientific report clearly stating that, 'Experiments with these two agents in British and American experimental bombs showed very clearly the superiority of one agent in one weapon, and the other in the other' by outlining how biological agent and weapon cannot be treated as separate entities.[112]

Rather contrarily to the results of the Cauldron and Hesperus trials, the Porton scientists claimed that they had gathered 'convincing evidence with Br.suis and Bact.tularense,'[113] advancing the argument that it was therefore

---

107 Ibid. p. 7.
108 The bacterium Br. suis affects the reproductive organs of female pigs and causes humans to become incapacitated once inhaled.
109 TNA, DEFE 5/47/310, Ministry of Defence Chiefs of Staff Committee, Memorandum – Operation Cauldron, 1952, Summary of Scientific Report by the Biological Warfare Sub-Committee, 7 July 1953, [n.p].
110 Ibid.
111 Bacterium tularense is a variant of the plague virus and tests showed that it was slightly more susceptible in terms of rates of infectivity.
112 TNA, Department of Defence (DEFE 55) DEFE 55/256, Operation Ozone 1954 Scientific Report by the Microbiological Research Department and Naval Report by the Naval Commander, p. (i).
113 Ibid. p. (i).

necessary to continue B.W. research in this area. At the request of the British Prime Minister, Winston Churchill, Operation Ozone was carried out during February–May 1954 followed by Operation Negation in 1955, in the waters of the Bahamas.[114]

Operation Ozone and Operation Negation: 1954–1955

Operation Ozone, followed in 1954–1955 by Operation Negation, also provided the opportunity to test an even more dangerous pathogen, Venezuelan Equine Encephalomyelitis (a progressive disease in horses that effects the central nervous system. In humans, flu-like systems appear which can eventually lead to death).[115] In Negation, an additional pathogen was added, Vaccinia Virus (a variant of small pox).[116] Another addition to the programmes that differed from the previous operations was the fact that it was deemed necessary to assess the behaviour of pathogens in 'natural conditions' using aerosol sprays, and how ultraviolet light affected the decay of bacterial and viral agents.[117] Alongside this, the team hoped to; '[S]tudy the influence of various methods of dispersal (high explosive and propellant explosive, compared with spray) on one or two well-known pathogens.'[118] Operation Ozone conducted trials in the daylight, whereas Negation took the opportunity to test infectious diseases at nightfall.[119] The animals used in these two studies were primarily guinea-pigs and mice, with fertilised chicken eggs being added to the mixture in Operation Negation. Incidentally, the fertilised eggs were not considered to be 'alive' as such.[120] To transport the animals from Allington Farm – Porton Down's own animal farm used for the purpose of breeding large quantities of experimental animals – a link by air was necessitated for Ozone, with transport by sea for Negation.[121]

The transport of the nonhuman animals to the British colony proved difficult and contentious at times. The intention of the British and Commonwealth governments was to keep the trials as secret as possible and away from the

114 Ibid. p. (i).
115 Ibid. p. (i).
116 TNA, DEFE 55/261, Operation Negation 1954–1955, Scientific Report by the Microbiological Research Department and Naval Report by the Naval Commander. p. i.
117 TNA, DEFE 55/256, Operation Ozone 1954: Small-scale Experiments with Biological Weapons Agents Over Water, Discussion of Results, p. 11.
118 Ibid. p. 11.
119 TNA, DEFE 55/261, Operation Negation 1954–1955, Scientific Report by the Microbiological Research Department and Naval Report by the Naval Commander, pp. 3–4.
120 See: TNA, DEFE 55/256, Operation Ozone1954: Small-scale Experiments with Biological Weapons Agents Over Water, Discussion of Results. And: DEFE 55/261, Operation Negation 1954–1955, Scientific Report by the Microbiological Research Department and Naval Report by the Naval Commander.
121 Ibid.

public gaze. Therefore, once the animals had arrived in the Bahamas in the town of Nassau, every effort was made so that the 'animals were specially handled to conceal their presence.'[122] This was indicative of the broader concerns about secrecy which surrounded all of these trials at the time: the use of live dangerous infective agents were to be kept hidden from the public. Concerns regarding press intrusion about the use of animals in these experiments were also evident. As noted by the Ministry of Supply in a letter addressed to the Prime Minster about undesirable publicity because of:

> ...The fact that we are experimenting with animals, a subject which the British public in general, and the Anti-vivisection Society in particular, are especially sensitive. The fitting out of Ben Lomond with animal cages is known to a wide circle of Dockyard Workmen at Chatham, naval ratings and some subcontractors. Replacements of animals arrive by air [...] and this cannot help being known to a number of civilians. [...] The danger of leakage is clear, but in view of the decisions last year the question of publicity has not been raised again at Ministerial level for this year's trial, and the position remains that there is a dormant statement in existence for the Chiefs of Staff to being up to the Minister of Defence if circumstances require[123]

To compensate for this, the Ministry of Supply drafted a press statement to release to journalists if certain events were suspected and eventually became public.[124] Even though the draft press release was written for Operation Cauldron and Hesperus, it was initally never released to the newspapers, and was kept until the government thought it may be needed, in 1954, at the time of the Bahaman trials[125]:

> In order that effective means of defence may be developed every possibility must be studied, not only in the laboratory but in the field. To this end, for example, highly specialised laboratory apparatus has been developed for the study of the mode of infection of many forms of respiratory disease. Furthermore, the results so obtained are to be tested

---

122 See: TNA, DEFE 55/256, Operation Ozone 1954: Small-scale experiments with biological weapons agents over water, Discussion of Results. And: DEFE 55/261, Operation Negation 1954–1955, Scientific Report by the Microbiological Research Department and Naval Report by the Naval Commander.
123 TNA Ministry of Aviation [AVIA 54] AVIA 54/2251, Policy: Operation Hesperus, Draft Statement to the Press on the General Purposes of Experiments at Sea During 1952, 27 May 1953. p. 2.
124 TNA, AVIA 54/2251, Policy: Operation Hesperus, Draft Statement to the Press on the General Purposes of Experiments at Sea During 1952, 27 May 1953.
125 Robert Harris, Jeremy Paxman, *A Higher Form of Killing: The Secret History of Chemical and Biological Warfare* (London: Red Arrow Books, 2002). p. 160.

this year by experiments in the open; for safety reasons this experiments will be carried out at sea. Only by such means can the risk from biological warfare attack be adequately assessed and specific defence measures perfected.[126]

This very bland statement from the Ministry of Supply, clearly aims to misguide the public in matters of the types of bacterium and viruses used in the experiments *and* that the nature of the trials was in fact for offensive reasons, not defensive measures. Not only that, by locating the trials within the broader social context of the Cold War and the heightened state of paranoia within Britain, the Ministry of Supply could hope to persuade the public of the necessity of the trials and the use of animals therein. In the Bahamas, news of the press release reached J. D. Morton who wrote:

> Our reaction [to the press release] was satisfaction at the easing of our problems at Nassau, tempered only by anxiety about the local feeling. There proved to be no very serious interest in our activities, though the Tourist Board declared, without evidence, that we would be bad for trade: mostly, there was welcome relief from 'you're from the Mystery ship, aren't you?' followed by curiosity as to our business, to a cheerful 'how are the germs today?' and a change of subject to something more interesting.[127]

Clearly, the press release had worked and the general public was unperturbed by the experiments. The nonhuman animals involved in the experiments were clearly and most 'officially' downplayed – not even mentioned. This allowed for the continuation of the use of hundreds of guinea-pigs and mice in Ozone and Negation.

With the public-led astray about the nature and content of the experiments, the trials of infective agents could continue as normal. For the scientists working on Ozone, the results were satisfactory. A total of 84 experiments were conducted for Operation Ozone; 27 with *Br suis*, 32 with Bacterium tularense and 18 with Venezuelan Equine Encephalomyelitis. The rest were 'unaccounted' for.[128] Operation Ozone demonstrated that ultraviolet light could rapidly decay the pathogenic organism and decrease the infection rate caused by the diseases when released through an aerosol spray, so 'their offensive use in such conditions would lose a great deal of its potential effect.'[129] Hence, Operation Negation aimed at testing the

---

126 TNA, AVIA 54/2251, Policy: Operation Hesperus, Draft Statement to the Press on the General Purposes of Experiments at Sea During 1952, 27 May 1953.
127 TNA, DEFE 55/256, Operation Ozone 1954: Small-scale Experiments with Biological Weapons Agents Over Water, 22 December 1954, p. 7.
128 Ibid. p. 12.
129 Ibid. p. 19.

pathogenic agents in both sunlight and twilight in order to compare infection rates and decay of the organisms.[130]

Despite the use of even more guinea-pigs for trials in Negation, the results were seen as lacking validity and were particularly 'ill-fated' when it came to the testing of Venezuelan Equine Encephalomyelitis.[131] Yet, 880 guinea-pigs were used in the experiments and 380 in laboratory tests. Mice were also bred and used on site, and rabbits were considered too but were not used because a batch of fertilised eggs could not be sourced on the town of Nassau:

> We took 24 rabbits so that at least a rough assessment of the vaccinia might be made by injection in the depilated skin: one rabbit would carry a day's assessment, so with a precautionary duplication each time we had enough for 12 days – more than we expected to do. One of the rabbits was injured on arrival in 'Ben Lomond' and was destroyed.... There was no need for the remainder to be used. They were kept however, mainly because they had acquired names, developed personalities, and became the cherished pets of the RAVC party. After six months of this idle luxury they were as large, sleek and contented as any rabbit could wish to be.[132]

As the rabbits were not needed for experimental purposes, they seemingly became doted-upon pets of the very staff who were using the nonhuman animals for testing. The incongruous and ambivalent nature of the treatment of nonhumans in these series of experiments acts as an analytical point of departure in this chapter. Animals were at once used as objects of study, but also treated with care and concern over their welfare. It is here where I will discuss the power–knowledge relationship embedded within these scientific discourses about the animals used in the Operations. Nonhumans were considered to be parts, not wholes, and kept healthy and well-fed, in order to infect them with virulent diseases so that the scientists could assess their decline in health and resultant physiological deterioration. A *discourse of lines*[133] is proposed, in order to understand the connection between scientific statements of 'truth' about biological weapons and the treatment of nonhuman animals in the trials.

Power in the making: Animal experiments and the production of knowledge

Within these series of trials lays a succession of discourses that hid behind a veil of purported scientific 'truth.' Michel Foucault asserts that the gaze of the scientific observer produces a knowledge which is based on the perceptual

---

130 TNA, DEFE 55/261, Operation Negation 1954–1955, Scientific Report by the Microbiological Research Department and Naval Report by the Naval Commander. p. 3.
131 Ibid. p. 13.
132 Ibid. p. 26.
133 Johnson, *Power, Knowledge, Animals*.

112 *Scientific intersections*

(what can be seen).[134] The focus on what can be observed excludes the other senses of touch, taste and smell, sight becomes the 'sense by which we perceive, extend and establish proof.'[135] The gaze beholding the infected nonhuman body enabled the scientists to categorise and generalise their experiments in terms of the effect dangerous pathogens had on parts of the nonhuman body. They did this through vivisection and the dissection of the animal into parts, or what sociologist Lisa Johnson, calls the 'discourse of lines.'[136]

Contained within the scientific reports, are precise details about the method employed to assess, analyse and recognise the uncontaminated nonhumans from the contaminated. Turning to Foucault,[137] the nonhuman animals used in the trials can be constituted by four historically contingent categories: the form of the elements, the quantity of those elements, the manner in which they are distributed in space in relation to each other and the relative magnitude of each element.[138] For example, the scientific reports describe in detail the effect of B.W. on animals, post-mortems were conducted, in order to enumerate the effect pathogens had on the different parts of an animal i.e. their liver, spleen, reproductive system, etc.[139] Alongside this was the ability to identify and define the effect and where the effect is distributed in the body.

The infected: The post-mortem as an exercise of power over the nonhuman

In order to determine the effect of dangerous pathogens on the body of the nonhuman, a rigorous post-mortem methodology was utilised, which was outlined in the report on Operation Cauldron. This technique was used throughout the series of trials, ending with Operation Negation. As will be shown, the nature and style of the conduct of the post-mortems became a site where the investigative and explanatory power of the human is exercised over the nonhuman. Furthermore, examining the manner in which vivisection was performed demonstrates how the interests of the scientists are interrelated with the concerns of the wider 'politico-technological' system in Britain at the time,[140] or what I would term the birth of the MAIC. In other

---

134 Foucault, *The Order of Things*. p. 144.
135 Ibid. p. 144.
136 Ibid. p. 145. Johnson, *Power, Knowledge, Animals*.
137 Foucault, *The Order of Things*. p. 146.
138 Ibid. p. 146.
139 TNA War Office [WO 195] WO 195/12213, Chiefs of Staff Committee: Biological Warfare Sub-Committee, Ministry of Supply, B.R.A.B., Operation Cauldron 1952, Scientific Report by the Microbiological Research Department, Porton and Naval Report by the Naval Commander.
140 Lindsay Prior, "Policing the Dead: A Sociology of the Mortuary," *Sociology* 21, no. 3 (1987): 355.

Animal experimentation at Porton Down 113

words, the investigative approaches to post-mortems were grounded in the socio-political apparatus rather than the biological. This was undergirded by a discourse of pathology[141] within which the animal body became a Cartesian material entity devoid of life, because the nonhuman 'cadaver [became] an object, a repository of disease and infection. It [was] a container, a shell; at once a solution to a riddle, and an obstacle to knowledge'[142]:

> The object of post mortem examination of trials animals… is to determine whether the animal is 'infected' with the specific organism … We have selected arbitrary conditions of examination which maybe expected to demonstrate invasion and substantial multiplication in the host.[143]

Hence, the visualisation of disease was imperative to determine infection. This was evident in the criteria chosen to determine abnormality, in terms of what was characteristic of infection with a specific disease and what was 'abnormal but not characteristic.'[144] The visual coalesced with the theoretical aspect of pathology. Consequently, the animals became objects of knowledge, and through the observational power of the scientists' gaze during post-mortems, the true nature of the efficacy of biological weapons could be determined:

> After exposure to a toxic agent all animals from trials and spray runs were held in the dirty hold for a period of observation. When the results of the laboratory assessment had been calculated, some of the animals which had obviously been outside the cloud [of released toxic agent] were killed off without post-mortem examination. The principle was to retain for further observations all animals at points whose…samples showed an even trace of agent and the animals from four further points, two right and two left of the cloud. The holding periods were 28 days for the animals exposed to US [Brucella suis] and 14 days for animals exposed to L [tularaemia]. Animals dying during the holding period were post-mortemed by the casual PM team.[145]

Clearly, the animals were made to live after attempted infection by a toxic bacterial agent. This was so deterioration of the physiology of the monkeys and guinea-pigs could be observed, and the intensity of the effect of the

---

141 Ibid. p. 355.
142 Ibid. p. 360.
143 TNA, WO 195/12213, Chiefs of Staff Committee: Biological Warfare Sub-Committee, Ministry of Supply, B.R.A.B., Operation Cauldron 1952, Scientific Report by the Microbiological Research Department, Porton and Naval Report by the Naval Commander. p. 19.
144 Ibid. p. 20.
145 Ibid. p. 37.

114 *Scientific intersections*

pathogen could be measured after the holding period. The autopsies were divided into two different kinds: 'casual autopsies' for animals that died during the holding period, and 'mass autopsies,'[146] where a team of six laboratory staff scientists and two veterinary staff engaged in the slicing and dicing of the body parts of guinea-pigs, monkeys and mice. All monkeys were post-mortemed, and most guinea-pigs, if they had survived the holding period.[147] In preparation for 'mass post-mortems,' there was, of course, a series of steps to follow to prepare the nonhuman animals:

> Two RAVC staff and one lab man enter the dirty hold and commence killing about one hour before the arrival of the post-mortem party. (Time adjusted according to number to be killed). Groups of 100–250 have been dealt with. The killed animals are placed in trays: each tray contains the group of animals from the cages which were exposed to the B. W. agent at a particular point of the layout [pontoon], or in a particular laboratory spray experiment. A label indicating Trial Number and exposure point is attached to each tray of dead animals.[148]

The bodies were quantified, but not only that, storage spaces were also to be referenced quantitatively, as well as an accurate time recorded for the euthanasia to happen prior to the post-mortem. The animals coalesced with the storage to become a 'thing' or object of the scientific enquiry:

> Monkeys are dealt with in a similar manner. A member of the laboratory staff kills the monkeys by an intraperitoneal injection [injection into the body cavity] of 10-20ml of 6.5 per cent Nembutal solution [a barbiturate drug which slows down the activity of the brain and nervous system]. They are injected 2-3 hours prior to the actual time scheduled for the commencement of post-mortems. For killing, a two vet party remove the animal from the cage (a four vet party if any large numbers of monkeys are required to be examined for a post-mortem); the animal is held extended so that the abdomen is fairly taut. After the injections the animal is returned to the cage and left until dead. The animals are inspected within 3-40 minutes after the Nembutal injection.[149]

The normativity of killing the nonhuman, by which these procedures are embedded in the daily practice of these series of Operations, enabled a language of 'distance' and a sense of ambivalence towards nonhuman animals in the B.W. trials.[150] The monkeys, guinea-pigs and mice became part of

---

146 Ibid. p. 37.
147 Ibid. p. 37.
148 Ibid. p. 78.
149 Ibid. p. 78.
150 Lynda Birke, "Structuring Relationships: On Science, Feminism and Non-Human Animals," *Feminism and Psychology* 20, no. 3 (2010): 341.

a 'generalised Other' – at once different from humans, but all of the same 'kind' when it came to the scientific observations and descriptions. The nonhumans were devoid of agency and individuality and were frequently referred to as an 'it,' or generally speaking 'the animals.' By deploying this discourse, the scientists held the mantle of neutrality and objectivity – they immediately became distanced observers, unattached and value-free: 'the object [became] objectified'[151] through the acts of killing, observation and reporting. The animals became numbers or 'tools of the trade' even.[152]

Once the killing was over, the autopsies used a 'mass production' style approach to enquiry.[153] The animals were labelled and passed from the 'dirty hold' in Ben Lomond to the post-mortem room. The rigour of the post-mortem methodology was the ultimate of capitalist production line techniques, one that mimicked the 'factory floor' approach: that of Taylorism. The bodies of the nonhumans were passed from one scientist to the next, round a rotating table, in what was described by Morten as the 'travelling Circus'[154]:

> The team prepare the post mortem table, a round revolving stainless steel table. Clips and chains are attached, beakers containing acetone or Lysol are placed in appropriate positions and instruments prepared... The two fixers (vet staff) who lay out the animal on the numbered towel on the tray in front of them and clip the animal out by its four limbs. Each animal thoroughly wetted with Lysol before the table is revolved to bring it in front of the *skinner* who opens the animal up from pubes to jaw, laying the skin back on each side. The animal is now moved round to the *Exposer* who removes the anterior portion of the thoracic cage, laying bare the heart and lungs, and opens up the abdominal cavity exposing the spleen for the *spleen plater* who removes a small portion of the spleen and smears its cut surface on the half of a plate labelled 'S,' handed to him by the *plate handler* who after marking the plate with the animal's number holds it for the *pathologist* who removes a portion of the lymphatic gland and smears it over the unmarked half of the plate. The pathologist reports to the recorder on the condition of the spleen, liver, cervical and bronchial glands in this order. A typically positive is plus, a typical negative –, E indicates enlarged, and A abnormal.[155]

Sounding rather like something out of a horror story, the dead animal is at first clipped to the table in 'chains,' with an identification number on the paper underneath them. The body is then rotated round and passed to the

---

151 Prior, "Policing the Dead: A Sociology of the Mortuary." p. 360.
152 Birke, "Structuring Relationships: On Science, Feminism and Non-Human Animals." p. 341.
153 http://www.youtube.com/watch?v=CPA_yce0Swg (accessed 12/05/14).
154 Ibid.
155 TNA, WO 195/12213, Chiefs of Staff Committee: Biological Warfare Sub-Committee, Ministry of Supply, B.R.A.B., Operation Cauldron 1952, Scientific Report by the Microbiological Research Department, Porton and Naval Report by the Naval Commander, p. 38.

116 *Scientific intersections*

first man who peels back the skin of the animal. The second man exposes the organs and the third takes a sample of one particular organ depending on the disease they were looking for.[156] All the scientists present are given names to assume their role, characters in a tragicomedy; they know their place and part, whether you become the '*skinner*' or the '*exposer*,' one assumes their role with utmost scientific authority and neutrality. Once the dissection is complete, the bodies of the nonhuman animals are then removed from the table, put into a dustbin, taken to an incinerator and burned.[157]

The autopsies not only vivisected the physical body of the nonhuman but they also acted as a process of scientific ideology. In this methodology of death is the discourse of pathology. Here, there are two aspects of dissection: the physical, as described above, and the ideological – that which is *a priori* to the evidence – the theoretical aspect.[158] Both facets rely on the gaze of the scientists and the ability to 'know' about nonhuman bodies. This is done through superimposing 'lines' upon the body,[159] to enable disassembly of *whole* living beings, and then to be categorised as 'abnormal' by a pathologist. The discourse of lines when taken in the context of the series of operations lead by the Porton scientists, gave the experiments the mantle of 'truth-telling power'[160] as it came from an 'office of authority to speak'[161] that of military science and the state:

> US [Brucella Suis] guinea-pigs were held at least 21 days: any dying during the holding period were examined, but results were accepted only from the 18th day onwards. Examination was normally confined to gross pathology of spleen and liver, and culture of spleen by smearing a cut surface over fortified tryptose agar containing methyl violet. The criterion normally adopted was positive or negative culture, except for one period when a batch of plates gave negative results from the animals indisputably positive. Having confirmed that the cultures were misleading, […] we had to interpret these trials another way: animals giving a visually positive spleen were taken as positive; animals giving liver only, or neither liver nor spleen, were taken as negative.[162]

Here, the guinea-pigs were divided into parts according to their organs, and how their organs *looked* according to the scientist's gaze upon the animal. The *whole* being of the guinea-pigs became obsolete; the organs became the important objects for discovery in the process. The pathologist's gaze was

---

156 Ibid. p. 38.
157 Ibid and WO 195/12213. p. 38.
158 Prior, "Policing the Dead: A Sociology of the Mortuary." p. 362.
159 Johnson, *Power, Knowledge, Animals*. p. 56.
160 Ibid. p. 56.
161 Ibid. p. 57.
162 TNA, DEFE 55/256, Operation Ozone 1954: Small-scale Experiments with Biological Weapons Agents Over Water, Discussion of Results. p. 27.

integral to assure the validity of the results for the trials conducted in the operations: one must *see* in order to understand and produce 'knowledge.' The results were negligible, but with the observation of specific parts of the animals, the scientists could acknowledge the nonhuman as being abnormal and contaminated with viruses. This developed into a methodology that was historically contingent upon the laws of science, as 'each visibly distinct part of... an animal is thus describable.'[163] In fact, the very act of seeing is built into the definition of autopsy: to examine, to *see*.[164]

Gendered violence towards nonhuman animals of war

It should be clear by know that the violence towards animals in the testing of these weapons of war was inherently gendered. As outlined at the beginning of this chapter, gendered violence does not always have to be so explicit, but can come in many guises, and some of these is through language, the written word and the underpinning philosophy upon which animal experimental science's methodologies rely upon. The scientific male gaze is clearly linked to how such scientific endeavours discussed in this chapter are communicated. The process of writing associated statistical techniques are enfolded within the masculine. The notion of objectivity and its associated mathematical calculations all represent the world in a particular way, one that stems from the male gaze. For example, the value of quantitative techniques during the testing of B.W. was essential in order to validate the scientist's findings, even when results were often negligible and erroneous:

> Two groups of three trials each with undiluted suspensions of Br.suis in the B/E.1 bomb were done with monkeys and guinea-pigs. The monkey was believed to be less susceptible (*though there were no good quantitative data*). So a layout of monkeys flanked by a few guinea-pig points were employed. The intention was to expose monkeys to the heavier dosages and guinea-pigs to the fringes of the clouds (to check against earlier guinea-pig results), this worked very well.[165]

In order to test biological bombs, monkeys had to be given higher dosages, as previous statistics were seen as invalid. Guinea-pigs were used alongside the monkeys in order to compare earlier work. The monkeys and guinea-pigs in Cauldron were transformed into statistical assemblages: mere numbers in the name of war, and this formed an important part of B.W. research. In

---

163 Johnson, *Power, Knowledge, Animals.* p. 57. Foucault, *The Order of Things.* p. 146.
164 Prior, "Policing the Dead: A Sociology of the Mortuary." p. 362.
165 TNA, WO 195/12213, Chiefs of Staff Committee: Biological Warfare Sub-Committee, Ministry of Supply, B.R.A.B., Operation Cauldron 1952, Scientific Report by the Microbiological Research Department, Porton and Naval Report by the Naval Commander. p. 7. [My emphasis.]

118 *Scientific intersections*

Hesperus, Ozone and Negation, once again the animals are collapsed into single entities of numbers. For example, in Negation:

> Guinea-pigs were exposed in a number of trials in an attempt to determine any loss of virulence, i.e. whether the number of viable cells required for a given degree of infection was greater after downwind travel. ... For infectivity calculations it is of course essential to get results in the range of partial infection: that is, between one to four animals in a group five. Points with 0–5 infected are of practically no use. ... It will be seen that the UL (Bacterium Tularense] trials were particularly ill-fated, for only one point gave a dosage that was in the measurable range (and that too high_, and only 3 points gave other than none or all guinea-pigs infected. We must rely on results from previous trials to support the belief that virulence is not lost in downwind travel.[166]

Calculations of infectivity rates seemed to be disappointing, but all were collated in numerical format. The language of mathematics in this case was important to convey the objectivity of the experiments in terms of the viability of biological agents. This was essential to be able to order the world in such a way so as to produce results that displayed a 'most gratifying linearity.'[167] In all the reports of the operations, these results were also coupled with graphs, charts and tables. The nonhuman animal in these statistics disappeared, became and 'data.' This too emphasises the experimenters' distance and scientific 'objectivity.'[168] Additionally, the use of mathematical analyses in these trials seemingly generated an ideology of value-freedom where the experimental results were apparently free from social influence and grounded in rationality. However, these assumptions about the objectivity of statistics and the use of them in this research are based in the based in the binary oppositions previously mentioned in this chapter. At the beginning of this chapter, the results display a hidden bias, and an underlying set of assumptions that were grounded in the androcentric. Hence, this in turn corresponds to the 'masculine' but not the 'feminine' way of knowing about the world.[169]

Likewise, the focus on statistical averages reinforces the illusion of objectivity because it obliquely denies the nonhuman individual as being an active agent. Another example of the kind of objectification of the nonhuman that denies their agency, and is considered a part of scientific objectivity, is through the language employed to describe the animals in all of the reports. The language of objectivity denies individual agency of the

---

166 TNA, DEFE 55/261: Operation Negation 1954–1955, Scientific Report by the Microbiological Research Department and Naval Report by the Naval Commander. p. 14.
167 Ibid. p. 14.
168 Joan Dunayer, *Animal Equality: Language and Liberation* (Maryland: Ryce Publishing, 2001). pp. 111–112.
169 Harding, *The Science Question in Feminism*. p. 51.

nonhuman animals, and transforms the animal body into objects: words such as 'batch' and 'consignment,' further, if an animal had to be euthanised, they were systematically 'destroyed.'[170] All signify an objectification of them grounded in the language of positivism, that gave the reports a masculinised 'language of depersonalised authority.'[171]

We must also note the kinds of virus used to test on nonhuman animals. Note how such viruses as Br. suis was used on experimental animals. As noted, this causes abortion in pigs and complete incapacitation in humans. The use of such a virulent virus which effects female nonhuman bodies is another example of how gender and power are linked in the oppression and exploitation of nonhuman animals. Carol J. Adams expresses this as the absent referent,[172] implicit in the choice of virus is the absent female (I would argue human and nonhuman), whose bodies can be vectors of disease yet ripe for scientific testing.

Conclusion

The B.W. trials of Porton Down in the late 1940s and early 1950s signify a significant historical formation in Britain regarding animal experimentation. After the Second World War and the looming crisis of the Cold War which shortly followed it, nonhuman animals, both dead and alive, became integral to rebuilding Britain's reputation as a nation which can lead in scientific developments and have enviable military prowess. Ultimately, the trials of Porton can be a signifier for the early formation of Britain's MAIC.

In the chapters that follow, I outline the qualitative nature of this complex, focusing on the development of laboratory welfare in Britain, and its gendered entanglements. It is important to note that animal welfare in Britain became integral to experimental practices and remains so to this day. For me, this is to ensure that Britain can maintain its MAIC in the neoliberal era. Nonhuman animals are essential for the maintenance of such a complex and I reveal the often-contradictory terrain of laboratory animal welfare, especially in regards to nonhumans confinement and psychological wellbeing.

During the Porton Down B.W. trials, the physical health of the animals was important in order to be able to test dangerous pathogens on them. Welfare was given a cursory glance in order to proceed with the animal experimentation. However, in this section of the book I demonstrate how, with the help of legal requirements, animal welfare moved from a focus on purely the physical health of nonhumans to their psychological health, asking why and how this is the case.

---

170 These words are used throughout the scientific reports on all five scientific trials – see previous references.
171 Hubbard, *The Poltics of Women's Biology*. p. 1.
172 Carol Adams, *The Sexual Politics of Meat* (Oxford, UK: Polity Press, 1990).

Coda

Historically, this chapter begins and finishes in the immediate aftermath of the Second World War (1945–1955). I have done this for two reasons; first, following Foucault, to denounce the 'universalising' tendency of normative histories. Foucault argues that traditional historical practices have totalising assumptions, whereby particular events are inserted into a unifying and total explanatory schema. This deprives specific events of the impact of their significance: 'the world as we know is not this ultimately simple configuration where events are reduced to accentuate their essential traits, their final meaning, or their initial and final value. On the contrary it's a profusion of entangled events.'[173]

Rather than falsely celebrate 'great moments' in history, this one highlights specific events, in detail. Second, and relatedly, by shifting the history away from the human (male) and centring it around nonhuman animals changes how we *do* history. This epistemological positioning of the thesis eschews the fixity of historical events, which traditionally focus around the human. The series of sea trials discussed above re-writes contemporary historical methodologies in terms of periodisation, as it centralises the events that had a huge impact on nonhuman animals in Britain at this point in time.

Bibliography

Adams, Carol. *The Sexual Politics of Meat*. Oxford, UK: Polity Press, 1990.

Adams, Carol J. *Neither Man nor Beast: Feminism and the Defense of Animals*. New York: The Continuum Publishing Company, 1995.

Agar, Jon. *Science in the Twentieth Century and Beyond*. Cambridge, U.K. and Malden, M.A.: Polity Press, 2012.

Balmer, Brian. *Britain and Biological Warfare: Expert Advice and Science Policy, 1930-65*. Basingstoke: Palgrave Macmillan, 2001.

———. "The Drift of Biological Weapons Policy in the UK, 1945–1965." *The Journal of Strategic Studies* 20, no. 4 (1997): 115–145.

———. "Killing 'without the Distressing Preliminaries': Scientists' Defence of the British Biological Warfare Programme." *Minerva* 40, no. 1, Special Issue: Ethics and Reason in Chemical and Biological Weapons Research (2002): 57–75.

———. *Secrecy and Science: A Historical Sociology of Biological and Chemical Warfare*. Surrey: Ashgate Publishing Ltd, 2012.

———. "The Uk Biological Weapons Programme." In *Deadly Cultures: Biological Weapons since 1945*, edited by Lajos Rózsa, Mark Wheelis, Malcolm Dando, 47–83. Cambridge M.A. & London U.K.: Harvard University Press, 2006.

Birke, Lynda. *Feminism, Animals and Science: The Naming of the Shrew*. Buckingham, UK: Open University Press, 1994.

———. "Structuring Relationships: On Science, Feminism and Non-Human Animals." *Feminism and Psychology* 20, no. 3 (2010): 337–349.

---

173 Paul Rabinow, ed. *The Foucualt Reader: An Introduction to Foucualt's Thought* (London: Penguin Books, 1984). p. 89.

Carter, G. B. *Porton Down: 75 Years of Chemical and Biological Research*. London: HMSO Publications, 1992.

Salter, Colin, Anthony J. Nocella II, Judy K. C. Bentley, ed. *Animals and War: Confronting the Military-Animal Industrial Complex*, Plymouth: Lexington Books, 2014.

Darnton, Robert. *The Great Cat Massacre and Other Episodes in French Cultural History*. New York: Basic Books, 1984.

Dunayer, Joan. *Animal Equality: Language and Liberation*. Maryland: Ryce Publishing, 2001.

Edgerton, David. *Warfare State: Britain, 1920–1970*. Cambridge, UK: Cambridge University Press, 2006.

Foucault, Michel. *The Order of Things*. 11 ed. Oxon and New York: Routledge, 2008.

Fox-Keller, Evelyn. *Secrets of Life, Secrets of Death: Essays on Language, Gender and Science*. London: Routledge, 1992.

Frewer, Andreas, Ulf Schmidt, ed. *History and Theory of Human Experimentation: The Declaration of Helsinki and Modern Medical Ethics*. Stuttgart: Franz Steiner Verlag Wiesbaden GmbH, 2007.

Hammond, Peter, Gradon Carter. *From Biological Warfare to Healthcare: Porton Down 1940-2000*. Basingstoke: Palgrave Macmillan, 2002.

Harding, Sandra. *The Science Question in Feminism*. Ithaca, USA: Cornell University Press, 1986.

Hubbard, Ruth. *The Poltics of Women's Biology*. New Jersey: Rutgers University Press, 1992.

Hunnicutt, Gwen. *Gender Violence in Ecofeminist Perspective: Intersections of Animal Oppression, Patriarchy and Domination of the Earth*. Abingdon & New York: Routledge, 2020.

Johnson, Lisa. *Power, Knowledge, Animals*. Basingstoke: Palgrave Macmillan, 2012.

Kean, Hilda. *Animal Rights: Political and Social Change in Britain since 1800*. London, UK: Reaktion Books Ltd, 1998.

Merchant, Carolyn. *The Death of Nature: Women, Ecology and the Scientific Revolution*. New York: Harper & Row Publishers Inc, 1983.

Millet, Piers. "Antianimal Biological Weapons Programs." In *Deadly Cultures: Biological Weapons since 1945*, edited by Lajos Rozsa Mark Wheelis, Malcolm Dando. Cambridge MA: Harvard University Press, 2006.

Mulvey, Laura. "Visual Pleasure and Narrative Cinema." In *Film Theory and Criticism: Introductory Readings*, edited by Leo Braudy, Marshall Cohen, 833–844. New York and Oxford: Oxford University Press, 1999.

Noske, Barbara. *Beyond Boundaries: Humans and Animals*. London, New York and Montréal: Black Rose Books, 1997.

Paxman, Jeremy, and Robert Harris. *A Higher Form of Killing: The Secret History of Chemical and Biological Warfare*. London: The Random House Group Ltd, 2002.

Prior, Lindsay. "Policing the Dead: A Sociology of the Mortuary." *Sociology*, 21, no. 3 (1987): 355–376.

Rabinow, Paul, ed. *The Foucualt Reader: An Introduction to Foucualt's Thought*. London: Penguin Books, 1984.

Salter, Colin. "Introducing the Military-Industrial Complex." In *Animals and War: Confronting the Military-Animal Industrial Complex*, edited by Anthony J. Nocella II, Judy K. C. Bentley, Colin Salter. Plymouth: Lexington Books, 2014.

Schmidt, Ulf. "Cold War at Porton Down: Informed Consent in Britain's Biological and Chemical Warfare Experiments." *Cambridge Quarterly of Healthcare Ethic* 15, no. 4 (2006): 366–380.

———. "Medical Ethics and Human Experiments at Porton Down: Informed Consent in Britain's Biological and Chemical Warfare Experiments." In *History and Theory of Human Experimentation: The Declaration of Helsinki and Modern Medical Ethics*, edited by Ulf Schmidt, Andreas Frewer. Stutgart: Franz Steiner Verlag Wiesbaden GmbH, 2007.

———. *Secret Science*. Oxford: Oxford University Press, 2015.

Twine, Richard. "Revealing the 'Animal-Industrial Complex' – a Concept & Method for Critical Animal Studies." *Journal for Critical Animal Studies* 10, no. 1 (2012): 8.

Wilson, Elizabeth. *Only Halfway to Paradise Women in Postwar Britain: 1945-1968*. London: Tavistock Publications Ltd, 1980.

5 Containing the laboratory animal
Laboratory spaces and gendered places, 1947–present

The main features of successful rat colonies, as observed in the 1947 edition of the Universities Federation for Animal Welfare's (UFAW) *Handbook on the Care and Management of Laboratory Animals*, 'are scrupulous cleanliness, strict attention to environmental temperature... adequate nutrition, and painstaking care in general management.' Further, an emphasis was laid upon the personnel who maintain and look after the rats, stating clearly that, preferably, these technical assistants should be *female*.[1] In highlighting this, I am arguing from the outset that the historical continuity of animal-dependent science is inherently gendered, with the values of it being shared with wider society, despite scientists' claims for its objectivity.[2]

This second section of the book focuses on the material practices of the animal-dependent science laboratory. If we recall, the Animals (Scientific Procedures) Act, 1986 provides a mandated set of guidelines which all research organisations and laboratory breeding and supply establishments have to abide by. Animal-dependent breeding and use institutions have to ensure that nonhuman animals are cared for both physically and psychologically. Despite this emphasis on their welfare, it was noted how the treatment of lab animals, as enshrined in law, only acted as a veil to perpetuate a very violent human-dominance hierarchy which continues to exploit nonhumans. This chapter outlines the material spaces nonhuman animals occupy and are contained within before, during and after experiment. However, this spatial confinement of experimental nonhumans is gendered. Their incarceration is shrouded in conscious and unconscious misogynistic relations which are historically contingent. Like the law, 'confinement technologies'[3] are inherently patriarchal.

1 Alastair N. Worden, ed., *The UFAW Handbook on the Care and Management of Laboratory Animals*, 1st ed. (London: Bailliere, Tindall and Cox, 1947). pp. 110–111.
2 Helen E. Longino, *Science as Social Knowledge: Values and Objectivity in Scientifc Inquiry* (Princeton, New Jersey: Princeton University Press, 1990). p. 15. Emily Martin, *The Woman in the Body: A Cultural Analysis of Reproduction* (Milton Keynes: Open University Press, 1989).
3 Zoë Sofia, "Container Technologies," *Hypatia* 15, no. 2 (2000): 181–201.

DOI: 10.4324/9780429461644-6

This patriarchal relationship between the nonhuman animal in the lab and their 'caregivers' (scientists and technicians) signifies a discrete set of power relations which both discipline the nonhuman body and contain it. In this instance, the experimental nonhuman body is read as a particular target of disciplinary power. Gender, particularly notions of the 'feminine' and 'female,' interact on a psychic and material level in the lab, to produce docile bodies. Containment historically plays out as a maternal-esque facilitating environment, where power masquerades as care. At the same time, the 'feminine' is patriarchally exploited as a 'container' for the physical and psychic lives of nonhuman animals. This is as much as it is essentialised and seen as a gendered characteristic necessary for the continued exploitation ('care') of nonhuman laboratory animals.

To illustrate this patriarchal containment and exploitation of nonhuman bodies and 'the feminine,' I draw on the research of Science and Technology Studies scholar, Zoë Sofia. She will be used to help me draw out the unconscious gendered dimensions of such 'containment technologies' used in laboratory animal welfare.[4] Sofia uses the work of psychoanalysts such as Donald Winnicott and Thomas Ogden, to explicate a feminist approach to the history of technologies centred around a variety of vessels associated with the 'feminine.'

Condemned bodies: The intersection of female human and laboratory nonhuman bodies

The body, according to Elizabeth Grosz, is a site of social inscription which cannot be understood without attention to its historicity, and cultural specificity. For Grosz, bodily representations and cultural inscriptions materially shape the body and enable its continual existence.[5] The sciences of biology and medicine have historically contributed to these various inscriptions. They have saturated the body in a variety of assumptions, both constructing it as a natural object of knowledge, ripe for investigation, and also giving it a pre-cultural status, which is immune to social and historical fact.[6] This scientific approach to the body is rooted in a philosophy that presents a particular way of understanding and seeing the world. It is grounded in an epistemology that dates back to seventeenth century scientists, Rene Descartes and Francis Bacon.[7] This 'way to knowledge' is labelled, in this sense, as 'objective,' the knowers are distinct from the known, all acquisition of information is through specific experimental methods, and the outcomes

---

4 Ibid.
5 Elizabeth Grosz, *Volitile Bodies: Towards a Coporeal Feminism* (Bloomington: Indiana University Press, 1994). p. x.
6 Ibid.
7 Carolyn Merchant, *The Death of Nature: Women, Ecology and the Scientific Revolution* (New York: Harper & Row Publishers Inc., 1983). p. xi.

thought of as a set of universal and absolute truths. Science has demarcated the world into binary categories that separate nature from culture, animal from human, and male from female.[8] These binary categories leave traces of gender labels that produce a powerful hierarchical structure.[9] With women occupying the 'underside' of the binary, inferior to men and placed alongside animals and nature.[10] In this case, women and animals become essentialised 'Others,' their bodies representing certain innate characteristics which deem them suitable for specific roles: mothering, care and objects of experimentation.[11]

Feminist animal studies scholar Carol J. Adams discusses this intersection of laboratory animals and women.[12] It is through the male gaze, or as she puts it, 'the arrogant eye,' that the intersection of woman and animal becomes an aspect of subject-object relations in the methodologies of animal experimentation.[13] If we refer back to the opening statement to this chapter, the rat and the woman become constituted as a scientific representation. The human, technical assistant who cares for the animal, must be female, the rat an experimental object – this, in Adams's terms, confirms 'the cultural role of the human male gaze that looks at women and animals.'[14] It is through such historical representations that women and animals' status as an object intersects and the two buttress each other within the discourses of science.

This chapter takes as its starting point Adams' thoughts on the human male gaze in animal experimentation but seeks to go further by situating it within the confines of the material spaces of the lab. For patriarchal power is not just a representation; it is also a very real material practice which has violent consequences for nonhuman animals and women.

Gender and the power of the unconscious

Nonhuman animals in the lab and women in the broader social world are subject to the same (but different) disciplinary practices. This is because of the dualistic assumptions outlined above. Historically, women have been constructed as both inferior beings and as foreboding entities to men.[15] As feminist Angela King argues, women throughout much of Western history

---

8   Evelyn Fox-Keller, *Secrets of Life, Secrets of Death: Essays on Language, Gender and Science* (London: Routledge, 1992). p. 18.
9   Val Plumwood, *Feminism and the Mastery of Nature* (London: Routledge, 1993).
10 Ibid.
11 Catherine Duxbury, "Of Monkeys, Men and Menstruation: Gendered Dualisms and the Absent Referent in Mid-Twentieth Century British Menstrual Science," *Journal of Historical Sociology* 32, no. 1 (2019): 94–107.
12 Carol J. Adams, *Neither Man nor Beast: Feminism and the Defense of Animals* (New York: The Continuum Publishing Company, 1995). pp. 39–54.
13 Ibid. p. 41.
14 Ibid. p. 43.
15 Grosz, *Volitile Bodies: Towards a Coporeal Feminism*.

have been in a perpetual need of containment and control.[16] Women, like nonhuman laboratory animals, have been condemned to particular disciplinary techniques. These disciplinary 'technologies of gender' are synonymous with 'containment technologies' used on the experimental animal in order to render them docile. Women's association with the 'underside' of the binary (body/animal), is reinforced by biological essentialism which defines the bodies of women as determined by their reproductive physiology.[17] Women become the literal repository for the desires of men and the 'container' of his offspring.[18] Nonhuman animals in the experimental world are contained in a 'nurturing' space.[19] Women and animals are thus exploited and contained, consciously and unconsciously (symbolically), because of the historical associations and constructions of their bodies.

Zoë Sofia exemplifies the unconscious gendered forces at play in 'Container Technologies.' She argues that objects of containment have been historically associated with the feminine and women's labours.[20] Containers then, are in this instance, interpreted as associated with the female.[21] For Sofia, containers are not passive receptacles but are dynamic and infinitely complex.[22] She draws on intersubjectivist psychoanalysis to explore the unconscious dynamics of container technologies:

> In the intersubjectivist model of subject formation, the self is understood as an entity given shape through various dynamic relationships of containment that both construct and occur in spaces that are interpersonal, imaginative, real, active, the products of conscious efforts as well as unconscious or automatic labours.[23]

The subjects, both human and nonhuman animals, are shaped by the relationships within their immediate environment. This includes the physical spaces of the lab: cages, restraining devices, etc., as well as the human workers themselves. The unconscious forces at work also permeate the makings of the laboratory animal, and this is where the gendered dimensions, noted above by Sofia take root. Laboratory houses are macro-containers, the cages of confinement which house nonhumans are the micro-containers.

---

16 Angela King, "The Prisoner of Gender: Foucualt and the Disciplining of the Female Body," *Journal of International Women's Studies* 5, no. 2 (2004): 29–39.
17 Duxbury, "Of Monkeys, Men and Menstruation: Gendered Dualisms and the Absent Referent in Mid-Twentieth Century British Menstrual Science."
18 King, "The Prisoner of Gender: Foucualt and the Disciplining of the Female Body." p. 31.
19 Dinesh Joseph Wadiwel, *The War against Animals* (Leiden & Boston: Brill Rodopi, 2015). p. 193.
20 Sofia, "Container Technologies." p. 182.
21 See also: ibid. p. 187.
22 Ibid. p. 185.
23 Ibid. pp. 184–185.

These containers are symbolically and unconsciously female. Psychically, they become 'the mother' who identifies with the living being and serves as their container and interpreter for their lived experiences.[24] There is a gradation of legitimacy at play in the lab. There is an exploitation of the symbolically 'feminine' container, and it is seen as a way to hold and discipline nonhumans – to make them docile. Nonhumans occupy the lowest rung of the patriarchal ladder; their bodies are exploited.

Deriving from the work of French psychoanalyst Jacques Lacan, the symbolic is the social and cultural order in which we live our conscious lives as gendered subjects. It is structured according to language, and as a result of this, the laws and institutions which comprise it.[25] The construction of sexual difference deeply permeates this symbolic dimension.[26] The symbolic order (our social and cultural worlds) are thus part of the phallocentric patriarchal order which fixes meanings according to binary oppositions discussed above.[27] This hierarchisation serves to subordinate women and animals, and thus renders them as inferior but necessary for relations of reproduction and production. They are defined according to the phallocentric patriarchal symbolic order of things – a sexual specificity which locates them in binary categories based on the 'presence or absence of a single term (the masculine).'[28]

Sofia's work acts as a framework to flesh out these intricate patriarchal symbolic power relations at play in the physical spaces of the lab. Containment technologies act as a 'caring' and 'nurturing' space, which allows for a typified kind of welfare to operate over nonhuman animals.[29] This in itself is symbolic and held within the phallocentric dominance hierarchy. She suggests a psychodynamically informed inventory to illustrate this.

First, is the 'facilitating environment,' this ensures smooth functioning of the area (scientific institution) while appreciating its dynamic rather than static interplay. Second, 'containment,' here Sofia claims this aspect of container technologies entails elements of projective identification. It is about what holds people and what kind of things we put 'stuff' into, what we identify with and 'what of ourselves we can and cannot contain.' Next is the 'primary maternal preoccupation and attunement.' The infant and

---

24 Ibid. p. 184.
25 Chris Weedon, *Feminist Practice and Poststructuralist Theory*, 6th ed. (Oxford: Blackwell Publishers, 1994). p. 52.
26 Stephen Frosh, "Psychoanalyitic Challenges: A Contribution to the New Sexual Agenda," *Human Relations* 50, no. 3 (1997): 231.
27 Weedon, *Feminist Practice and Poststructuralist Theory*. p. 63, p. 66.
28 Sheena J. Vachhani, "The Subordination of the Feminine? Developing a Critical Feminist Approach to the Psychoanalysis of Organizations," *Organization Studies* 33, no. 9 (2012): 1245.
29 Wadiwel, *The War against Animals*. p. 193.

128 *Scientific intersections*

caregiver act in synchronicity, correspondingly, container technologies adapt to us. The more a technological object is adapted to respond to or even anticipate our wishes and capacities, the more 'user-friendly' it seems. Fourth, the 'ruthlessness of infant,' where we take for granted the containers (like the mother) and the resources they supply. They become just spaces for our things to go in. Penultimately, the 'toy or tool as transitional object,' the tool is never just an inanimate object but has its origin in the inner world of the human. It is always meaningful and part of a set of individual purposes. Lastly, 'potential space' which corresponds to the infants play area, 'an imaginative space between inner and outer worlds.' These are workspaces for invention, such as the laboratory.[30]

In this framework, nonhuman animals act as the object, tool, and toy in the making of laboratory animal science. The spaces and containers are thus patriarchally attributed (the symbolic) as the 'feminine' (the 'mother' in Sofia's terms), and the scientists hold within themselves elements of the ruthless infant.[31] The interrelationship between human and nonhuman in the laboratory is a constructed one. This relationship is mediated by the psychodynamic energies outlined above. Consequently, these spaces of the laboratory act as an interceding force to enable the continuation of the production of binary distinctions between human and nonhuman. Those that are deemed suitable to test on and those that are not. These spatial confinements are dynamic, and in a perpetual state of tension, because of this, the dualistic assumptions that shape laboratory relations are always at risk of being ruptured. Spaces and containers have to be highly disciplined areas in order to avoid this rupture. They are always subject to the scrutinising (male) gaze of the scientist[32] in order to carry on containing the nonhuman animal and rendering them 'Other,' alongside women.

Post-war legitimation of laboratory animal science and the creation of 'the 3 Rs'

Towards the end of the nineteenth and beginning of the twentieth century, there was a transformation in biomedical science and the use of nonhuman bodies in experimental science. A multitude of substances was discovered which demonstrated their contribution to the functioning of the human body, most notably, insulin, vitamins and hormones.[33] These discoveries were made with the aid of animals – vivisection became the Gold Standard

---

30 Sofia, "Container Technologies." p. 185.
31 Ibid. King, "The Prisoner of Gender: Foucualt and the Disciplining of the Female Body."
32 "The Prisoner of Gender: Foucualt and the Disciplining of the Female Body." p. 31.
33 Robert G.W. Kirk and Michael Worboys, *Medicine and Species: One Medicine, One History?*, ed. Mark Jackson, The Oxford Handbook of the History of Medicine (Oxford: Oxford University Press, 2012). p. 569.

of laboratory methodology.[34] Nonhuman animals became essential to the experimental scientist, and thus by the mid-twentieth century, were embedded in a series of networks that included not only the laboratory but also the hospital, farm, slaughterhouse and government.[35] These networks of 'supply and demand' became more formalised in 1947 with the creation of the Laboratory Animals Bureau (L.A.B.) by the Medical Research Council (MRC).[36] This was coupled with the emergence of an ethics of scientist-animal relations. The publication of The UFAW *Handbook on the Care and Management of Laboratory Animals* contributed to this growing awareness.[37]

The creation of the L.A.B. and the resultant publications it inspired came at a crucial juncture in the advent of post-war British modernity. It was after the Second World War that science-government relations took on a new form. Scientists began to assume influential positions within state departments. They became key advisers to politicians with regards to the funding of scientific endeavours and in the formation of science policy.[38] Scientists amongst other specialists were integrated into the civil service in a way they had not been previously.[39] An Advisory Council on Scientific Policy was created, which had the function of advising high-ranking politicians on devising and implementing civil scientific policy, such as plans concerning contemporary medical research.[40]

The Labour government, under the leadership of Clement Attlee, won the 1945 General Election by a landslide and introduced a system of welfare reflective of the Keynesian model of governance.[41] They instituted free healthcare and education for all. This was as well as a system of benefits and housing to support those unemployed. As a consequence of all these political and economic factors, the British government were the driving

---

34 Richard D. French, *Antivivisection and Medical Science in Victorian Society* (Princeton, New Jersey: Princeton University Press, 1975).
35 Worboys, *Medicine and Species: One Medicine, One History?* p. 570.
36 The L.A.B. was created for scientists so that they could get information regarding laboratory animal supply. It also acted in a regulatory capacity, to facilitate the breeding of a standardised animal that could be used in laboratories all over Britain and internationally. See: Robert G.W. Kirk, "A Brave New Animal for a Brave New World: The British Laboratory Animals Bureau and the Constitution of International Standards of Laboratory Animal Protection and Use, Circa 1947–1968," *Isis* 101, no. 1 (2010): 62–94.
37 Ibid.; Worden, *The UFAW Handbook on the Care and Management of Laboratory Animals*. p. 62.
38 Philip Gummett, *Scientists in Whitehall* (Manchester, UK: Manchester University Press, 1980); ibid. p. 2.
39 Ibid. p. 28.
40 Ibid. p. 31.
41 Vicente Navarro, *Class Struggle, the State and Medicine: An Historical and Contemporary Analysis of the Medical Sector in Great Britain* (London, UK: Martin Robertson & Co. Ltd., 1978). p. 38.

130 *Scientific intersections*

force behind the increase in funding and resources being directed into medical research and its allied services.[42] Government subsidies to the MRC increased exponentially between the years 1945–1965, rising from £0.3m in 1945–1946 to £7m in 1963–1964.[43] Nonhuman animals became integral to this *modus operandi*.

As we saw in section one, the UFAW and their associated publications were highly influential in this era. They pioneered the ethical principles of laboratory animal care and welfare. Aspects of these were eventually enshrined in law under the Animals (Scientific Procedures) Act, 1986 (ASPA), and thus, are a legal requirement still in use today. Forming part of these ethical principles are detailed requirements for the housing of laboratory animals, and the associated accoutrements that come with that (heating, lighting, ventilation, etc.). These now mandatory stipulations can be traced back to the first edition in 1947 of *The UFAW Handbook on the Care and Management of Laboratory Animals*.

The most influential aspect of the UFAW's work on laboratory animal welfare is the now internationally recognised notion of the 'The 3 Rs.' The 3 Rs were created by W.M.S. Russell, University College London scholar and UFAW Research Fellow; and R.L. Burch a research assistant with the UFAW in their 1959 UFAW book *Principles of Humane Experimental Technique*.[44] In order to diminish or remove 'inhumanity' in experiments, Russell and Burch advocated the notion of 'Replacement, Reduction, Refinement.'[45]

> Replacement means the substitution for conscious living higher animals of insentient material. Reduction means reduction in the number of animals used to obtain information of given amount and precision. Refinement means any decrease in the incidence or severity of inhumane procedures applied to those animals which still have to be used.[46]

The 3 Rs are now an internationally recognised laboratory practice and were initially implemented indirectly in the Animals (Scientific Procedures) Act, 1986. During the review of this legislation, they were then explicitly placed on the face of the Act. Now the 3 Rs are a fundamental component to the legal practice of animal experimentation in both Britain and Europe (see Chapters 1 and 2). This chapter is mainly interested in the practice of *Refinement* as it relates to laboratory animal housing and accommodation.[47]

---

42 Ibid. pp. 39–40.
43 Gummett, *Scientists in Whitehall*. p. 39.
44 W.M.S. Russell, R.L. Burch, *The Principles of Humane Experimental Techinque* (London: Methuen & Co Ltd, 1959).
45 Ibid. p. 64.
46 Ibid.
47 RSPCA, "Housing, Husbandry and Care," https://science.rspca.org.uk/sciencegroup/researchanimals/ethicalreview/functionstasks/housingandcare.

Spaces of segregation: Making laboratory animals' metaphorical 'mother' 1947–1986

Alastair Worden, Professor and Director of research in animal health at the University College of Wales compiled and edited the first edition of *The UFAW Handbook on the Care and Management of Laboratory Animals*.[48]. Chaired by Major C.W. Hume and with Professor Edward Hindle of the Zoological Society of London as its President, the UFAW sought to approach the nonhuman in ways that absented the 'emotional or sentimental' yet served the interests of science by building a 'realistically humane policy based on objective fact.'[49] The book provided guidance and advice on a variety of laboratory practices and animal husbandry, including; food preparation, cages and cage-equipment, experimental techniques, as well as information regarding a host of experimental animals from rabbits, guinea pigs, rats and mice, to pigeons, fish and ferrets.[50] This was followed up in chapters devoted to the ideal laboratory conditions and clear instructions for animal technicians and assistants.

The book was well received and was praised for its insight and philosophical approach to the science of animal welfare. A review in the *British Medical Journal* by A.L. Bacharach praised Worden for his 'common sense' approach towards animals and their use for experiments.[51] Bacharach hailed the book as 'indispensable' due to its 'practical blend of economics and humanitarianism.'[52] Emphasis was placed upon the economic rewards that would be reaped by scientists if they treated their laboratory species' with 'kindness.' Bacharach also made a sly dig at the antivivisectionists, exclaiming that the *Handbook* was a 'common sense' approach to animals, as opposed to a 'sentimental' one. 'Healthy contented animals' would provide 'more information than sick and miserable animals.' For Bacharach, the book had hidden depths, as behind the technical descriptions of keeping animals, lay 'shrewd tactics' utilised by the book's 'level-headed planners, who are willing to run with the laboratory hares in the most friendly association, provided they are not also expected to hunt with the anti-vivisectionist hounds.'[53] This book deflected the antivivisectionist critique by claiming scientific rationality, humanitarianism and care towards animals.

The book is now in its eighth edition, and it still covers such topics. However, it was in the 1947 edition that the gendered division of labour within the laboratory was explicitly highlighted, and asserted 'many workers

---

48 Worden, *The UFAW Handbook on the Care and Management of Laboratory Animals*.
49 Ibid. inset.
50 Ibid. p. xi.
51 A.L. Bacharach, "Review: Laboratory Animals," *British Medical Journal* 4617 (1949): 20.
52 Ibid.
53 Ibid. p. 21.

prefer women to men as animal assistants.'[54] The UFAW's attribution of care with that of women helped to imbue animal welfare with the *idea* of the 'feminine.' This facilitated the generation of an ideology of the laboratory as a 'nurturing' space, reminiscent of 'primary maternal attunement.' The 'feminine' (the mother) is identified as the model of care to be delivered by the laboratory workers. She becomes sufficiently separate to serve symbolically as the container, and interpreter, for the experiences of the worker and nonhuman animals of the laboratory.[55]

Subsequent editions of the *Handbook* do not explicitly tie women to the role of animal assistants. The role of the female eventually becoming symbolically (unconsciously) present in the guise of objective scientific language. Interestingly, in the post-war era, the emphasis was placed on standardisation of laboratory practices; as a result of this, the work gradually became more implicitly masculinised. For instance, in the 1957 edition, importance was placed on the role of a *qualified* technician. These technicians were required to have been trained specially in this area because 'the demand for more animals of a higher quality produced urgent need for skilled personnel.'[56] Once qualified, they were assigned a membership level: Students, Associates or Fellows.[57] We can assume here that the standardisation of laboratory practice aimed to masculinise the role of the animal technician. Standardisation is a form of control over laboratory life. It is associated with the phallocentric philosophy of positivism (science).[58] The sciences in post-war Britain remained firmly located within this phallocentric domain, as the state wanted to attract *male* science graduates into the post-war scientific officer classes of government.[59] Correspondingly, there was no increase of women being recruited onto science, technology and medicine courses in the late 1940s and 1950s: the notoriously masculinised subject of science was firmly entrenched to the exclusion of women.[60]

Standardisation was also to be enacted in the very spatial practices of the animal house in the guise of homogeneity of confinement. To standardise scientific research and its apparatuses meant that the results of experiments

---

54 Worden, *The UFAW Handbook on the Care and Management of Laboratory Animals*. p. 41.
55 Sofia, "Container Technologies." pp. 184, 185.
56 A.E. Mundy, "The Animal Technician," in *The UFAW Handbook on the Care and Management of Laboratory Animals*, ed. Alastair Worden, W. Lane-Petter (London: UFAW, 1957). p. 183.
57 Ibid. p. 184.
58 Philipa Rothfield, "Alternative Epistemologies, Politics and Feminism," *Social Analysis: The International Journal of Anthropology* 30 (1991). p. 63. Evelyn Fox-Keller, Helen E. Longino, "Introduction," in *Feminism and Science* (Oxford: Oxford University Press, 1999).
59 David Edgerton, *Warfare State: Britain, 1920-1970* (Cambridge, UK: Cambridge University Press, 2006). p. 179.
60 Ibid. pp. 176–177.

could be generalised to wider populations – both human and nonhuman.[61] One example of such attempts to standardise in the post-war period is with 'The Animal House.' The animal house is where nonhuman animals are contained before, and after they have been experimented on (if they survive). It is where they live and die. What emerges in the *Handbook* is a method to create particular kinds of places. The animal house, in this instance, acts as an integral component in the creation of valid scientific knowledge. The *Handbook* details how this knowledge can be created through 'careful and considerate management'[62] of laboratory spaces, the keeping of animals, how the animals are tested and the gendered divisions of labour within the laboratory.[63] By neglecting to do this, it would:

> [S]eem futile to expect reliable results from the use of animals of mixed or unknown origin... housed in inadequate, dirty, parasite-infested, unevenly heated, badly ventilated, draughty, noisy or otherwise unsuitable surroundings, handled with fear or distaste and fed irregularly on diets containing bulky or rapidly spoiling foods of which the nutritive value has never been ascertained.[64]

Highly structured and sterile spaces were advocated as they were considered to facilitate valid experiments. Nevertheless, these spaces sought to constrain the behaviours of nonhuman animals living in them and they too were considered to be standardisable. With the emergence of the LAB in 1947, the next couple of decades aimed to establish national and international networks of breeders of specific pathogen-free laboratory animals, with their own set of standards and regulations that linked explicitly to the UFAW recommendations for the care and housing of such animals.[65] Dr William Lane-Petter led the way in devising such standards of control over nonhuman bodies and their breeders.

Dr William-Lane Petter was a qualified medical doctor, and during the Second World War served in the Royal Army Medical Corps. After leaving the army, he became a Home Office Inspector under the 1879 Cruelty

---

61 Lynda Birke, "Telling the Rat What to Do: Laboratory Animals, Science and Gender," in *Gender and the Science of Difference: Cultural Politics of Contemporary Science and Medicine*, ed. Jill A. Fisher (United States of America: Rutgers, the State University, 2011). p. 101.
62 Worden, *The UFAW Handbook on the Care and Management of Laboratory Animals*. p. 21.
63 Birke, "Telling the Rat What to Do: Laboratory Animals, Science and Gender." p. 98.
64 Worden, *The UFAW Handbook on the Care and Management of Laboratory Animals*. p. 21.
65 Kirk, "A Brave New Animal for a Brave New World: The British Laboratory Animals Bureau and the Constitution of International Standards of Laboratory Animal Protection and Use, Circa 1947–1968."

to Animals Act. In 1949 he helped to establish, and became Director of the LAC and was Secretary-General of the International Committee on Laboratory Animals (ICLA).[66] Petter's work for LAC took him around the world promoting laboratory animal research and its standardisation. This international work and his role at the LAC led to the formation of the ICLA, which aimed to standardise laboratory animals and regulate breeders and suppliers of these animals worldwide.[67]

The 1957 edition of the *Handbook* had a chapter written by William Lane-Petter. It was devoted entirely to the design of the animal house. He stressed that the layout, whether serving 'a small hospital laboratory or that of a large research institute,' should have four basic departments.[68] These departments acted as the 'facilitating environment' for the laboratory and would ensure its smooth running.[69] According to Petter, there should be four departments of a functioning scientific establishment. They are given the titles of 'normal animals,' 'experimental animals,' 'washing and sterilising' and 'food, bedding and clean cage stores.' The interrelationship of these departments demonstrates containers as dynamic entities, which are in a constant state of movement and flux.[70]

The spatial layout of the animal house signifies the contradictory nature of the human-animal relationship: one of absolute control and astute discipline and segregation. On the other hand, a relationship which is dynamic and changing due to the interrelationships of the segregated departments.

For the department of 'normal animals,' Lane-Petter emphasised its splitting into two, one for breeding animals and one for receiving animals from outside sources(suppliers). A 'breeding house rule' was recommended in terms of complete isolation of the animals in order to produce 'one-way traffic of animals going out but never in (except to found new lines).'[71] The quarantining of animal bodies was especially deemed essential to the functionality of the entire system, as was the avoidance of the placement of more than one single species in the same room. Interestingly, the 'normal' animal house acted as an area of conscious and unconscious 'containment.' Lane-Petter could be seen to be arguing for the containment of something which can, and at the same time, cannot be contained. For instance, the strict segregation of those animals used for breeding (on the whole female animals).

---

66 William Lane-Petter, "The Place of Laboratory Animals in the Scientific Life Og a Country," *Impact of Science on Society* 9 (1959). p. 178.
67 Kirk, "A Brave New Animal for a Brave New World: The British Laboratory Animals Bureau and the Constitution of International Standards of Laboratory Animal Protection and Use, Circa 1947–1968." p. 2.
68 W. Lane-Petter, "The Animal House," in *The UFAW Handbook on the Care and Management of Laboratory Animals*, ed. Alastair Worder, W. Lane-Petter (London: UFAW, 1957). p. 16.
69 Sofia, "Container Technologies." p. 185.
70 Ibid.
71 Lane-Petter, "The Animal House." p. 16.

They would be separated according to their sex and species, due to them being unable to contain (restrain) their natural breeding and behavioural habits. As Sofia argues, containment is not merely just about holding 'stuff' but is also about what we identify with.[72] Heteronormative sexual behaviour was being imposed upon the life of the nonhuman laboratory animals. This is a thoroughly human value in what was considered a scientifically objective spatial organisation of nonhuman laboratory animals.

The department of 'Experimental Animals' is another example of a container technology which becomes part of the 'potential space' of scientific endeavours.[73] This too was recommended to be subdivided into several rooms. Part of this department would be the 'potential space' whereby experiments took place. Space for a post-mortem room was advised, and isolation rooms where the 'toys/tools' (nonhuman animals) could be placed when they are infected and under investigation.[74]

The other two departments emphasise the importance of hygiene in running the animal house and enabling experiments on animals to take place. Here, evidences the 'ruthlessness of the infant.' Space was needed to allow for the cleaning and maintaining of hygiene of the animal house, in the guise of the 'Washing and Sterilising Department' and the 'Clean Stores Department.'[75] This infantile mercilessness plays under the pretext of the taken-for-grantedness of the containers. They are merely spaces to place the necessary laboratory 'tools.' In the former, a space for the incineration of carcasses would need to be present. Here the laboratory animal becomes the 'toy or tool as transitional object'; it has a human purpose until it can be discarded.[76]

In 1972, a fourth edition of the *Handbook* was published. Lane-Petter embellished his previous chapter on the Animal House from both the second and third edition (published 1967)[77] by adding three additional departments to the 'original' four. These additions were 'an office for administration,' 'a room for mechanical plant' and 'corridors giving access to all these areas.'[78] Lane-Petter stressed the necessity of these spaces to be flexible:

> In most laboratories, a variety of species of animals will be in use, and the relative numbers of each will not remain constant from year to year. As far as possible, therefore, this fact should be taken into account, so

---

72 Sofia, "Container Technologies." p. 185.
73 Ibid.
74 Lane-Petter, "The Animal House." p. 17.
75 Ibid.
76 Sofia, "Container Technologies." p. 185.
77 UFAW, ed. *The UFAW Handbook on the Care and Management of Laboratory Animals*, 3rd ed. (Edinburgh & London: E & S Livingstone Ltd, 1967).
78 W. Lane-Petter, "The Animal House and Its Equipment," in *The UFAW Handbook on the Care and Management of Laboratory Animals*, ed. UFAW (Edinburgh and London: Churchill Linvingstone, 1972). p. 74.

that a room that is used for rabbits one year can be converted easily to house mice or rats the next. Certain species, such as dogs and monkeys, have such special requirements that their rooms cannot be easily turned over to other species. Yet even in these cases the special requirements should not be so permanently built into the structure of the house that it can never be dismantled or adapted for any other purpose.[79]

To ensure that the nonhuman animals used for experiments produced valid results, it was necessary to house them appropriately. Standardisation of the animal house was just one aspect of ensuring validity in animal-dependent scientific tests. Lane-Petter insisted on creating an environment which was conducive to ensuring quality science. Consequently, he claimed that such facilitative environments were flexible. Accommodations could be dismantled and adapted; different animals could be housed, just as long as space was homogenous yet dynamic.

Containing nonhuman laboratory animals: Primary maternal attunement and sexual seclusion

The idea of the standardisation of dynamic departments in the animal house was also transferred to the cages confining nonhuman animals. From the immediate post-World War II era to the 1970s, the *idea* of standardisation of laboratory life was promulgated by both the LAB, especially Lane-Petter,[80] and the work of the UFAW. On a broader scale, the ideology and subsequent practice of standardisation reflected a new kind of social order, one that was radically different from the one before the war.[81] This new order was the welfare state and its associated left-wing ideologies. As Robert Kirk rightly points out, the study of best practice with regards to laboratory life was done against a back-drop of 'socialist-influenced state planning.'[82] Alongside the growing (international) momentum for the standardisation of germ-free and genetically similar laboratory animals,[83] was the need for homogenous laboratory spaces and an increase in the necessity for harmonised practices of care. The Welfare State ushered in not only a new kind of care over human life but also acted as the impetus behind

---

79 Ibid. p. 73.
80 Kirk, "A Brave New Animal for a Brave New World: The British Laboratory Animals Bureau and the Constitution of International Standards of Laboratory Animal Protection and Use, Circa 1947–1968."
81 Steven Shapin; Simon Schaffer, *Leviathan and the Air-Pump: Hobbes, Boyle, and the Experimental Life*, 2 ed. (Princeton, NJ: Princeton University Press, 2017). p. 342.
82 Kirk, "A Brave New Animal for a Brave New World: The British Laboratory Animals Bureau and the Constitution of International Standards of Laboratory Animal Protection and Use, Circa 1947–1968." p. 62.
83 Ibid.

the growing concern over the welfare of laboratory animals. The welfare of nonhuman animals became inextricably tied to the overall health of the post-war national economy.[84]

Cages that 'care' helped sustain this economic promulgation, and were seemingly seen as synonymous and integral to the implementation of legal regulations of animal welfare that was to come later on in the twentieth century. This ran alongside notions of the post-war woman being a stay-at-home mother in order to ensure the secure attachment of their infant.[85] Psychologist John Bowlby led the way in this dynamic aspect of maternal care, with his theory on 'maternal deprivation,'[86] as much as the UFAW and LAB advocated it in laboratory practices and the 'care' of nonhuman animals. Society feared the 'latch-key' child who was left to fend for themselves, just as much as animal-dependent science feared that their test objects would cause invalid results if not contained or looked after appropriately.

The cages to house the nonhuman animals were stark and basic. The 1947 UFAW *Handbook* advised them to be stored in racks – piled high on top of each other – and numbered to identify the individuals living in them.[87] Both the apparatus and nonhumans in the experimental laboratories were transforming scientific practice. In effect, this was another way for scientists to control 'nature' by the use of technocratic management techniques, and preventing variation and individual difference amongst animals through standardisation and numbering.[88] Furthermore, the book advised that the animals be segregated according to sex and kept in small groups such as 'mothers with litters.'[89] The book asserts the fact that in rabbits 'unless the sexes are separated when 3 ½ to 4 months old, fighting and unwanted matings occur.'[90] For guinea-pigs, 'the sexes may be mixed in the proportion of one male to five females.'[91] To segregate animals, according to sex, reflected the social assumptions of the time concerning gender differences. These assumptions determined the right way that laboratory animals were to be kept and tested. Thus, the advice in the *Handbook* was replete with social and cultural values that the authors were trying to obviate in the first place. The limited housing conditions and laboratory spaces, how and by *whom* they were handled would have affected the nonhumans' behaviour and physiology. Thus, the constrained laboratory animal became a distortion

---

84 Ibid. pp. 68–69.
85 Elizabeth Wilson, *Only Halfway to Paradise Women in Postwar Britain: 1945–1968* (London: Tavistock Publications Ltd, 1980).
86 Inge Bretherton, "The Origins of Attachment Theory: John Bowlby and Mary Ainsworth," *Developmental Psychology* 28, no. 5 (1992).
87 Worden, *The UFAW Handbook on the Care and Management of Laboratory Animals*. p. 38.
88 Birke, "Telling the Rat What to Do: Laboratory Animals, Science and Gender." p. 100.
89 Worden, *The UFAW Handbook on the Care and Management of Laboratory Animals*. p. 22.
90 Ibid. p. 73.
91 Ibid. p. 97.

138 *Scientific intersections*

and re-construction of their actual behaviour in the wild. The information given in the *Handbook* is itself a distortion of the nonhuman, alongside the very behaviour the book was trying to categorise – the use of reductionist logic, binary divisions and gender-specific practices.[92]

Sex seclusion and cages of confinement were elaborated on by Lane-Petter in the 1972 edition of the *Handbook*. According to Lane-Petter, a cage must have four functions: the ability to confine, bring comfort, be economically efficient and provide experimental validity.[93] In the first instance, nonhumans' recalcitrance was noted:

> The cage must be made of a material which the animal cannot break, distort or destroy, e.g. by gnawing or pulling apart. The mesh of the wire or bars must be small enough to prevent the animal, or its young, from escaping; in this respect particular attention must be paid to well-fitting doors and food baskets or other openings. Door-fastenings must be secure, for many animals are persistent and ingenious fiddlers, and will worry apart quite safe-seeming closing-devices. Monkeys are particularly liable to release themselves, and a padlock is the only really trustworthy answer; but rabbits also show a surprising aptitude for undoing catches. Rats and even mice can lift off the lids of boxes in which they are confined, unless these are held firmly in place either by their own sufficient weight or by fasteners.[94]

For Lane-Petter, the cage must be strong enough to restrain nonhuman animals and completely obliviate their agency. Monkeys, rabbits, mice and rats were seen as particularly capable of escaping human modes of confinement. Nonhuman animals were seen as initially having agency and ability to react to human ways of constraining them. However, by ensuring high standards of caging, this would eventually facilitate *[maternal] attunement*. This attunement would quash any sign of nonhuman obduracy. Thus, they would eventually adapt to human scientists in a 'user-friendly' manner.[95]

Cages also had to allow the animal to live in 'comfort.' For Lane-Petter, this directly related to its overall size and the length of time the experimental animal was to be kept in it.[96] The nonhuman (predominantly mammalian) need to experience their naturally occurring circadian rhythm with varying degrees of provision of light and darkness was also mentioned. This ran alongside an in-depth exposition on breeding, and the housing of breeding animals and mated pairings. Lane Petter recommended rabbits and ferrets

---

92 Birke, "Telling the Rat What to Do: Laboratory Animals, Science and Gender." p. 102.
93 Lane-Petter, "The Animal House and Its Equipment." pp. 87–89.
94 Ibid. pp. 87–88.
95 Sofia, "Container Technologies." p. 185.
96 Lane-Petter, "The Animal House and Its Equipment."

be provided with a darkened cloister to birth, 'but guinea-pig sows have no obstetrical shyness, and will farrow happily in an open pen among a group of their fellows.'[97] This wry remark by Lane-Petter highlights the slippage between what sociologist Michael Lynch calls the 'analytic' and 'naturalistic' animal in the lab. Lynch found that there are two coexisting constructions of the guinea-pig in laboratories. The 'naturalistic' animal appearing tacitly throughout daily interactions in the lab, often in humour-filled anecdotes (like Lane-Petter's), but not presented in scientific reports. Instead, that is when the 'analytic' animal comes to the fore, the intention being to construct the guinea-pig as an object to be tested on – the very methodology of science dictating the terms unto which the scientist *inscribes* the laboratory animal with any sense of meaning: as a subject or object.[98]

Lynch goes on to argue that the simple act of writing up the results from experiments helps to enable this transformation of the animal from 'naturalistic' to the 'analytic.' Anthropomorphism is assumed to disappear in the very act of 'objective' inscription.[99] Nevertheless, this is not as simple as Lynch claims. Philosopher Vinciane Despret argues that this transformation in the construction of the laboratory animal happens way before the process of writing occurs.[100] She claims that there is a denial of anthropomorphism occurring in all aspects of laboratory life, and even in the writing up of research results; it is neither restricted nor absent, just invisible.[101] There are two reasons for this, first, not affording agency to nonhuman animals is something already implicit in scientific practice. According to Despret, scientists do not ask the laboratory animal if they are interested in the task at hand. Second, as a result of this, they do not think about the fact that the nonhuman may not be interested in doing what the experimenter demands.[102]

Contra to Despret, I would not account for the fact that agency is indeed ignored, it is recognised but highly regulated and thus, disciplined. This suppression of individual acts of agency is a form of psychic *denial,* which runs alongside the repudiation of anthropomorphism in laboratory life. Denial is an unconscious defence mechanism which aims to deliberately mislead us without us noticing, and it also goes hand-in-hand with projective identification.[103] Despret seems to infer that the denial of anthropomorphism is consciously made. It could be taken as a shift which becomes habitual once

---

97 Ibid. p. 88.
98 Michael E. Lynch, "Sacrifice and the Transformation of the Animal Body into a Scientific Object: Laboratory Culture and Ritual Practice in the Neurosciences.," *Social Studies of Science* 18 (1988).
99 Ibid.
100 Vinciane Despret, *What Would Animals Say If We Asked the Right Questions?* (Minneapolis & London: University of Minnesota Press, 2016). p. 90.
101 Ibid.
102 Ibid. p. 91.
103 Ian Craib, *Psychoanalysis: A Critical Introduction* (Cambridge: Polity Press, 2001). p. 43.

140 *Scientific intersections*

the scientist has practised their profession over time (rather like the muscle memory of an athlete!). However, this denial is also unconscious *and* projective. It is not just anthropomorphism which is at stake here, but also the belief in nonhuman animals to have a life of their own outside of laboratory conditions away from the scrutinising gaze of the (male) scientist.

Hence, if we take Lane-Petter's jest about the obstetric life of the guinea-pig, we can see how Lynch's distinctions between the 'analytic' and 'naturalistic' animal are more complex than he admits. We can also acknowledge Despret's account of anthropomorphism as a normative cultural practice in *all* aspects of laboratory life. However, this anthropomorphism is tied up with both the unconscious psychic forces at play and the very physical and spatial containers of the lab – not just human-animal interactions as espoused by Lynch and Despret. Cages, especially those recommended by Lane-Petter, involve the *containment*[104] of laboratory animals in order to create *primary maternal attunement*.[105] That enables the guinea-pig to adapt to unnatural conditions so that they become 'user-friendly.'[106] Alternatively, in Lynch's terms, they are enabled so as to become the 'analytic animal.'[107] Lane-Petter jokes about the birthing habits of the guinea-pig yet he is projecting an entirely male imaginary of the life-world of the guinea-pig based on his views of female genitalia, pregnancy and birth. He cannot contain the laboratory animal, but the cage can. The cage acts as a 'warm,' 'nurturing' womb-like space to enable the 'analytic' animal to come forth and synchronise (maternal attunement) with the scientists.

Mandating the metaphorical mother: The legalisation and standardisation of laboratory container technologies, 1986–present

The UFAW handbooks before the Animals (Scientific Procedures) Act, 1986 (ASPA), helped to furnish animal-dependent science with a code of ethics and practice which seemed to demonstrate care for experimental animals. As we will recall from section one, the period from 1945–1986 saw the emergence of the animal rights movement, and a strong public discourse against animal experimentation (particularly in the 1970s). The scientific community responded to this by taking on board the recommendations made by the UFAW. This was evidenced by their connections to the Research Defence Society (RDS). However, this next part of the chapter moves on to the legislated codes of ethics from 1986 onwards. Here we can ask: what differences are there between the non-legalised and legalised requirements

---

104 Sofia, "Container Technologies." p. 185.
105 Ibid.
106 Ibid.
107 Lynch, "Sacrifice and the Transformation of the Animal Body into a Scientific Object: Laboratory Culture and Ritual Practice in the Neurosciences."

of laboratory spaces? Are the practices still gendered? And, what, if any, unconscious psychic forces help to shape these mandated spaces.

The review of the 1876 Cruelty to Animal Act in 1965 by the Littlewood Committee acted as a precursor to the eventual legalisation of ethical laboratory practice in 1986. In the Littlewood Report, not only was there a wealth of analysis presented on the Pain Condition (see Chapter 1) but also much of the Report was dedicated to discussing the accommodation and husbandry of experimental animals.[108] Here, the Committee linked their new conception of the Pain Condition: stress, distress and nonhumans' wellbeing, to their housing and handling. In the memorandum sent to the Committee, the RDS strongly emphasised this aspect of laboratory life. They recommended that the Home Office should be 'concerned in the care of animals in some way over and above its duties as outlined in the present Act.'[109] Animal care was underscored to be beyond the experimental manipulations. It was to include their handling and care before and after the testing. Consequently, the Report presented a rationalisation of care. This included the recommendation for the standardisation of the laboratory spaces and their associated container technologies.

The rationalisation of laboratory spaces and the 3 Rs

As we have seen the calls for the professionalisation of welfare in animal-dependent science went hand-in-hand with the ideology of care being integral to nonhuman animals' *experience* in the laboratory. By fostering an ethos of care in laboratory workers, the animals would be healthy enough to take part in the experiment. As the RDS stipulated '…animals in the laboratory are entirely dependent on those who care for them for all necessities of life and health – they are deprived of all opportunity of fending for themselves'[110]. In chapter one, I showed that the review of the 1876 Act was part of a broader ideology for the rationalisation of this care in the life of the laboratory. This rhetoric of welfare only became a mandated practice with the passing into law of the ASPA in 1986. The Council of Europe (CoE) and the European Union (EU),[111] played an integral role, alongside British law-makers, scientists, animal welfarists and politicians in shaping the official guidelines for the recommendations of this approach.

How laboratory animal welfare was to be done was communicated via a written document entitled: *Guidance on the Operation of the New Legislation*

---

108 Sydney Littlewood, "Report of the Departmental Committee on Experiments on Animals," ed. Home Office (London: Her Majesty's Stationery Office, 1965). pp. 129–142.
109 The Welcome Library [Well], PP/CLE/C.3.: Box 3. Research Defence Society, 1963–1965.Draft Memorandum to send to Home Office Committee of Inquiry, 21 October 1963.
110 Well, PP/CLE/C.3.: Box 3. Research Defence Society, 1963–1965. Memorandum Preparedfor Home Office Committee of Inquiry. January 1964.
111 Then the European Economic Community (EEC).

to *Replace the Cruelty to Animals Act 1876*.[112] It was jointly written by the UFAW and the MRC, who also published a *Code of Practice* (CoP).[113] As we noted in Chapters 1 and 2, the ASPA was both influenced by and influenced a variety of European organisations. The most prominent being the CoE's Treaty Series 123, of which Britain played a leading role in creating. This was transposed into EU law in the guise of ECC Directive 86/609 and subsequently EU Directive 2010/63, elements of which ultimately became enfolded within the ASPA in 1986 and its 2012 update.[114]

One of these elements was the explicit command for the implementation of Russell and Burch's 1959 idea of 'The 3 Rs.' Reduction, Replacement and Refinement were all but explicitly mentioned in the 1986 ASPA. Now, with its revision in 2012 and under the provisions of EU Directive 2010/63, animal-use organisations have to explicitly aim to reduce, refine and replace experimental animals and procedures in their practice. Section 2A of the 2012 ASPA declares:

> For the purposes of this Act—
>
> a the principle of replacement is the principle that, wherever possible, a scientifically satisfactory method or testing strategy not entailing the use of protected animals must be used instead of a regulated procedure;
> b the principle of reduction is the principle that whenever a programme of work involving the use of protected animals is carried out the number of protected animals used must be reduced to a minimum without compromising the objectives of the programme;
> c the principle of refinement is the principle that the breeding, accommodation and care of protected animals and the methods used in regulated procedures applied to such animals must be refined so as to eliminate or reduce to the minimum any possible pain, suffering, distress or lasting harm to those animals.[115]

The principle of refinement includes the accommodation and care of protected animals to prevent unnecessary pain, suffering, distress or lasting harm. This is taken in conjunction with Section 5B 4(d) whereby the

---

112 Home Office, "Guidance on the Operation of the New Legislation to Replace the Cruelty to Animals Act 1876," HMSO, https://webarchive.nationalarchives.gov.uk/19970429190800/http://www.open.gov.uk:80/home_off/aspag.htm.
113 TNA HO 285/189 Government proposals for legislation to replace the Cruelty to Animals Act 1876: White Paper on Scientific Procedures on Living Animals; Home Secretary's briefing. Memo from N.M. Johnson E4 Division to Mr Head and Mr Davidson. 16 November 1984. p. 1.
114 HM Government Animals in Science Regulation Unit, "Code of Practice for the Housing and Care of Animals Bred, Supplied or Used for Scientific Purposes," ed. Home Office (London: OGL Crown Copyright, 2014).
115 HM Government, "The Animals (Scientific Procedures) Act 1986 Amendment Regulations 2012" (2012).

Secretary of State in their evaluation of a programme of work to determine the granting of a licence must consider 'expertise in animal husbandry and care in relation to the species of protected animals that are intended to be used.'[116] This legally recognised animal husbandry refers to techniques currently mandated and practiced in the UK. The central bodies associated with disseminating 'good' methods of husbandry include the RSPCA and their Research Animals Team's *Guidance Notes*. They make a clear connection between confinement technologies and refinement of laboratory animal science[117]:

> Housing and care has a major impact on the welfare of animals and consequently on the quality of scientific data. All establishments should therefore aim to refine housing and care as far as possible. Consideration of the natural habitat, biology and behaviour of each species can provide useful insights into appropriate refinements to housing and husbandry, including environmental enrichment.[118]

Alongside the work of the RSPCA, the UFAW also acts as a significant organisation informing the legal and practical aspects of British laboratory life. The CoP also being informed by the UFAW's eighth edition of the *'The UFAW Handbook on the Care and Management of Laboratory and Other Research Animals.'*[119] A supranational body which Britain is a part of is The European Cooperation in Science and Technology (COST) group. COST is an intergovernmental panel which promotes animal-dependent science and coordinates funded research across Europe, the key scientific areas being Biomedicine and the Molecular Biosciences. Countries who are not members of the EU can be members of COST. Their latest manual *'The COST Manual of Laboratory Animal Care and Use: Refinement, Reduction and Research'* draws on EU Directive 2010/63 and the revised appendix A to the European Convention's ETS 123 (see Chapters 1 and 2). The book aims to advise on laboratory animal welfare through drawing heavily on Russell and Burch's '3 Rs.'[120] The 2014 CoP issued by the British government embodies these recommendations made by these groups, and it is this current guidance which concerns us the most in this section.

---

116 Ibid.
117 RSPCA, "Housing, Husbandry and Care."
118 Ibid.
119 Robert Hubrecht, James Kirkwood, ed. *The UFAW Handbook on the Care and Management of Laboratory and Other Research Animals*, 8th ed. (Chichester John Wiley & Sons, 2010).
120 Bryan Howard, Timo Nevalainen, Gemma Perretta, ed., *The Cost Manual of Laboratory Animal Care and Use: Refinement, Reduction, and Research* (Boca Raton, U.S.A.: CRC Press, Taylor and Francis Group, 2011).

144 *Scientific intersections*

The 2014 CoP was implemented in 2017 and issued under Section 21 of the 2012 amended ASPA.[121] Alongside this was EU Directive 2010/63 and requires member states to ensure that:

> The establishments of breeders, suppliers and users should have adequate installations and equipment in place to meet the accommodation requirements of the animal species concerned and to allow the procedures to be performed efficiently and with the least distress to the animals. The breeders, suppliers and users should operate only if they are authorised by the competent authorities.[122]

Recital 5 of Directive 2010/63 incorporated the European Commission's recommendations of animal welfare and housing, entitled *European Commission Recommendation on Guidelines on the Accommodation and Care of Animals Used for Experimental and Other Scientific Purposes*.[123] The recommendation is still in force and has been adapted to the UK context as outlined in the British Government's CoP.[124] The impetus behind the EU guidance and subsequent CoP is to ensure member states' animal experiments are standardised at a level to ensure harmonisation of practices and procedures across the EU (see Chapters 1 and 2). In Directive 2010 it was stated that differences in requirements across the Member States could 'distort the internal market.'[125] Therefore the reason behind the continued striving for standardisation of laboratory animal housing and equipment is an economic one (see Chapters 1 and 2). The British Government's CoP of 2014 aims to fulfil the requirements laid out by both Annex III of the EU Directive 2010/63 (informed by the European Commission's Recommendations) and the ASPA:

> The purpose of the CoP is to ensure that the design, construction and method of functioning of the installations and equipment of licensed establishments – along with their staffing, care and practices – allow procedures to be carried out as effectively as possible, in order to obtain reliable results using the minimum number of animals and causing the minimum degree of pain, suffering, distress or lasting harm.[126]

---

121 Government, "The Animals (Scientific Procedures) Act 1986 Amendment Regulations 2012."
122 Council of the European Union, "Directive 2010/63/EU of the European Parliament and of the Council of 22 September 2010 on the Protection of Animals Used for Scientific Purposes," *Official Journal of the European Union* (2010). Recital 29. p. 36.
123 European Commission, "Recommendation on Guidelines for the Accommodation and Care of Animals Used for Experimental and Other Scientific Purposes," *Offical Journal of the European Union* (2007).
124 Unit, "Code of Practice for the Housing and Care of Animals Bred, Supplied or Used for Scientific Purposes." See p. 5.
125 Union, "Directive 2010/63/EU of the European Parliament and of the Council of 22 September 2010 on the Protection of Animals Used for Scientific Purposes." Recital 35. p. 36.
126 HM Government Animals in Science Regulation Unit, "Code of Practice for the Housing and Care of Animals Bred, Supplied or Used for Scientific Purposes." p. 3.

The CoP is divided into sections, with sections one and two being mandatory and section three acting as advisory points for areas not covered in the first two sections.[127] However, how does this contemporary mandatory guidance and advice demonstrate the gendered nature of laboratory space and unconscious notions of 'feminine' containment? As we have seen, the unconscious forces at play in the material spaces of the lab are both one and at the same time, gendered and patriarchal. Here I follow the work of Lynda Birke who stresses the importance of context (and lack of it) in the laboratory/animal house, whereby nonhuman animals are stripped of their 'wildness,' standardised and held in cages under tightly controlled conditions. As a consequence, this restricts the social world of nonhuman animals and aides in the regulation of their behaviour, which has an impact on inherently gendered research outcomes.[128]

Laboratory animal becomings: Creating contained nonhuman worlds in the 21st century

The current Home Office CoP stresses that the physiological and behavioural needs of nonhuman animals of the laboratory should be restricted only for the minimum necessary time.[129] Given this, it is now standard practice to house those social animals together to replicate their natural behaviours (generally referring to rodents, rabbits, cats, dogs and nonhuman primates). In recent years a whole host of research and literature has emerged, highlighting the importance of caging specific animals in their natural social groups and specifying how the container can be adapted to meet these needs.[130] It is this section where we address the containers of the 21st century laboratory animal.

The definition of 'enclosure' outlined in the European Commission's *Recommendations*, acts as our starting point for this exploration of contemporary containment technologies. Here we can notice the diversification of laboratory containers compared to laboratory and animal house standards of Lane-Petter's day:

> 'animal enclosure' means the primary accommodation in which the animals are confined, such as:
>
> a 'cage' — a permanently fixed or movable container that is enclosed by solid walls and, at least on one side, by bars or meshed wire or, where appropriate, nets, and in which one or more animals are kept or

---

127 Ibid. p. 6.
128 Birke, "Telling the Rat What to Do: Laboratory Animals, Science and Gender." p. 99.
129 Unit, "Code of Practice for the Housing and Care of Animals Bred, Supplied or Used for Scientific Purposes."
130 Penny Hawkins, Anne McBride, Giles Paiba, Rita Rose, Mark Prescott, John Mulley, Sam Izzard, Deborah Ridley, Luca Melotti, Sarah Kappel, Robert Hubrecht, "Report of the 2017 Rspca/UFAW Rodent and Rabbit Welfare Group Meeting," *Animal Technology and Welfare* 17 (2018): 75–83.

146 *Scientific intersections*

transported; depending on the stocking density and the size of the container, the freedom of movement of the animals is relatively restricted;

b 'pen' — an area enclosed, for example, by walls, bars or meshed wire in which one or more animals are kept; depending on the size of the pen and the stocking density, the freedom of movement of the animals is usually less restricted than in a cage;

c 'run' — an area closed, for example, by fences, walls, bars or meshed wire and frequently situated outside permanently fixed buildings, in which animals kept in cages or pens can move freely during certain periods of time in accordance with their ethological and physiological needs, such as exercise;

d 'stall' — a small enclosure with three sides, usually a feed-rack and lateral separations, where one or two animals may be kept tethered.[131]

The variety of the containment technologies have changed since Lane-Petter's advice given in the UFAW Handbooks noted earlier. One thing they do have in common is that they all have the overriding aim to keep nonhuman animals confined by fences, walls, metal bars or wire. Aside from acting as a *facilitating environment*[132] for the production of scientific facts, the definitions given of the various containers also make a statement about ontology. Without this set of recommendations for the 'nurturing' of the laboratory animal, the actual laboratory animal itself cannot come into being. The facilitating environment of the cage, pen, run or stall acts to *create* the lab animal and allow for its emergence as a specific scientific *object* that is eventually put to work in the *potential space*.[133]

The fact that these containers allow for differing degrees of 'freedom' of movement for nonhumans demonstrates the humancentric dialectic of container and contained. Nonhuman lab animals are still contained but, if allowed to be placed in say, a run, they 'can move freely during certain periods of time in accordance with their ethological and physiological needs.' The enclosure is sufficiently separate from the nonhuman to serve as both the container and interpreter of their experiences of the world. Yet, the laboratory animal is held *within it*, and their movement restricted. This is analogous to the infant-mother relationship; the mother allows her infant a certain degree of separation but still acts as the container for the infant's experiences.[134]

Nonhuman animals are thus given shape through the various *relationships* of containment offered in the European Commission's *Recommendations*.

---

131 European Commission, "Recommendation on Guidelines for the Accommodation and Care of Animals Used for Experimental and Other Scientific Purposes." p. 9.
132 Sofia, "Container Technologies." pp. 183–184.
133 Ibid. p. 185.
134 Ibid. For example, see, p. 184.

The British CoP emphasises the importance of this 'nurturing relationship' by stating:

> All animals shall be provided with space of sufficient complexity to allow expression of a wide range of normal behaviour. They shall be given a degree of control and choice over their environment to reduce stress-induced behaviour. Establishments shall have appropriate enrichment techniques in place, to extend the range of activities available to the animals and increase their coping activities including physical exercise, foraging, manipulative and cognitive activities, as appropriate to species. Environmental enrichment in animal enclosures shall be adapted to the species and individual needs of the animals concerned.[135]

The space allocated is supposed to allow for the expression of 'normal behaviour.' Signalling acknowledgement of agency, the CoP aims to demonstrate how the laboratory animal can have choice over 'their environment.' The container is thus structurally necessary, and a precondition for the nonhuman laboratory animal's *becoming*. Nonhuman laboratory animals are encouraged to be active agents but within the confines of the allocated enclosures. Expressed behaviour of nonhumans is based on *a priori* classifications of the 'natural' animal to convert them into the 'analytic' animal.[136] This is part of what Sofia deems 'primary maternal attunement,' whereby the nonhuman becomes one with the container. They adapt to the technological space, thus adjusting to the humancentric way of being making them more 'user-friendly' for scientific procedures.[137]

Container technologies play a vital part in forming the laboratory animal. Sofia states that container technologies 'withdraw from attention,' and are 'exploited but not noticed.'[138] I would say that in contemporary laboratory animal science, this withdrawal from visibility is contrary to Sofia's suggestion. To a certain extent, that is. Rather, legislation, such as the ASPA, and the mandated Codes of Practice have positioned containers at the forefront of laboratory animal welfare. But, at the same time its capacity to confine and 'nurture' is designed to be as unobtrusive as possible. Containers of laboratory animals may not 'produce' some heroic scientific discovery to be in awe of, but they do act as an integral part to the makings of such sciences. At the same time, they are at the forefront of lab animal welfare but also remain firmly in the background. The very material spaces of the

---

135 Unit, "Code of Practice for the Housing and Care of Animals Bred, Supplied or Used for Scientific Purposes." p. 17.
136 Lynch, "Sacrifice and the Transformation of the Animal Body into a Scientific Object: Laboratory Culture and Ritual Practice in the Neurosciences."
137 Sofia, "Container Technologies." p. 185.
138 Ibid. p. 188.

laboratory/animal house are designed to be unobtrusive. They form part of a disciplined and highly ordered space which can be 'taken as a background for other activities.' Not too dissimilar from the idea of the exploited 'environment mother.'[139]

Containment of laboratory animals serves many functions: it is a 'nurturing' force, it is a way to allow them to express themselves as far as reasonably possible and at the same time, in its obverse, it acts as a restraining device. The enclosure is designed to only allow for minimal psychological and physical movement. Dinesh Joseph Wadiwel sees container technologies as having an ideologically benign representation, and this acts to shelter the very real acts of violence held within it. For Wadiwel, the container 'contains what would otherwise be seen as violence, by renaming it as something else.'[140] The definition of enclosures mentioned above best illustrates this. The CoP instructs user establishments to design and build containers which do not damage the health of nonhuman animals.[141] All facilities to house animals:

> Shall be constructed to provide an environment which takes into account the physiological and ethological needs of the species kept in them. Facilities shall also be designed and managed to prevent access by unauthorised persons and the ingress or escape of animals.[142]

At first glance, it seems that the containers accede to the needs of nonhuman animals – all facilities have to address the animals' physical and psychological needs. However, this notion of welfare provides a veneer of respectability to the purpose of the cage. It has to be designed to prevent 'unauthorised persons' from entering and also to stop nonhuman animals moving between containers. This is a covert form of violence, which restricts agency of nonhuman animals as much as it hopes to facilitate conformity of behaviour and allow for the production and reproduction of a particular type of animal: the laboratory animal.

The specific requirements of nonhumans used for breeding illustrate this particularly well. The CoP stresses that the environmental needs of breeding animals will be different from those 'of stock and experimental animals.'[143] Advice is given regarding the longer lifespan breeding animals will have over experimental ones, stating that females will be vulnerable to an increase of stress due to their reproductive capacities. It is suggested that close attention

139 Ibid.
140 Wadiwel, *The War against Animals*. p. 195.
141 Unit, "Code of Practice for the Housing and Care of Animals Bred, Supplied or Used for Scientific Purposes." p. 17.
142 Ibid. p. 15.
143 Ibid. p. 79.

should be paid to designing an environment which takes these reproductive physiological and behavioural characteristics into account:

> Animals give birth during the time of day when they are usually quiescent and will often seek or create a secure place for parturition and the raising of offspring; typically a nest or den in the case of rodents, cats, dogs and birds. Such behaviour is strongly motivated. The breeder should ensure that the animals' need for privacy is considered. This can be achieved by the provision of nesting material, nest boxes or a secluded and sheltered area within the pen or cage. Nesting material also allows the animal to partially control its own environment (e.g. noise, temperature and humidity). Given the means for controlling its own microenvironment, the appropriate range of room temperatures may be wider than would otherwise be the case.[144]

Breeding cages further separate the animal of the laboratory from nature.[145] Females become the invisible backbone to the production and reproduction of animal dependent science. This is of course against the framework of standardisation. Even the provision of a 'private' space to birth and rear their young is indeterminably regulated by the additional materials specifically recommended suitable for nesting. Nonhumans do not have a choice in the type of nesting and bedding material they receive; even this is highly regulated due to the effects it can have on the experimental results and the animals themselves.[146] The allusion to nonhumans' agency with regards to nesting material is also problematic given that cage space is strictly limited. For breeding rodents, mice have a minimum floor area of 330 cm^2 and rat mothers and their litter 880 cm^2 with an additional 400 cm^2 added to the cage for each other adult animal.[147]

One example of the latest technologies for housing laboratory rats are designed and built by the company 'Techniplast,' they demonstrate the contemporary mandated space allowed for rats in terms of their breeding and keeping. There is an emphasis on the cage's versatility, its ability to 'house a higher number of rats for stock, as well as breeding purposes.' Furthermore,

---

144 Ibid.
145 Birke, "Telling the Rat What to Do: Laboratory Animals, Science and Gender." p. 100.
146 Hannah-Marja Voipio, Ping Ping Tsai, Heinz Brandsetetter, Marcel Gyger, Hansjoachim Hackbarth, Axel Kornerup Hansen, Thomas Krohn, "Housing and Care of Laboratory Animals," in *The Cost Manual of Laboratory Animal Care and Use: Refinement, Reduction, and Research*, ed. Bryan Howard, Timo Nevalainen, Gemma Perretta (Boca Raton: CRC Press, Taylor and Francis Group, 2011). p. 55.
147 Ibid. p. 32. And see European Union, "Directive 2010/63/EU of the European Parliament and of the Council of 22 September 2010 on the Protection of Animals Used for Scientific Purposes." Annex II. p. 57–58.

150 *Scientific intersections*

the container is advertised as being designed with humans in mind rather than rats, as it allows for 'an easier access' to them. Techniplast also celebrates their ability to make space-saving cage racks which make a breeding/ animal houses run more efficiently. Like the cage rack designs from 1947, small mammals such as rats and mice are housed in 'tower blocks' where they will live out their life and give birth to future 'stock' rodents:

> Techniplast has developed some specific Housing Breeding Systems for small rodents and rabbits to give customer solutions compliant with new international standards. 11 rows high (and above) to achieve the highest density, the racks are completely configurable in terms of watering solutions, number of rows and columns and layout. Cages are available in a wide range of plastic materials: Polycarbonate, Polysulfone and Polyphenylsulfone.[148]

Plastic materials have replaced metal ones to contain the animal of the laboratory. Breeding females are housed in a high-density structure to ensure maximum efficiency and to save on space. The new technical standards Techniplast refers to are included in Section 2 of the Home Office's CoP, which came into force on 1 January 2017.[149]

Nonhumans are raised and bred in laboratories and houses which are reminiscent of what sociology of science scholar, Karin Knorr-Cetina calls 'production facilities.'[150] For example, laboratory animals are bred explicitly as commodities and put on the market to be bought and sold. Specific strains and types of animals are created. Once animal use organisations have purchased them for testing, they are put into an animal house for further breeding and reproduction.[151] Males and females are designated for mating, litters are separated from their parents, and any 'surplus' nonhumans that are not deemed useful are killed or transferred elsewhere.[152]

Females are the *containers*[153] and this is especially the case with the now widespread practice of creating transgenic and genetically modified (GM) experimental animals, such as mice and rats. GM animals contain genes which have been artificially inserted rather than gained through natural methods of reproduction, transgenic organisms are a specific example of GM but contain genes which have been inserted from a completely different

---

148 Ibid.
149 Unit, "Code of Practice for the Housing and Care of Animals Bred, Supplied or Used for Scientific Purposes." pp. 39–66.
150 Karin Knorr Cetina, *Epistemic Cultures: How the Sciences Make Knowledge* (Cambridge, MA & London, UK: Harvard University Press, 1999). p. 145.
151 Ibid.
152 Ibid.
153 Ibid. p. 152.

species.¹⁵⁴ The COST manual explains several ways of creating GM animals, the most straightforward being via a method called 'pronuclear microinjection.'¹⁵⁵

In pronuclear microinjection, fertilised eggs are removed from 'donor' females that are superovulated. The eggs are then genetically manipulated and injected into another 'host' female. These females are turned pseudopregnant by breeding them with sterile or vasectomised males.¹⁵⁶ The COST manual is at pains to stress the influencing factors on the productivity of this method. It declares 'embryo quality, survival after microinjection and the host background strain influence the overall efficiency.'¹⁵⁷ The whole repertoire of breeding depends heavily on the quality of the female and the production of quality embryos. This is a production process which emphasises 'overall efficiency.' The female body is 'donated' for the process, especially their reproductive organs. Their very bodies become container technologies, their bodies transformed into parts – *toys/objects*¹⁵⁸ – to be manipulated. The involvement of the different nonhuman animals and the differentiated roles they play indicate that they are reproductive containers, joined together to create a factory of laboratory animals.¹⁵⁹

Female animals of the laboratory which are used for breeding are in fact containers which are contained. The cages of breeding racks illustrate the 'ruthlessness of the infant' scientists who see them as spaces to be filled efficiently. The breeding females are thus a result of 'projective identification,' they are bodies which can be genetically modified and therefore something which humans cannot contain.¹⁶⁰ They are reified as female breeding machines and objectified as an economic resource. Here, female nonhumans are made 'present' in the sense of being integral to the production of scientific animal dependent research; but this is also the site of their complete annihilation as subjects. The contained container of the laboratory is a staged representation according to 'exclusively 'masculine' parameters' that is part of the symbolic phallocratic order.¹⁶¹ In other words, it is the 'feminine' which is excluded from the binary opposition and hence, where

---

154 Donna Haraway, Modest_Witness@Second_Millenium.Femaleman_Meets_Oncomouse: *Feminism and Technoscience* (New York: Routledge, 1997).
155 Belen Pintado; Marian van Roon, "Creation of Genetically Modified Animals," in *The Cost Manual of Laboratory Animal Care and Use: Refinement, Reduction, and Research*, ed. Bryan Howard, Timo Nevalainen, Gemma Peretta (Boca Raton: CRC Press, Taylor & Francis Group, 2011). pp. 183–185.
156 Also see: Cetina, *Epistemic Cultures: How the Sciences Make Knowledge*. p. 152.
157 Roon, "Creation of Genetically Modified Animals." pp. 184–185.
158 Sofia, "Container Technologies." p. 185.
159 Cetina, *Epistemic Cultures: How the Sciences Make Knowledge*. p. 153.
160 Sofia, "Container Technologies." p. 185.
161 Luce Irigaray in Margaret Whitford, *Luce Irigaray: Philosophy in the Feminine* (London: Routledge, 1991). p. 118.

they are represented in this economy is 'precisely the site of their erasure' as sentient beings.[162]

Conclusion: The fetishised container of laboratory animal science

In every sense of the word then, one could argue that container technologies in animal-dependent science are spaces of covert violence and oppression. These covert violent spaces are far from the idea of them being a maternal and nurturing container for nonhuman animals. However, what I am positing in this chapter is the notion of container technologies being *symbolic* of the 'feminine' and therefore simultaneously creating the erasure of women's and nonhumans subjectivity.

What I have shown is that the symbolic dimension of language and discourse, which represents culture and social life in general, is inherently patriarchal. Accordingly, the symbolic represents the father who metaphorically intervenes in the imaginary ties of the mother and child.[163]

The intervention of animal welfare and its standardisation into the life of the laboratory is patriarchal because of the nature of its unconscious symbolism and material-semiotic activities. The very structures of the laboratory and its spatial layout forms the symbolic world of animals of the laboratory. The design of cages and legal recommendations all work together to produce an episteme which reproduces socially constructed differences of sex and sentiency in order to secure a male identity. As psychoanalyst Elizabeth Weed argues 'terms like woman, matter, mother, nature are indeed stand-ins for fetishising operations, they cannot carry 'truly' positive meanings outside of their symbolic history.'[164] Consequently, women, animals and nature belong to a phallocentric discourse which enables scientific exploration at their expense.

By drawing on the work of Zoë Sofia, I demonstrated how cages were masculine representations of 'feminine' vessels for the confinement of laboratory animals. A whole array of psychic forces are at play in order to confine and subdue nonhuman animals. The work of the UFAW and William Lane-Petter in the immediate Post-War era set the standard for what was to follow in the world of animal-dependent science. Lane-Petter advocated dynamic containers (the animal house) which created *facilitating environments*. Nonhuman animals were constructed as *toys/objects* ('tools of the trade') to manipulate for experimental purposes. The cages to house animals of the laboratory advocated animal health and welfare in order to

---

162 Judith Butler, *Bodies That Matter*, 2nd ed. (Oxon, UK: Routledge, 2011). p. 37.
163 Vachhani, "The Subordination of the Feminine? Developing a Critical Feminist Approach to the Psychoanalysis of Organizations." p. 1240.
164 Elizabeth Weed, "The Question of Style," in *Engaging with Irigaray*, ed. Carolyn Burke, Naomi Schor, Margaret Whitford (New York: Columbia University Press, 1994). p. 100.

enable nonhumans to adapt to humans and become user-friendly *(primary maternal attunement)*.

Eventually the ideas of the UFAW and Lane-Petter were enshrined in the Animals (Scientific Procedures) Act, 1986, alongside the work of EU bodies and the CoE. Standardisation of spaces and containers were legally mandated and became an essential prerequisite for the carrying out of scientific experiments and procedures. This legal turn in animal welfare, in terms of their housing and accommodation, still follows the trajectory of patriarchal power relations. I illustrated this with a focus on animals used for breeding, particularly GM and transgenic breeding programmes. These female nonhumans were the containers and enfolded within this discourse was Sofia's idea of the *ruthlessness of the infant* – small GM mammals are seen as just spaces (containers) to allow for scientific creative expression (the *potential space* of the lab to emerge).

The next chapter develops this understanding of gender, animals of the laboratory and their welfare. I focus on the psychological and behavioural discourses concerning their care and welfare and how this runs parallel to discourses about women's mental ill health and stress.

Bibliography

Adams, Carol J. *Neither Man nor Beast: Feminism and the Defense of Animals*. New York: The Continuum Publishing Company, 1995.

Bacharach, A. L. "Review: Laboratory Animals." *British Medical Journal* 4617 (1949): 20–21.

Birke, Lynda. "Telling the Rat What to Do: Laboratory Animals, Science and Gender." In *Gender and the Science of Difference: Cultural Politics of Contemporary Science and Medicine*, edited by Jill A. Fisher. NJ: Rutgers, The State University, 2011.

Bretherton, Inge. "The Origins of Attachment Theory: John Bowlby and Mary Ainsworth." *Developmental Psychology* 28, no. 5 (1992): 759–775.

Burch, R.L., W.M.S. Russell. *The Principles of Humane Experimental Techinque*. London: Methuen & Co LTD, 1959.

Butler, Judith. *Bodies That Matter*. 2nd ed. Oxon, UK: Routledge, 2011.

Cetina, Karin Knorr. *Epistemic Cultures: How the Sciences Make Knowledge*. Cambridge, MA & London, UK: Harvard University Press, 1999.

Commission, European. "Recommendation on Guidelines for the Accommodation and Care of Animals Used for Experimental and Other Scientific Purposes." *Offical Journal of the European Union* (2007): 1–89.

Council of the European Union. "Directive 2010/63/EU of the European Parliament and of the Council of 22 September 2010 on the Protection of Animals Used for Scientific Purposes." *Official Journal of the European Union* (2010).

Craib, Ian. *Psychoanalysis: A Critical Introduction*. Cambridge: Polity Press, 2001.

Despret, Vinciane. *What Would Animals Say If We Asked the Right Questions?* Minneapolis, U.S. & London: University of Minnesota Press, 2016.

Duxbury, Catherine. "Of Monkeys, Men and Menstruation: Gendered Dualisms and the Absent Referent in Mid-Twentieth Century British Menstrual Science." *Journal of Historical Sociology* 32, no. 1 (2019): 94–107.

Edgerton, David. *Warfare State: Britain, 1920–1970*. Cambridge, UK: Cambridge University Press, 2006.

Fox-Keller, Evelyn. *Secrets of Life, Secrets of Death: Essays on Language, Gender and Science*. London: Routledge, 1992.

French, Richard D. *Antivivisection and Medical Science in Victorian Society*. Princeton, New Jersey: Princeton University Press, 1975.

Frosh, Stephen. "Psychoanalyitic Challenges: A Contribution to the New Sexual Agenda." *Human Relations* 50, no. 3 (1997): 229–239.

Grosz, Elizabeth. *Volitile Bodies: Towards a Coporeal Feminism*. Bloomington: Indiana University Press, 1994.

Gummett, Philip. *Scientists in Whitehall*. Manchester, UK: Manchester University Press, 1980.

Haraway, Donna. *Modest_Witness@Second_Millenium.Femaleman_Meets_Oncomouse: Feminism and Technoscience*. New York: Routledge, 1997.

HM Government. "The Animals (Scientific Procedures) Act 1986 Amendment Regulations 2012." 2012.

"HM Government Animals in Science Regulation Unit." *Code of Practice for the Housing and Care of Animals Bred, Supplied or Used for Scientific Purposes."* edited by Home Office, 1–212. London: OGL Crown Copyright, 2014.

Hubrecht, Robert, Penny Hawkins, Anne McBride, Giles Paiba, Rita Rose, Mark Prescott, John Mulley, Sam Izzard, Deborah Ridley, Luca Melotti, Sarah Kappel. "Report of the 2017 Rspca/Ufaw Rodent and Rabbit Welfare Group Meeting." *Animal Technology and Welfare* 17 (2018): 75–83.

King, Angela. "The Prisoner of Gender: Foucualt and the Disciplining of the Female Body." *Journal of International Women's Studies* 5, no. 2 (2004): 29–39.

Kirk, Robert G.W. "A Brave New Animal for a Brave New World: The British Laboratory Animals Bureau and the Constitution of International Standards of Laboratory Animal Protection and Use, Circa 1947–1968." *Isis* 101, no. 1 (2010): 62–94.

Kirkwood, James, Robert Hubrecht, ed. *The UFAW Handbook on the Care and Management of Laboratory and Other Research Animals*. 8th ed. Chichester John Wiley & Sons, 2010.

Krohn, Thomas, Hannah-Marja Voipio, Ping Ping Tsai, Heinz Brandsetetter, Marcel Gyger, Hansjoachim Hackbarth, Axel Kornerup Hansen. "Housing and Care of Laboratory Animals." Chap. 3, In *The Cost Manual of Laboratory Animal Care and Use: Refinement, Reduction, and Research*, edited by Bryan Howard, Timo Nevalainen, Gemma Perretta, 29–73. Boca Raton: CRC Press, Taylor and Francis Group, 2011.

Lane-Petter, W. "The Animal House." Chap. 2, In *The UFAW Handbook on the Care and Management of Laboratory Animals*, edited by Alastair Worder, W. Lane-Petter. London: UFAW, 1957.

———. "The Animal House and Its Equipment." In *The UFAW Handbook on the Care and Management of Laboratory Animals*, edited by UFAW. Edinburgh and London: Churchill Livingstone, 1972.

Lane-Petter, William. "The Place of Laboratory Animals in the Scientific Life Og a Country." *Impact of Science on Society* 9 (1959): 178–196.

Littlewood, Sydney. "Report of the Departmental Committee on Experiments on Animals." edited by Home Office. London: Her Majesty's Stationery Office, 1965.

Longino, Helen E, Evelyn Fox-Keller. "Introduction." In *Feminism and Science*. Oxford: Oxford University Press, 1999.

Longino, Helen E. *Science as Social Knowledge: Values and Objectivity in Scientific Inquiry*. Princeton, New Jersey: Princeton University Press, 1990.

Lynch, Michael E. "Sacrifice and the Transformation of the Animal Body into a Scientific Object: Laboratory Culture and Ritual Practice in the Neurosciences." *Social Studies of Science* 18 (1988): 265–289.

Martin, Emily. *The Woman in the Body: A Cultural Analysis of Reproduction*. Milton Keynes: Open University Press, 1989.

Merchant, Carolyn. *The Death of Nature: Women, Ecology and the Scientific Revolution*. New York: Harper & Row Publishers Inc., 1983.

Mundy, A. E. "The Animal Technician." In *The UFAW Handbook on the Care and Management of Laboratory Animals*, edited by Alastair Worden, W. Lane-Petter. London: UFAW, 1957.

Navarro, Vicente. *Class Struggle, the State and Medicine: An Historical and Contemporary Analysis of the Medical Sector in Great Britain*. London, UK: Martin Robertson & Co. Ltd, 1978.

Office, Home. "Guidance on the Operation of the New Legislation to Replace the Cruelty to Animals Act 1876." HMSO, https://webarchive.nationalarchives.gov.uk/19970429190800/http://www.open.gov.uk:80/home_off/aspag.htm.

Perretta, Gemma, Bryan Howard, Timo Nevalainen, ed. *The Cost Manual of Laboratory Animal Care and Use: Refinement, Reduction, and Research*. Boca Raton: CRC Press, Taylor and Francis Group, 2011.

Plumwood, Val. *Feminism and the Mastery of Nature*. London: Routledge, 1993.

Roon, Marian van, Belen Pintado;. "Creation of Genetically Modified Animals." In *The Cost Manual of Laboratory Animal Care and Use: Refinement, Reduction, and Research*, edited by Bryan Howard, Timo Nevalainen, Gemma Peretta, 179–204. Boca Raton: CRC Press, Taylor & Francis Group, 2011.

Rothfield, Philipa. "Alternative Epistemologies, Politics and Feminism." *Social Analysis: The International Journal of Anthropology* 30 (1991): 54–67.

RSPCA. "Housing, Husbandry and Care." https://science.rspca.org.uk/sciencegroup/researchanimals/ethicalreview/functionstasks/housingandcare.

Schaffer, Simon, Steven Shapin. *Leviathan and the Air-Pump: Hobbes, Boyle, and the Experimental Life*. 2nd ed. Princeton, NJ: Princeton University Press, 2017.

Sofia, Zoë. "Container Technologies." *Hypatia* 15, no. 2 (2000): 181–201.

Techniplast. "Housing: Breeding and Stock." https://www.tecniplast.it/en/product/breeding-and-stock-at-breeders-solutions.html.

UFAW, ed. *The UFAW Handbook on the Care and Management of Laboratory Animals*. 3rd ed. Edinburgh & London: E & S Livingstone Ltd, 1967.

Vachhani, Sheena J. "The Subordination of the Feminine? Developing a Critical Feminist Approach to the Psychoanalysis of Organizations." *Organization Studies* 33, no. 9 (2012): 1237–55.

Wadiwel, Dinesh Joseph. *The War against Animals*. Leiden & Boston: Brill Rodopi, 2015.

Weed, Elizabeth. "The Question of Style." In *Engaging with Irigaray*, edited by Carolyn Burke, Naomi Schor, Margaret Whitford, 79–111. New York: Columbia University Press, 1994.

Weedon, Chris. *Feminist Practice and Poststructuralist Theory*. 6th ed. Oxford: Blackwell Publishers, 1994.

Whitford, Margaret. *Luce Irigaray: Philosophy in the Feminine*. London: Routledge, 1991.

Wilson, Elizabeth. *Only Halfway to Paradise Women in Postwar Britain: 1945–1968.* London: Tavistock Publications Ltd, 1980.

Worboys, Michael, Robert G. W. Kirk. Medicine and Species: One Medicine, One History? *The Oxford Handbook of the History of Medicine.* Edited by Mark Jackson. Oxford: Oxford University Press, 2012.

Worden, Alastair N, ed. *The UFAW Handbook on the Care and Management of Laboratory Animals.* Edited by Alastair Worden. 1st ed. London: Bailliere, Tindall and Cox, 1947.

6 Anxious animals, monstrous menstruating women and the science of stress, 1947–present

Feminists have long been documenting how discourses of mental ill health have historically been used to control women due to their constructed closeness to nature.[1] As outlined in the previous chapter, women are on the underside of the binary with nonhuman animals.[2] This renders them as being constituted as a part of nature, emotional rather than rational, animal not human, and therefore historically making us seem more fragile and prone to mental distress.[3] This chapter illuminates the biopolitical relationship between women, animals and madness via the discourses of stress and pre-menstrual stress (PMS) To explore this, we remain firmly situated amongst the spaces and material practices of the laboratory – amidst the cages, racks and experimental devices that are the life worlds of nonhuman animals. This will help us to flesh out the intricate intersections between laboratory animal stress, welfare and the biomedical researches used to pathologise menstrual disorders. This chapter critically explores the intersectional biopolitical relationship of women and animals via the discourses of stress and distress in both laboratory animal welfare and psychiatry.

I follow on from work presented in the previous chapter to reconstruct the historical rise of psychological mechanisms of control over nonhuman animals in the laboratory under the rubric of the three Rs, or replacement, reduction and refinement of animal experimentation. This is coupled with an analysis of the psychiatric classification and treatment of women's PMS.

---

1 Heather Fraser, Nik Taylor, "Women, Anxiety, and Companion Animals: Towards a Feminist Animal Studies of Interspecies Care and Solidarity," in *Animaladies: Gender, Animals and Madness*, ed. Lori Gruen, Fiona Probyn-Rapsey (New York & London: Bloomsbury Academic, Bloomsbury Pulbishing Inc., 2019). p. 161.
2 Val Plumwood, *Feminism and the Mastery of Nature* (London: Routledge, 1993); Carolyn Merchant, *The Death of Nature: Women, Ecology and the Scientific Revolution* (New York: Harper & Row Publishers Inc., 1983).
3 Taylor, "Women, Anxiety, and Companion Animals: Towards a Feminist Animal Studies of Interspecies Care and Solidarity."

DOI: 10.4324/9780429461644-7

158 *Scientific intersections*

The rise and eventual legalisation of psychological care over nonhuman laboratory animals is the site of emergence of the modern laboratory animal. Correlatively, it is also the site where the 'female' body became constituted and 'cared' for.[4] Discourses of laboratory care over nonhuman animals are entangled both literally and metaphorical with a psychiatric discourse of care over menstruating 'distressed' women.

'Animalmaladies': The biopolitics of domestication and subordination

The term 'animaladies' was first coined by feminist animal studies scholar Fiona Probyn-Rapsey to describe the worsening human–animal relationships in the current destructive epoch of the Anthropocene. But for her, it is a gesture towards how awareness of such 'dis-ease' can be a stimulus for positive change.[5] Later, Probyn-Rapsey and fellow feminist animal studies researcher Lori Gruen extended the term's conceptual meaning to enfold within it the relationship between gender, animals, and mental health (maladies).[6] The words 'animal' and 'maladies'; 'animal' and 'ladies make up the concept 'animaladies.'[7] I take this latter interpretation to explore the biopolitical interrelationship between laboratory animals and the medicalisation of women's mental health via the discourses of stress and PMS.

For me, biopolitics enfolds within it animaladies. Here, animaladies are strategically convened to subjugate and control 'abnormal' (gendered) bodies and nonhuman animals. As we know from the previous chapters, biopolitics is not limited to human populations but also extends into the realm of nonhuman life.[8] For Foucault, a society's dawn of biological modernity is located

---

4 Lynda Birke, Arnold Arluke, and Mike Michael, *The Sacrifice: How Scientifc Experiments Transform Animals and People* (West Lafayette IN: Purdue University Press, 2007); Lynda Birke, "Telling the Rat What to Do: Laboratory Animals, Science and Gender," in *Gender and the Science of Difference: Cultural Politics of Contemporary Science and Medicine*, ed. Jill A. Fisher (United States of America: Rutgers, the State University, 2011); *Feminism, Animals and Science: The Naming of the Shrew* (Buckingham, UK: Open University Press, 1994).
5 Fiona Probyn-Rapsey, "Review Article: Multispecies Mourning: Thom Van Dooren's Flight Ways: Life and Loss at the Edge of Extinction by Thom Van Dooren," *Animal Studies Journal* 3, no. 2 (2014): 16.
6 Lori Gruen, Fiona Probyn-Rapsey, "Distillations," in *Animalmaladies: Gender, Animals, and Madness*, ed. Lori Gruen, Fiona Probyn-Rapsey (New York & London: Bloomsbury Academic, 2019). p. 1.
7 Ibid.
8 Dinesh Joseph Wadiwel, *The War against Animals* (Leiden & Boston: Brill Rodopi, 2015); Matthew Chrulew, Dinesh Joseph Wadiwel, "Introduction: Foucault and Animals," in *Foucault and Animals*, ed. Matthew Chrulew, Dinesh Joseph Wadiwel (Leiden & Boston: Brill, 2017); Kristin Asdal, Tone Druglitrø, Steve Hinchcliffe, ed., *Humans, Animals and Biopolitics: The More-Than-Human Condition*, Multispecies Encounters (Oxon: Routledge, 2017).

at the point at which the human species and the person as a biological entity become part of its political strategies.⁹ This threshold of the modern era is termed biopolitics, and it involves the conversion of biological processes, such as reproduction, into the mechanisms and calculations of State power.

Hans Selye and the general adaptation syndrome

> What is this one mysterious condition that the most different kinds of people have in common with the animals and even with individual cells, at times when much – much of anything – happens to them? What is the nature of stress?¹⁰

The constituent discourses of stress and distress in the mid-twentieth century is where we start our journey in this chapter. The two World Wars propelled British medical research into a new era, and the State increasingly turned to science in the search for medical cures.¹¹ For instance, it was acknowledged that the typically 'feminine' disease of hysteria also manifested in men, and was coined as 'Shell-Shock' (a form of post-traumatic stress as a result of soldiers' experiences on the battlefield).¹² In 1950s Britain, it became commonplace to declare that there was an increase in mental health issues due to the changes in living conditions bought about by war, economic conditions and technological advances.¹³ One of the main conceptual apparatuses that accompanied these industrial and military descriptions about mental ill health in the immediate post-war period was stress.¹⁴

For the Hungarian physiologist Hans Selye (1907–1982), the 'one mysterious condition' which both human and nonhuman animals become afflicted with at certain times in their lives, is stress.¹⁵ Selye was the originator of the concept, and he promulgated a universal theory about human nature which he considered was a 'natural philosophy of life.'¹⁶ Despite his views about the human mind and body being largely rejected by physiological scientists

---

9 Michel Foucault, *The History of Sexuality Vol 1: The Will to Knowledge*, 5th ed. (London: Penguin Books Ltd., 1998). pp. 140–143.
10 Hans Selye, *The Stress of Life*, 2nd ed. (New York: McGraw-Hill, 1976). p. 3.
11 Philip Gummett, *Scientists in Whitehall* (Manchester, U.K.: Manchester University Press, 1980).
12 Elaine Showalter, *The Female Malady*, 17th ed. (London: Virago Press, 1985; repr., 2014).
13 Robert G.W. Kirk, "The Invention of the "Stressed Animal" and the Development of a Sceicne of Animal Welfare, 1947-1986," in *Stress, Shock and Adaptation in the Twentieth Century*, ed. David Cantor, Edmund Ramsden (Rochester, NY: University of Rochester Press, 2014). p. 241.
14 Russell Viner, "Putting Stress in Life: Hans Selye and the Making of Stress Theory," *Social Studies of Science* 29, no. 3 (1999). p. 392.
15 Ibid. p. 391.
16 Mark Jackson, "The Pursuit of Happiness: The Social and Scientific Origins of Hans Selye's Natural Philosophy of Life," *History of the Human Sciences* 25, no. 5 (2012): 14.

during the interwar and immediate post-war years; in Britain, his work was influential in the development of a science of animal welfare at this time.[17] It was not until the 1970s when his research on stress in laboratory animals translated into human experiences of the modern world made an impact, and he became internationally renowned in both scientific and lay circles.[18]

In 1907, after completing his medical degree and a doctorate in organic chemistry, Hans Selye later settled in the Department of Biochemistry at McGill University.[19] It was here that his earlier experiments on female rats – analysing ovarian hormones – paved the way for his development of the concept of the general adaptation syndrome (GAS).[20] Selye's first foray into major publication about his GAS came in a short article published in the science journal *Nature* in 1936. It referred to a host of external and internal 'nocuous agents' that caused a change in the living being's body and mind.[21] As a result of these various harmful agents, the living body responded in a series comprised of three stages. Firstly, the response is the 'general alarm reaction' then resistance to 'invasions' and the final stage being adaptation. Towards the end of the article, Selye notes how 'since the syndrome as a whole seems to represent a generalised effort of the organism to adapt itself to new conditions, it might be termed the general adaptation syndrome.'[22] This short and subdued article did not mention the word 'stress' at all.

Selye's most explicit description of his theory was in 1946 in a comprehensive article published in the *Journal of Endocrinology*.[23] Over one hundred pages long and featuring diagrams, photographs and charts, this article facilitated the general acceptance and use of the term 'stress' within medical circles and eventually in broader society, if not yet entirely accepted by most laboratory biologists.[24] It was his use and extension of contemporary hormonal and physiological theories that formed the bedrock of his GAS concept. Stress was seen as an acute reaction to external and internal incompatibilities with the body, and Selye claimed it could be anything from 'diet, temperature [and] light' to 'heredity' and general 'constitution.'[25] He named these causes 'conditioning factors' and claimed that the adaptation

---

17 Kirk, "The Invention of the 'Stressed Animal' and the Development of a Sceicne of Animal Welfare, 1947-1986." pp. 250–252.
18 Viner, "Putting Stress in Life: Hans Selye and the Making of Stress Theory." p. 392.
19 Mark Jackson, *Evaluating the Role of Hans Selye in the Modern History of Stress*, in David Cantor, Edmund Ramsden, ed. *Stress, Shock and Adaptation in the Twentieth Century* (Rochester, USA: University of Rochester Press, 2014). pp. 23–24.
20 Ibid.
21 Hans Selye, a Syndrome Produced by Diverse Nocuous Agents, *Nature*, 4 July 1936. p. 32.
22 Ibid.
23 Hans Selye, "The General Adaptation Syndrome and the Diseases of Adaptation," *Journal of Clinical Endocrinology* 6, no. 2 (1946). pp. 117–230.
24 Viner, "Putting Stress in Life: Hans Selye and the Making of Stress Theory." p. 396.
25 Hans Selye, *The Story of the Adaptation Syndrome Told in the Form of Informal, Illustrated Lectures* (Montreal Canada: Acta Inc, Medical Publishers, 1952). P. *Leitmotiv*.

syndrome was an 'indispensable physiologic defence reaction to damage.'[26] Influenced by the world-renowned Harvard physiologist Walter B Cannon's concept of homeostasis[27] and popular hormonal theories of the body,[28] Selye's concept of stress influenced a diverse array of intellectual bodies from sociology to psychology, cybernetics and endocrinology.[29] Stress offered a unifying concept to explain non-specific disturbances in the human and nonhuman body, as well as instabilities occurring in wider society.[30]

> With the concept of the General Adaptation Syndrome we have attempted to integrate a number of seemingly quite unrelated observations into a single unified biologic system... The keynote of this unification was the tenet that all living organisms can respond to stress as such, and that in this respect the basic reaction pattern is always the same, irrespective of the agent used to produce stress. We called this response the general adaptation syndrome, and its derailments the diseases of adaptation.[31]

Stress provided the theoretical ground for transdisciplinary discussions about how scientists could come to understand a variety of biological and psychological behaviours that were contrary to 'normal' functioning in living beings.[32]

It was in 1958 when Selye's scientific credence began to take shape in Britain. The Mental Health Fund convened a conference to discuss 'research on stress in relation to mental health and mental illness.'[33] Held at Lincoln College, Oxford, the meeting comprised of delegates from the behavioural and animal-dependent sciences, including Selye himself, psychologist John Bowlby, zoologist Robert Hinde and psychobiologist Howard Liddell.[34] The aim was to use Selye's concept of stress to 'arrive at a synthesis of the concepts used in different branches of the behavioural sciences when discussing

---

26 Ibid.
27 Hans Selye, "Stress and the General Adaptation Syndrome," *British Medical Journal*, no. 4667 (1950): 1383–1392.
28 Mark Jackson, *The Age of Stress: Science and the Search for Stability* (Oxford, U.K.: Oxford University Press, 2013). pp. 82–83.
29 "The Pursuit of Happiness: The Social and Scientific Origins of Hans Selye's Natural Philosophy of Life."
30 Ibid.; Viner, "Putting Stress in Life: Hans Selye and the Making of Stress Theory."
31 Hans Selye, "Stress and the General Adaptation Syndrome," *British Medical Journal* 1, no. 4667 (1950): 1382.
32 Kirk, "The Invention of the "Stressed Animal" and the Development of a Sceicne of Animal Welfare, 1947-1986." p. 241.
33 Special Correspondent, "Adaptation to Stress: Conference of Behavioural Scientists," *British Medical Journal* 2, no. 5092 (1958): 382.
34 James M. Tanner, ed. *Stress and Psychiatric Disorder: The Proceedings of the Second Oxford Conference of the Mental Health Research Fund* (Oxford, U.K.: Blackwell, 1960).

162 *Scientific intersections*

stressful situations and stress effects.'[35] What is particularly fascinating about this conference with regards to the premise of this book, is some of its focus was on the role of women as mothers and the use of nonhuman laboratory animals in exploring mother–child dyads of the human and nonhuman type:

> Professor Liddell reported that kids [young goats] which have been separated from their dams [mothers] for an hour or two immediately after birth suffer a very high mortality subsequently, the majority dying within a year. All these psychosocial Stressors demand from the individual a "role transition" and a reorganization of social relationships, which may be successfully accomplished; otherwise illness and even death result.[36]

Liddell went on to state the impact the mother had on maintaining low stress levels, using his research on sheep to demonstrate:

> How the presence of the mother reduces the effects on lambs of monotonous, reinforced stimulation. Lambs so tested in the presence of their mothers move freely and actively about the pen; lambs separated from their mothers become virtually immobile.[37]

Other participants of the conference echoed this emphasis on mother–child attachment and its relationship to childhood stress. Most notably was Bowlby, who was renowned for his theory on human kinship 'disorders.' He made links between his theory of attachment and the stressful effects of separation of the young child from the mother.[38] Aside from attachment disorders signifying a form of Selyian stress syndrome, mental ill health, in the form of 'mental neurosis' was debated. The evidence illustrated this garnered from Ivan Pavlov's behaviour experiments whose restraining 'harness and frame' facilitated the onset of such mental illness in pigs, sheep and goats.[39]

The conference characterises the biopolitical rationality of mid-twentieth-century Britain. The idea that parallels could be drawn between experimental animals and women (as mothers in this instance), signifies a postwar scientific shift from an emphasis on eugenic social engineering seen during the interwar period, to sociological, ethological and psychological theories.[40] The delegates at the conference, including Selye, presented their research against a backdrop of functionalist and behaviourist theories of social order. These theories were integral to the rebuilding of social life after

---

35 Special Correspondent, "Adaptation to Stress: Conference of Behavioural Scientists." p. 382.
36 Ibid. p. 383.
37 Ibid.
38 Ibid.
39 Ibid.
40 Jemima Repo, *The Biopolitics of Gender* (New York: Oxford University Press, 2016). p. 19.

the atrocities of the Second World War.[41] The behavioural and psychiatric sciences became a new technology of social control. To keep pace with the quickening economic and technological progress of the era, bodies had to be disciplined. This was done via scientific management techniques such as psychiatric therapy and scientific policy.[42] Functionalism, behaviourism and the imminent rise of sociobiology in this era aimed to scientifically manage and regulate 'inefficient, maladaptive, obsolescent' bodies by updating 'our biology through social control.'[43]

As we have just seen, Selye's concept of stress influenced not only intellectual discussion on mental illness but also the highly gendered role of the mother in post-war British society. Nonhuman animals were integral to the making of these theories, and for Selye, they were the *sine qua non* of his experimental work. Without them, the GAS and his subsequent permutations on the stress syndrome, would not have happened. In his many writings, Selye was a passionate advocate of the use of animals for experimentation - rats, and later monkeys were an integral part of his laboratory *modus operandi* throughout his entire career. He certainly did not question the use of them in his pursuit of professional recognition. In his 1956 book, *The Stress of Life*, he came across as a zealous advocate of the use of nonhumans in experiment:

> If we want to learn something about any aspect of life, we first need a sample of its pattern as expressed in the body of an animal or man. The structural organisation of living beings can often be studied by dissection after death, but vital processes can only be explored during life. Since it is not justified to perform dangerous operations on man, experimental animals are quite indispensable for such studies.[44]

With Selye's passionate opinions on the matter, he went on further to outline why the use of nonhuman animals was necessary for medicine. Over two pages he described the medical breakthroughs made over the past one hundred years from using animals in experiments, claiming that 'a major step of progress in medicine has been based, at least partly, on animal experiments.'[45] He ended with a personal pronouncement on the matter:

> The better one understands the nature of life, disease and suffering, the more one becomes incapable of brutality. This thought was not the least important among the motives which led me to write a book on the

---

41 Donna Haraway, *Primate Visions: Gender, Race, and Nature in the World of Modern Science* (New York: Routledge, 1989).
42 *Simians, Cyborgs, and Women: The Reinvention of Nature* (London: Free Association Books, 1991). p. 35. Repo, *The Biopolitics of Gender*. p. 29.
43 Haraway, *Simians, Cyborgs, and Women: The Reinvention of Nature*. p. 35.
44 Selye, *The Stress of Life*. p. 87.
45 Ibid. p. 88.

nature of disease for those who are not professionally concerned with medicine. In our Institute last year, we used about 1400 rats a week for research, but not one of them exposed to unnecessary pain because of carelessness.[46]

Animals were integral to Selye's theories on stress and gave him the capacity to question nature. He published his lectures in a book entitled *The Story of the Adaptation Syndrome*. In the book, Selye elaborated on the relationship of science to nature (and thus nonhumans). It was reminiscent of Francis Bacon's treatise on the philosophy of science, as in it he emphasises that he derived great 'intellectual satisfaction... from *forcing one's way*, step by step, into the confidence of Nature' to 'understand her.'[47] For Selye 'nature' was 'the source of all knowledge – [and] rarely replies to questions unless they are put to her in the form of experiments to which she can say 'yes' or 'no.' She is not loquacious; she merely nods in the affirmative or in the negative.'[48] In Selye's eyes, nature was female, and science is there to uncover the secrets that *she* beholds. Passive and shy, 'she will silently show us a picture'[49] of the world at large. And, it was through this perception of the natural world and his experiments on rats, that he could establish his theory on stress and the GAS, catapulting him to scientific fame in mid-twentieth century Britain.

The UFAW Handbook: New beginnings in animal welfare, 1947–1959

The publication of Selye's 1946 article was a watershed moment in accepting that physiological disturbances in the body caused both psychological shock and stress to a living organism. It helped to inaugurate a science of animal welfare into the practice of British biological and medical research over the coming decades.[50] How did Selye's concept of stress provide the impetus for the revisioning of the practice of animal experimentation? Historian Robert Kirk documents how the zoology trained pharmacologist Robin Alexander Chance transmuted Selye's ideas into the control of psychosomatic stresses of lab animals.[51] Chance's work emphasised how laboratory scientists and

---

46 Ibid. pp. 89–90.
47 Selye, *The Story of the Adaptation Syndrome Told in the Form of Informal, Illustrated Lectures.* p. 15. [emphasis added].
48 *The Stress of Life.* p. 19.
49 Ibid. p. 19.
50 Kirk, "The Invention of the "Stressed Animal" and the Development of a Sceicne of Animal Welfare, 1947–1986."
51 Robert G.W. Kirk, "Between the Clinic and the Laboratory: Ethology and Pharmacology in the Work of Michael Robin Alexander Chance, C. 1946–1964," *Medical History* 53 (2009). pp. 528–534. Kirk, "The Invention of the "Stressed Animal" and the Development of a Sceicne of Animal Welfare, 1947–1986."

their staff comprised aspects of the 'social environment' of the animal in the laboratory, and this affected the processes of experimental technique and design.[52] It was this acknowledgement of the psychosomatic and psychosocial experienced by nonhuman animals of the laboratory which led the UFAW to sponsor Chance to develop a programme of 'humane experimental technique' and thus was the start a science of animal wellbeing and welfare in British laboratory animal research.[53]

As we have seen from the previous chapter, the standardisation of laboratory equipment, nonhuman experimental animals and their housing became integral to the development of British lab science after the Second World War. The publication in 1947 of *The UFAW Handbook on the Care and Management of Laboratory Animals* paved the way for the beginnings of a science of animal welfare. As Kirk rightly observes, it was through these tactics that the UFAW reshaped laboratory relations between the human and animal in this period, and challenged the current legislation on animal experiments, especially in regards to pain.[54] As we know from chapters one and four, up until 1986, the 1876 Cruelty to Animals Act was the legislation which governed the regulation of animal experiments in Britain. The Cruelty to Animals Act defined pain in strictly physiological terms; *The UFAW Handbook* provided scope for a redefinition of pain and acknowledged the psychological dimensions of pain animals of the laboratory suffered.[55]

In 1954, the UFAW funded another research project that intended to outline a welfarist approach towards laboratory animal science.[56] Buoyed by the success of the *Handbook*, the UFAW enlisted two scientists to continue its work into laboratory animal welfare: W.M.S. Russell, UFAW research fellow, Department of Zoology and Comparative Anatomy, University College London, and, R.L. Burch UFAW research assistant. This time the focus was not going to be on animal husbandry and laboratory spaces, but rather, the very methodologies employed by scientists to conduct their experiments.

With contributions from several distinguished scientists in the fields of ethology, physiology and zoology, including Professor P.B. Medawar, as chair of the Consultative Committee for the book,[57] and Dr Lane-Petter

---

52 "The Invention of the "Stressed Animal" and the Development of a Sceicne of Animal Welfare, 1947–1986." p. 249.
53 Ibid.
54 Ibid. p. 243.
55 Alastair N Worden, ed. *The Ufaw Handbook on the Care and Management of Laboratory Animals*, 1st ed. (London: Bailliere, Tindall And Cox, 1947). p. 19.
56 Kirk, "The Invention of the "Stressed Animal" and the Development of a Sceicne of Animal Welfare, 1947–1986."; W.M.S. Russell and R.L. Burch, *The Principles of Humane Experimental Techinque* (London: Methuen & Co LTD, 1959). p. xiii (P250 – Kirk).
57 *The Principles of Humane Experimental Techinque*. Ibid. p. xiii.

166 *Scientific intersections*

head of the Laboratory Animals Bureau,[58] the book was intended to be a contribution towards the celebrations of the centenary of Charles Darwin's *The Origin of Species*.[59] With Russell taking the main editorial lead,[60] the book became known as *The Principles of Humane Experimental Technique*. The book recognised that:

> It has sometimes seemed that there is an irreconcilable conflict between the claims of science and medicine and those of humanity in our treatment of lower animals... The conflict disappears altogether on closer inspection, and by now it is widely recognised that the humanest possible treatment of experimental animals, far from being an obstacle, is actually a prerequisite for successful animal experimentation.[61]

The aim was to demonstrate the links between 'humanity and efficiency,' in the treatment of animals during the experiment – the very methodologies of experimental science were being questioned.[62] The book's authors suggested that it represented the starting point of a 'new science' of humane experimentation because of its interdisciplinary approach, and its establishment of a set of 'general principles' for this 'new subject.'[63] However, the humane principles were only applied to a certain kind of nonhuman, the vertebrates, for reasons of 'simplicity and clarity.'[64] It was against this background that the book proposed different ways of assessing pain, measuring subjectivity and imparting guidance for a more humane approach towards those nonhumans with a backbone.

'Stress without distress': The scientific basis of kindness to animals, 1954–1959

What the UFAW did in the 1950s was to rationalise and objectify animal emotions in the laboratory. They moved away from philosophical and emotive descriptions of pain, fear and distress in the animal, as favoured by the antivivisectionists, and developed a new discourse of animal morality. This discourse was deployed to legitimate the continued use of even more animals in experimental procedures. As has been mentioned, it was this organisation that led the way in fashioning a language of animal-use as 'humane,'[65] which

---

58 Kirk, "The Invention of the "Stressed Animal" and the Development of a Sceicne of Animal Welfare, 1947–1986." p. 250.
59 Burch, *The Principles of Humane Experimental Techinque*. p. xiv.
60 Kirk, "The Invention of the "Stressed Animal" and the Development of a Sceicne of Animal Welfare, 1947–1986." p. 250.
61 Burch, *The Principles of Humane Experimental Techinque*. pp. 3–4.
62 Ibid. pp. 4–5.
63 Ibid. pp. 5–6.
64 Ibid. pp. 6–7.
65 Ibid.

legitimated animal experimentation. Further, the idea of animal psychological-stress prompted the consideration of a change in scientific methodologies and practices associated with medical experiments on animals.

Influenced by Selye's GAS concept, Russell and Burch proposed a 'psychosomatic' approach to this new construction of the lab animal.[66] This was a branch of medicine which stipulated the link between the mind and the body and rejected the historical propositions of the Cartesian idea of the mind-body binary. The authors claimed that 'the mind-body dichotomy is an entirely pathological fantasy... first thrust upon science by Descartes.'[67] The repudiation of Cartesian principles was first suggested in the *Handbook* and echoed by Hume in the *Humane Experimental Technique*.[68] The book was replete with Selyian ideas and language associated with stress and the nervous system, and the hormonal and endocrine changes the body underwent during periods of ill health. But, as the authors suggested, 'it is regrettable on humane and scientific grounds that so large a proportion of the study of psychosomatics in animals has so far been carried out with the bludgeon of 'stress' of the more severe kinds.'[69] It was at this point that the authors emphasised the importance of assessing more 'subtle interactions' between behavioural and physiological states in lab animals.[70]

Interestingly, the studies mentioned the more indirect stressful states in nonhumans as a result of experiments conducted to understand the reproductive system. Russell and Burch claimed that in this particular branch of medical research 'we know most about the complex effects of the physical and social environment on endocrine control units.'[71] Furthermore, the exploration of these subtle states was justified by Russell and Burch regarding modes of synchronisation in reproductive states of mating and ovulation in female nonhuman animals. The authors refer to scientific literature which demonstrates the psychosomatic effects of reproduction on the female and their oestrous cycle. Accordingly, 'the female will only mate (or is only attractive) at a period suitably timed with her own spontaneous ovulation' and this depends on their social environment.[72]

The Selyian ideas of hormones interacting with the social environment were the precursor to understanding stress in nonhuman animals. As Evelyn Fox-Keller asserts, in the mid-twentieth century, biology and its related disciplines became accepted members of the scientific community through the idea of

---

66 Ibid. p. 10. Also see: Kirk, "The Invention of the "Stressed Animal" and the Development of a Sceicne of Animal Welfare, 1947–1986." p. 250.
67 Burch, *The Principles of Humane Experimental Techinque*. p. 11.
68 Worden, *The Ufaw Handbook on the Care and Management of Laboratory Animals*. p. 18.
69 Burch, *The Principles of Humane Experimental Techinque*. p. 12.
70 Ibid.
71 Ibid.
72 Ibid.

168 *Scientific intersections*

the body – both human and nonhuman – as a 'chemical machine.'[73] Selye's powerful pronouncements about the role of environmental stressors and hormones contributed to the shaping of discourses of laboratory animal welfare.

> The psychosomatics of experimental animals is perhaps the most important single subject for the development of humane and efficient technique in animal experiments. If we may by this time use the tag without fear of Cartesian implications, the motto of the experimenter in his dealings with his subjects must be *mens sana in corpore sano*, and he will not get the one without the other.[74]

Mens sana in corpore sano: 'sound mind in a sound body.' Hence, the lip service paid to the rejection of Cartesian principles. The idea of having a sound mind *in* a sound body renders visible the discourse of the body as a machine with the mind, although part of the body, still dependent on physiological mechanisms for 'its' use, rather than the two being interdependent.

This is most explicitly recognised when the authors discuss pain, fear and distress in nonhumans. The authors describe this as a 'the sequence of moods in a lower animal... is rigidly controlled by internal and external changes according to a code of rules, largely pre-set for a given species.' Of course, 'in this respect, animals are functionally similar to neurotic humans.'[75] To ascertain these moods of stress Russell and Burch postulated the possible existence of a measurement scale of wellbeing to distress so that:

> [W]e are led to set our sights high in removing inhumanity, and to attempt always to drive the animal up to the highest possible point on the scale. Thus we can aim at well-being rather than at mere absence of distress. We may then, define distress of a certain degree (of whatever origin) as a central nervous state of a certain rank on a scale, in the direction of mass autonomic response *which, if protracted, would lead to the physiological stress syndrome.*[76]

By moving from a notion of pain to one of distress, the idea was for medical science to emphasise wellbeing of the animal. This would allow for the embedding of quantifiable techniques both before the use of the animal in an experiment.[77] Distress and consciousness became a variable for measurement

---

73 Evelyn Fox-Keller, "Language and Ideology in Evolutionary Theory: Reading Cultural Norms into Natural Law," in *Feminism and Science*, ed. Evelyn Fox-Keller, Helen E. Longino (Oxford, U.K.: Oxford University Press, 1999). p. 154.
74 Burch, *The Principles of Humane Experimental Techinque.* p. 13.
75 Ibid. p. 17.
76 Ibid. pp. 23–24.
77 Kirk, "The Invention of the "Stressed Animal" and the Development of a Sceicne of Animal Welfare, 1947–1986." Ibid. p. 251.

and accountable to the experimenter. What Burch and Russell did was recommend ways of reducing distress and enhancing wellbeing through a discussion on ways to reduce, replace and refine animal experiments.[78]

These 3 R's acted as a foundation from which medical science could reshape laboratory relations and re-construe the nonhuman. For Replacement, the authors continued to justify the use of nonhuman animals through the concepts of absolute and relative replacement.[79] The teleological endpoint for Russell and Burch was to replace vertebrate animals with either invertebrates or plants eventually wholly. In the meantime, the focus remained on relative replacement where animals were still required but 'in actual experiment they are exposed, probably or certainly, to no distress at all.'[80] Replacement was defended as being in:

> [T]he case of non-recovery experiments on living and intact but completely anaesthetized animals. Provided the anaesthesia is general and sufficiently deep, and its time-course properly synchronised with the treatment itself, such experiments are totally free from inhumanity.[81]

Using animals would fit the criteria of Replacement if they were painlessly killed afterwards. For the UFAW this 'already constitutes a further advance' in humane experiments 'provided the euthanasia is satisfactory and provided there is substantial reduction in numbers, such experiments are beyond reproach.'[82] Reduction and refinement of the use of animals were consequently justified by the nature of the experimental technique used and the ability to quantify the results of experiments.

Ironically, in the 3 R's, what the authors were proposing was a way to perceive nonhumans differently, not just as passive objects but active agents in the world. However, animals were re-shaped into an active *object*, a new form of tool, for a new version of science, one that had to be made more efficient in a post-war world of medical research. Thus, this new approach to the study of biological science was achieved through still seeing the nonhuman body as a *machine-like-object*. This is most evident in the discussion concerning direct and contingent inhumanity. Direct inhumanity was seen as the infliction of 'distress' as an 'unavoidable consequence' of the experiment. In contrast, contingent inhumanity was the 'infliction of distress as an incidental and inadvertent by-product' of the experiment.[83]

---

78 The 3R's, still used today in laboratories and enshrined in current animal experimentation legislation.
79 Burch, *The Principles of Humane Experimental Techinque*. pp. 70–75.
80 Ibid. p. 70.
81 Ibid. p. 71.
82 Ibid.
83 Ibid. p. 54.

It is here that we can perceive the historical continuity of the influence of the Cartesian method, as argued elsewhere in the book. Despite the UFAW's rebuke of Descartes, the mechanistic nature of the conceptions of nonhuman animals of the laboratory extended into the new epistemologies of scientific welfarism. This post-Cartesian epistemology[84] established a claim to the authority of medical science in a post-war world. It became a way of disciplining bodies, most notably nonhuman bodies, but also, as we shall see gendered human ones, via a biopolitical animalady. This form of control was a product of the broader social and cultural milieu of the time, one which embedded and embraced a notion of modernity which was drawing on historical paternalistic modes of thought and practice.[85] These paternalistic impulses were at once entrenched in wider society and the laboratory, through the persistence of the scientific discourses of hierarchy, both within the animal kingdom, and in human society in the form of hierarchies of stratification according to social class, gender and race.

'Brains or sawdust?'[86]: The royal society's ethical working party on animal experiments, 1979–1986

Both Selye's and the UFAW's influence continued into the 1980s with the most overt evidence of their presence being in the Animals (Scientific Procedures) Act, 1986 (see chapter two). What helped to establish Selye's influence further with regards to the persistence of the use of his GAS concept in understanding animal wellbeing, was the Royal Society.

Established in 1660 and receiving royal approval in 1663, The Royal Society was founded to promote Britain's scientific research.[87] In the nineteenth century, with the creation of the Parliamentary Grant System, the society was able to receive government funding for a host of its fellows and researches; for instance, from 2015 to 2016, the Society received a government grant of £47.101 m.[88]

In October of 1979, around the time when the EU began to draft the Convention for the Protection of Vertebrate Animals; and when discussions

---

84 Naomi Scheman, "Though This Be Method, yet There Is Madness in It: Paranoia and Liberal Epistemology," in *Feminism and Science*, ed. Evelyn Fox-Keller and Helen E. Longino (Oxford, U.K.: Oxford University Press, 1999). p. 210

85 Jon Lawrence, "Paternalism, Class and the British Path to Modernity," in *The Peculiarities of Liberal Modernity in Imperial Britain*, ed. Simon Gunn and James Vernon (California: California Press, 2011). p. 147.

 NB: The definition of Paternalism simply means a way of managing populations and individuals in the manner of a father dealing with children. Inevitably this is a form of patriarchy and biopolitics.

86 Well, PP/WDP/E/4/: Box 60, Royal Society Committee on Animal Experiments, 1978-1983. Ethics of Animal Experimentation in Physiology, Appendix B, Brains – or Sawdust?. n.d. 1982/3?

87 "The Royal Society," https://royalsociety.org/about-us/history/.

88 Ibid.

abounded about the introduction of new legislation to regulate animal experiments, the Royal Society created a working party on the use of animals in science.[89] Its primary purpose was to present the 'scientists' point of view' to the various actors responsible for the proposals for the new regulations. It was also committed to ensuring that a 'proper balance would be struck between limitations of pain and distress to experimental animals… and the progress of medical science and experimental biology.'[90]

A host of prominent scholars were part of the group, including Andrew Huxley, physiologist and biophysicist; biologist Marian Stamp Dawkins; physiologist Dennis Noble and philosopher Bernard Williams. Many other foremost British academics contributed to the committee and all submitted papers discussing various aspects of animal pain and distress from the perspective of their respective disciplines. These papers were compiled into a discussion booklet and sent to the Secretary of Scientific Societies on 27 May 1983, in the hope of convening a private meeting, with 'no press representation,' for the authors to discuss their work.[91]

It was biologist Marian Stamp Dawkins who provided a comprehensive essay on the psychological suffering of nonhuman animals. For Dawkins, suffering in nonhuman animals was difficult to measure but, she argued 'we can build up a great deal of indirect evidence as to what it might be feeling.'[92]

> There are three commonly used indications that an animal is suffering. The first, and most obvious, is its state of physical health. If an animal is diseased or injured, then there are good grounds for suspecting that it is suffering… the second measure of suffering…is based on physiology. Long before clear-cut disturbances of health become apparent on the outside of an animal, it may be possible to detect changes going on beneath the skin, changes in hormone levels, brain state, heart rate, body temperature and so on…A third source of suffering is the behaviour of the animal. Many animals have a rich repertoire of signs which can, with care, be used to infer something about their mental state.[93]

In Dawkins's stipulation of three common signs of suffering, she inferred that one must understand animals in order to alleviate their suffering. Dawkins recognises nonhuman animals as active agents in the world by acknowledging their 'experience,' and stating how we can only approximate

---

89 Well, PP/WDP/E/4/: Box 60, Royal Society Committee on Animal Experiments, 1978-1983. A. F. Huxley, The Royal Society Ad Hoc Committee on Animal Experiments – Background to the Work of the Ad Hoc Committee. 9 July 1982. p. 1.
90 Ibid.
91 Well PP/WDP/E/4: Box 60, Royal Society Committee on Animal Experiments, 1978-1983. Letter to Secretary of Scientific Societies with Interest Directly Related to Experiments on Animals. R.W.J Keay, Executive Secretary of the Royal Society. 27 May 1983. p. 1.
92 Ibid. Methods of Assessing Suffering in Animals, Marian Stamp Dawkins. N.d. 1982/3? p. 1.
93 Ibid. pp. 1–4.

what they are feeling by relying on 'analogy with ourselves.' Yet, she argues that this analogy is prone to error compared to one that 'makes full use of biological knowledge of the animal – the conditions under which it is healthy, what it chooses, its behaviour and physiology.'[94] For Dawkins, biological science was the key to understanding nonhuman suffering via the three indications quoted above. Yet, in her essay, she combined a scientific understanding of nonhuman animals with qualitative aspects of their lived experience – at once acknowledging their phenomenology of existence and integrating that with quantitative measurements of pain.

Selye played a large part in Dawkins' essay, which seemed to be in part informed by her writing for her 1980 book *Animal Suffering: The Science of Animal Welfare*.[95] Both in the article and book, Selye's GAS concept was referred to and discussed in light of animal pain and distress. Dawkins acknowledges that Selye's concept has 'had a major impact on ideas about the physiological assessment of welfare.'[96] Although critical in her discussion of Selye, she does acknowledge the usefulness of his GAS and its positive influence when assessing aspects of physiological suffering in *some* animals. She also states that Selye's work has led to the concept of 'stress' having different interpretations existing at the same time; consequently, there is 'no universal agreement' as to its definition or function.[97]

> Whether suffering is actually occurring has to be established by independent means. These independent means include the physical health of the animals and physiological measurements. The problem here is to decide how much of a physiological change an animal can tolerate before we say that it is suffering. Many physiological changes occur as quite normal features of an animal's daily life. They are indications that the animal's body is functioning properly. Some degree of 'stress' seems to be beneficial to animals.[98]

For Dawkins, some level of physiological 'stress' on the animal body is beneficial to their overall health. Here, she quotes Selye again, stating that 'some lesser stress symptoms may be a sign that an animal's body is coping with its environment.'[99] Yet, because of the differentiated application of the concept of 'stress' Dawkins claims that physiological measurement of wellbeing is difficult to measure and simultaneously, to relate what is measured

---

94 Ibid. p. 5.
95 Marian Stamp-Dawkins, *Animal Suffering: The Science of Animal Weflare* (Bungay: The Chaucer Press Ltd, 1980).
96 Ibid. p. 57.
97 Ibid. pp. 59–60.
98 Ibid. p. 110.
99 Ibid. p. 62.

to the degrees of suffering an animal is experiencing.[100] To overcome this, she recommends a checklist for animal wellbeing which includes: the animals' living conditions, their general physical state, assessing the difference in behaviour, physiology and overall general appearance of the captive animal compared to its genetically similar wild counterpart; and lastly, looking for evidence of severe physiological disturbance as well as accounting for animals' preferences. Dawkins concludes the book by saying:

> Inevitably, this evaluation will contain a subjective element. There is a subjective element, for example, in deciding how much fear, conflict etc. constitutes 'suffering.' There is, unfortunately, no formula for giving a clear yes/no answer to the question of whether the animal is suffering; that must in the end be based on analogies with our own feelings. However, the point of the book is not to eliminate subjective judgements altogether from our analysis of whether animals are suffering. *The point has been to put those judgements on a scientific footing and to base them on biological knowledge of the animals concerned.*[101]

At first glance, this rather obverse embrace of subjectivity compared to biology's well-known reverence for objectivity seems quite brave. Yet what gives animal suffering its intelligibility and identity was not necessarily the result of nonhuman animals' recalcitrance against human interference, but rather Dawkins' own 'knowledgeable manipulations'[102] by which suffering was identified. Dawkins never questions animal experimentation in her work, but instead uses a host of animal dependent research to substantiate her claims. This *knowledge* of the captive nonhuman, in a sense, *creates* suffering and allows it further. Nonhuman animals are depicted as something one studies, something one disciplines. Animals are thus also constrained and represented by dominating frameworks of suffering as characterised by Dawkins and her colleagues in the Royal Society working party.

The Royal Society's ad hoc committee on animal experiments illustrates the ineradicable distinction between human superiority and nonhuman inferiority. These discussions on animal pain and suffering, a vast majority of which became enshrined in law, did not eradicate suffering but instead ensured its continuation; and deepened the distinction between human and nonhuman bodies. Drawing on Agamben's ideas of biopolitics, nonhuman animals of the laboratory are the *homo sacer* of the scientific world; their feelings simultaneously included and excluded when it comes to assessing their tolerance for the experiments they form a significant part of. Dawkins

---

100 Ibid. p. 110.
101 Ibid. pp. 115–116. [emphasis added]
102 Edward Said uses this phrase in the context of the colonisation of the 'near-East' (Egypt in particular). See: Edward Said, *Orientalism*, 5th ed. (London: Penguin Classics, 2003).

provides the most pertinent example of this state of exception the nonhuman resides. Correlatively, thanks to Selye and the UFAW, the laboratory in this era was becoming 'the pure, absolute, and impassable biopolitical space (insofar as it is founded solely on the state of exception)'[103] for the modern-day practice of animal dependent science. As we will see presently, these notions of pain and suffering in lab animals continue to this day, and have parallels with the study of women's bodies in biomedical research. First, I must turn briefly to the contemporary understanding of pain and distress in the modern laboratory subject.

Sacred animals: The integration of science and politics in the theorisation of pain

For Giorgio Agamben, the Nazi Reich marked the point at which medicine and politics fused to form one of the essential characteristics of modern biopolitics.[104] This is also the case for the contemporary practice of animal dependent science. The Animals (Scientific Procedures) Act, 1986 (ASPA) was the watershed moment whereby the 'wellbeing' of the laboratory animal became enshrined in law (see Chapter 2). Scientists and politicians work together in their role as sovereign to decide on the value or nonvalue of nonhuman laboratory life. For Agamben, the camp contributes to an indistinguishable hybridisation of law and fact; we could argue here that it is the laboratory which now becomes this ambiguous space of confluence for the two.[105] This is illustrated most clearly in the current standards for the assessment of pain, as discussed in the *COST Manual of Laboratory Animal Care and Use*:

> Animal suffering has both emotional and physical connotations… Although it is not possible to measure direct feelings (or mental experiences) in animals, they can be deduced directly through behavioural and physiological observations… Adverse states often occur in combination; for example, an animal that experiences chronic pain or is physically disabled may be anxious and fearful, even aggressive and consequently suffering mentally as well as physically. Some animals in captivity show signs of boredom and frustration (mental distress), often revealed as abnormal or unnatural behaviours that are not normally seen in the wild and, depending on how long they have been present, may be reversed by enriching their environment.[106]

---

103 Giorgio Agamben, *Homo Sacer: Sovereign Power and Bare Life* (Stanford: Stanford University Press, 1998). p.123.
104 Ibid. p. 143.
105 Ibid. p. 170.
106 Bryan Howard; Timo Nevalainen; Gemma Perretta, ed. *The Cost Manual of Laboratory Animal Care and Use: Refinement, Reduction, and Research* (Boca Raton: CRC Press, Taylor and Francis Group, 2011). p. 334.

Anxious animals 175

The legacies of Selye, Russell and Burch of the UFAW, and Dawkins are evident in this definition of animal suffering. Psychological and physical suffering is accepted as part of nonhuman animals' qualitative experience. Yet, all of this suffering can be alleviated by regulating the animals' environments and 'enriching' it. The state of exception (the psychological *and* physical life of nonhumans) is now the norm, and care must be taken to continue to have sovereign power over animals. This historical trajectory of stress demonstrates the integration of science with politics to produce a modern form of laboratory animal biopolitics. For instance, take this extract from the Home Office guidance of 2014 on the operation of ASPA:

> You must not allow an animal to experience severe pain, suffering or distress that is likely to be long-lasting and cannot be ameliorated. You should act at all time in a manner consistent with the principles of the 3Rs – replacement, reduction and refinement. You are responsible for the welfare of the animals you work on.[107]

Pain and distress are enfolded within the confines of a discourse on welfare, and the 'care' of nonhuman animals' rests solely with the scientist. This welfare also includes ensuring that after the procedure, the animals are monitored in terms of their health and wellbeing, and:

> Taking precautions to prevent, or reduce to a minimum consistent with the purposes of the procedure, any pain, suffering, distress or discomfort to the animal which may or may not lead to lasting harm. This may include using medication where appropriate, such as sedatives, tranquilisers, analgesics or anaesthetics, as well as other appropriate methods such as husbandry measures, which increase animal comfort or improve access to food and water.[108]

This exclusion of pain and distress in the lab also acts as its inclusion. Whereby, it is expected that nonhuman suffering will take place regardless of the measures put in place for reducing 'unnecessary suffering.' This forms part of the discourse of law and what is first brought into law is the state of exception itself, in this case, nonhuman pain and suffering. Consequently, as Agamben argues 'the state of exception is "willed", it inaugurates a new juridico-political paradigm in which the norm becomes indistinguishable from the exception.'[109]

---

107 Home Office, "Guidance on the Operation of the Animals (Scientific Procedures) Act, 1986," ed. Home Office (London: Crown Copyright, 2014). p. 35.
108 Ibid. p. 36.
109 Agamben, *Homo Sacer: Sovereign Power and Bare Life*. p. 170.

176 *Scientific intersections*

The state of exception thus becomes naturalised. Nonhuman animals of the laboratory, via scientific-political discourses of pain and suffering, become normalised as laboratory objects. They are simultaneously included and excluded in the political realm in terms of their care. This parallels the state of exception occupied by the gendered female body. Once again, what raises to the fore here is the power–pain nexus.

*

WHEN THE DISTRESSED ANIMAL BECAME THE NEUROTIC WOMAN: ANIMALADIES IN THE POST-WAR ERA

As will be recalled, within the writings of the *Principles of Humane Experimental Technique* reference was made likening the distressed laboratory animal to the neurotic human.[110] It was in the 1950s and early 1960s that Selye's ideas of stress were synthesised with psychological markers of distress in the human. These ideas of stress overlapped with notions of women's health and mental health, sex-appropriate behaviour, sexual intercourse and the role of hormones in the development of sex differences. With the introduction of the contraceptive pill to British women in 1961,[111] it would seem that medicine and science revolutionised cultural life by giving women more control over their bodies. However, that in itself did not transform the power relationships between men, women and scientific constructions of sex, gender and incidentally, animality.

This section explores Selye's ideas of stress and how it links to the intersection between animals and women, specifically concerning discourses on PMS. For instance, it should come as no surprise to know that nonhuman animals were used before the first wide-scale human trials of the contraceptive pill. Mostly rabbits and mice, because of their varied but equally similar oestrous cycles to female humans' reproductive ones. Experiments were conducted throughout the 1950s to find out the levels of toxicity of the different substances and their propensity to inhibit ovulation.[112] Furthermore, some of the initial human trials of the contraceptive pill in the United States used psychotic women who had been diagnosed with schizophrenia and depression, and who were confined to asylums.[113] It is here, then, that we can begin to explore the dependency that medical research had on women and

---

110 Burch, *The Principles of Humane Experimental Techinque*. p. 17.
111 Sue Bruley, *Women in Britain since 1900* (Hampshire and New York: Palgrave, 1999). p. 137.
112 Lara V. Marks, *Sexual Chemistry: A History of the Contraceptive Pill* (New Haven and London: Yale University Press, 2001). pp. 91–92.
113 Ibid. p. 100. Anne Fausto-Sterling, *Sexing the Body: Gender Politcs and the Construction of Sexuality*, 2 ed. (New York: Hachette Book Group, 2020).

animals for both the testing of new drugs and the contribution it made to the construction of broader cultural ideas about sex, gender and animality.

Them raging hormones!

It was from the early twentieth century to the 1940s that the discovery and idea of hormones, and more specifically sex hormones, became the new paradigm for a whole gamut of the biological sciences to operate from.[114] I have documented elsewhere the history of the sex hormones and menstruation in relation to the bodily transmutations of women and animals during the interwar years.[115] Yet, as we will see presently, this hormonal dependency on understanding women's periods and sex-specific behaviours continues to this day.[116] To elucidate the connections between animals and women in scientific research on stress, we must first address this idea of hormones.

Androgen, oestrogen and progesterone were discovered in the early twentieth century by British scientist Ernest Starling and his colleagues; followed in 1935 by the androgen testosterone.[117] It is these hormones which help to determine the development of the sex organs and help to regulate reproduction; as well as influencing the functioning of a whole host of other organs in the body.[118] Yet, it will come as no surprise that the [male] scientists who discovered these hormones assigned them a gender: oestrogens were given the name of 'female sex hormones' and androgens 'male sex hormones.'[119] This gendering of the hormones ultimately leads to the demarcation of the human body and its biochemical messengers into binary opposites: male or female. Nonhuman animals were integral to the discovery of such chemicals in the body – from castrated roosters being injected with testosterone to regain their 'masculinity,' to the injection of oestrogen in male rats to

---

114 Marks, *Sexual Chemistry: A History of the Contraceptive Pill*. p. 43.
115 Catherine Duxbury, "Of Monkeys, Men and Menstruation: Gendered Dualisms and the Absent Referent in Mid-Twentieth Century British Menstrual Science." *Journal of Historical Sociology* 32, no. 1 (2019): 94–107.
116 There is plenty of feminist scholarship on the link between the science of hormones and sexism towards women. See for example: Angela Sani, *Inferior: How Science Got Women Wrong and the New Research That's Rewriting the Story* (London: 4th Estate, 2017); Cordeila Fine, *Testosterone Rex: Unmaking the Myths of Our Gendered Minds*, 2 ed. (London: Icon Books Ltd, 2018); Gina Rippon, *The Gendered Brain: The New Neuroscience That Shatters the Myth of the Female Brain* (London: Penguin, 2019); Fausto-Sterling, *Sexing the Body: Gender Politcs and the Construction of Sexuality*.
117 Celia Roberts, *Messengers of Sex: Hormones, Biomedicine and Feminism* (Cambridge: Cambridge University Press, 2007).
118 Nelly Oudshoorn, *Beyond the Natural Body: An Archeology of Sex Hormones* (London: Routledge, 1994). Fausto-Sterling, *Sexing the Body: Gender Politcs and the Construction of Sexuality*.
119 Rippon, *The Gendered Brain: The New Neuroscience That Shatters the Myth of the Female Brain*.

stimulate 'female' behaviour– sex hormones were, and still are, thought to determine our gender.[120] It was in the early twentieth century where this hormonal gendering began. Hormones created the perfect opportunity for scientists to respond to the nascent feminist movement and its resultant agitations in the public sphere. Social and political ideas about femininity, masculinity, sexuality and the body became entangled in scientific discourses about the role of hormones in regulating our gendered bodies.[121]

This hormonal gendering continued well into the inter-war years and beyond, despite it being discovered in the 1930s by numerous German, U.S. and British scientists, that both 'male' and 'female' hormones were present in all human bodies regardless of gender.[122] Endocrinologists, reproductive scientists and biologists continued to assign gender to hormones and demarcate the sexes and their hormones into two distinct binary opposites. This hormonal naming legacy is very much still present with us today. For instance, I recently typed into an internet newspaper search engine, the words 'female sex hormones' and in less than a second, 158,000 results were displayed. Headlines ranged from 'female sex hormone could offer protection against Covid, says study by Kings College London'[123] to 'sexual dimorphism in body clocks,' which emphasises how males and females have differential circadian rhythms due to their primary male or female sex hormones.[124] Despite us animals (human and nonhuman alike) having a combination of the supposedly 'male' and 'female' hormones in all of us, (they are just present at differing levels), this sexing of the body in terms of these biochemicals, is very much part of our culture and persists to this day.[125] Science and culture combine to represent female and male bodies as gender specific. Take the Kings College study mentioned above. Despite it stating that 'higher levels' of oestrogen may help females to have a more robust immune response to the latest coronavirus, Covid-19, they still refer to it as the 'female sex hormone'[126]:

120 Ibid.
121 Fausto-Sterling, *Sexing the Body: Gender Politcs and the Construction of Sexuality.*
122 Duxbury, "Of Monkeys, Men and Menstruation: Gendered Dualisms and the Absent Referent in Mid-Twentieth Century British Menstrual Science."
123 Bismee Taskin, "Female Sex Hormone Could Offer Protection against Covid, Says Study by King's College London," https://theprint.in/india/female-sex-hormone-could-offer-protection-against-covid-says-study-by-kings-college-london/477348/.
124 Garret A. FitzGerald Seán T. Anderson, "Sexual Dimorphism in Body Clocks," https://science.sciencemag.org/content/369/6508/1164.
125 Rippon, *The Gendered Brain: The New Neuroscience That Shatters the Myth of the Female Brain.*
126 Karla A. Lee Ricardo Costeira, Benjamin Murray, Colette Christiansen, Juan Castillo-Fernandez, Mary Ni Lochlainn, Joan Capdevila Pujol, Iain Buchan, Louise C Kenny, Jonathan Wolf, Janice Rymer, Sebastien Ourselin, Claire Steves, Timothy Spector, Louise Newson, Jordana Bell, "Estrogen and Covid-19 Symptoms: Associations in Women from the Covid Symptom Study," https://www.medrxiv.org/content/10.1101/2020.07.30.20164921v3.

Men and older women have been shown to be at higher risk of adverse COVID-19 outcomes. *Animal model studies* of SARS-CoV and MERS suggest that the age and *sex difference* in COVID-19 symptom severity may be due to a *protective effect of the female sex hormone estrogen.* Females have shown an ability to mount a stronger immune response to a variety of viral infections because of more robust humoral and cellular immune responses.[127]

The persistence of sexual dimorphism and the naming of oestrogen as a female sex hormone is still prevalent in today's scientific world. Previous studies using animals were mentioned to validate the authors' claims. Their study comprised of participants who were pre-menopausal and taking the contraceptive pill, post-menopausal and post-menopausal but taking Hormone Replacement Therapy. The study has to date, not yet been peer-reviewed. Nevertheless, it indicates to us two things: how biological and medical science is entangled within our social world and how nonhuman animals are integral to the perpetuation of binary sex difference and hormonal dimorphism.

Rivers of blood: Science, Pre-menstrual stress and controlling the animal within

As we have seen, the history of a vast majority of biological science depends on the use of nonhuman animals as test subjects, the gendering of hormones and women's reproductive capacities. All three seem to become enmeshed within discourses that perpetuate the subjugation of both women and animals in science and society. This is because a series of philosophical dichotomies that separates nature from culture, man from woman, animal from human, and reason from irrationality underpins a vast majority of biological science.[128] In turn, these binary opposites, although not consciously presented in medical research, are still imposed upon it.

The UFAW presented discourses of animal welfare that hoped to resolve the human/nature dualism by constructing nature, animals and the human within a mechanistic framework and in reductionist and essentialised terms.[129] But animals within the medical research laboratory still encapsulate these binaries. The interplay of scientific discourses introduced by the UFAW saw the nonhuman as being the 'same but different' from humans – with a tendency to oscillate between the two poles.[130] This treatment and implicit construction of the natural as separate from the cultural also has

---

127 Ibid. p. 2. emphasis added.
128 Plumwood, *Feminism and the Mastery of Nature*. p. 43. Also see: Ludmilla Jordanova, *Sexual Visions: Images of Gender in Science and Medicine between the Eighteenth and Twentieth Centuries* (Wisconsin: The University of Wisonsin Press, 1989). p. 19.
129 Plumwood, *Feminism and the Mastery of Nature*. p. 121.
130 Ibid. p. 123.

180 *Scientific intersections*

implications for those humans who read as female. The discourses surrounding a science of animal welfare, surprisingly and for some of us, weirdly, overlap with discourses of sex and gender promulgated by science. Historically, women were seen by biological and psychological (psychiatric) science to be more susceptible to neurosis as a result of their gender and their biological disposition to certain illnesses.[131] In the modern era, stress and hormonal response are the connective tissues that bind women and animals together as biological 'Others.' This is most notable when we look at stress which is, historically, thought to be brought on through the monthly occurrence of menstruation.

In the early to mid-twentieth century, menstruation was scientifically conceptualised thanks to the discovery and naming of the hormones.[132] Various psychological and physiological changes in the body associated with it were labelled as 'pre-menstrual syndrome' (PMS).[133] Not only did this occur within the medical field but also the notion of PMS permeated into the cultural milieu and had a massive impact on how people perceived the female body.[134] In particular, PMS and menstruation were tied to notions of the psychological and hence contributed to a form of regulation and control over the female body through the practice of medicine.[135] This regulation over the body helped shape popular discourses of womanhood and manhood, with various rites of passage associated with each.

PMS was first diagnosed in 1931 by medical man Robert T Frank. He termed it Pre-menstrual tension, and it was later renamed by Katharina Dalton (a character we will get to know very well in a moment) as Pre-menstrual syndrome (PMS).[136] Frank postulated the link between the hormonal changes women's bodies underwent during the menstrual cycle and their negative emotional state.[137] For Frank, premenstrual tension was both physiological and psychological. It was a direct result of 'the continued circulation of an excessive amount of female sex hormone in the blood' which 'in labile persons produces serious symptoms.'[138] To express the nature of

---

131 Showalter, *The Female Malady*.
132 Duxbury, "Of Monkeys, Men and Menstruation: Gendered Dualisms and the Absent Referent in Mid-Twentieth Century British Menstrual Science."
133 Helen E. Longino, *Science as Social Knowledge: Values and Objectivity in Scientifc Inquiry* (Princeton, New Jersey: Princeton University Press, 1990).
134 Jane Ussher, *Women's Madness: Misogyny or Mental Illness?* (Hemel Hempstead: Harvester Wheatsheaf, 1991).
135 Julie-Marie Strange, "'I Believe It to Be a Case Depending on Menstruation': Madness and Menstrual Taboo in British Medical Practice, C. 1840–1930," in *Menstruation: A Cultural History*, ed. Andrew Shail and Gillian Howie (Hampshire: Palgrave Macmillan, 2005). p. 103.
136 Peter Zachar; Kenneth Kendler, "A Dsm Insiders' History of Premenstrual Dysphoric Disorder," in *Philosophical Issues in Psychiatry III: The Nature and Sources of Historical Change* ed. Kenneth S. Kendler; Josef Parnas (Oxford, U.K.: Oxford University Press, 2015).
137 Frank Rt. The Hormonal Causes of Premenstrual Tension. *Arch NeurPsych*. 1931; 26(5): 1053–1057
138 Ibid. p. 1056.

these symptoms, Frank drew on his patients' accounts, claiming that the women become 'reckless' and their actions 'reprehensible.' 'Not only do they realise their suffering, but they feel conscience-stricken towards their husbands and families, knowing well that they are unbearable in their attitude and reactions.'[139]

An immediate comparison with 'the sexual cycle of the lower animals' was also integral to Frank's theoretical postulations about the human female body. He claimed that women and animals had the same hormonal action when it came to the sexual cycle. The release of a specific hormone for estrus was dependent upon the function of the pituitary gland in both 'lower' mammals and humans. Overproduction of the female sex hormone would result in the human female experiencing PMS.[140] This 18lavor18onalise of women and animals' cycles helped to establish a biologically defined linear psychological cause and effect model for menstrual disorders. Frank's work marked a significant turning point in the scientific exploration of women's psychological experience. Women's psychological wellbeing became explicitly tied to her menstrual *cycle*. The use of the metaphor of cyclicity and the study of the fluctuations of the 'female' hormones could help explain this often irrational and emotional female human mind.

Frank naturalised the cyclicity of human menstrual cycles with that of the estrus of the nonhuman female.[141] During Franks era, women and animals' subjectivities became obsolete in the name of science. Their objectification in experiments accentuated their biological similarities. Their differences radically bifurcated from [human] males.

'Mickey mouse in his club house'[142]: Selye's female derangement

After the publication of Hans Selye's (1946) paper on the GAS, scientific theories surrounding the responses of the body during times of trauma directly related to the concept of stress. It was in Selye's 1956 book *The Stress of Life* that he fully articulated the link between stress, women and animals:

> Clinical studies have confirmed the fact that people exposed to stress react very much like experimental animals in all these respects. In women, menstruation becomes irregular or stops altogether, and during lactation milk secretion may become insufficient for the baby.[143]

---

139   Ibid. p. 1054.
140   Ibid.
141   Susan. E. Bell, "Gendered Medical Science: Producing a Drug for Women," *Feminist Studies* 21, no. 3 (1995): 469–500.
142   A euphemism for being on your period, see: Emma Barnett, *Period* (London: HarperCollins Publishers Ltd, 2019). p. 280.
143   Selye, *The Stress of Life*. p. 256.

182 *Scientific intersections*

Despite also noting how men's 'sexual urge and sperm count diminished' during times of stress, the emphasis was very much placed on the woman being abnormal. For the rest of the chapter, Selye discusses PMS and characterises it as being 'among other things, nervous tension and the desire to find relief in uncustomary, compulsive actions which are difficult to restrain.'[144] He went on to assert that:

> [T]he derangement deserves serious attention because it is frequently accompanied by a number of disturbing mental changes such as: periods of abnormal hunger, general emotional instability, and occasionally, a morbid increase in the sexual drive. It is particularly noteworthy that, according to extensive statistical studies, 79 per cent to 84 per cent of all crimes of violence committed by women occur during, or in the week, before their period.[145]

So, for Selye men could have a sex drive, and there was danger of it diminishing during times of stress, but women who showed signs of wanting to have sex were seen as abnormal. It was within the framework of Selye's theory of stress and the body that PMS could be articulated as a mental disorder. Other scientists sought too to investigate the disorder using the language of stress as a theoretical backdrop to their research. For instance, in 1951 a psychiatrist named Joseph Henry Rey made an application for a licence to use animals in an experiment. The aim was to assess the role of hormones for the 'treatment of patients suffering from disorders of the menstrual cycle, together with mental illnesses, and to investigate the psycho-physiological mechanisms in such states.' The certificate to perform such experiments was granted on 12 February 1952 by the Under Secretary of State for the Home Office.[146]

After successfully applying for licence, Rey went on to produce several papers about the role of hormones in PMS. This included studies of 'menstrual disorders in psychiatric illness' through experimentation on female psychiatric patients.[147] Here, a clear distinction between normal and abnormal was made. Rey claimed that 'there are certain abnormalities of behaviour and changes in mental state coinciding with certain phases of the [menstrual] cycle,'[148] listing depression, a higher incidence of suicides

---

144 Ibid.
145 Ibid. p. 257.
146 TNA: Home Office Registered Papers (HO285): HO285/15, Joseph Henry Ray Application for Licence under the Cruelty to Animals Act 1976: Eligibility of a Professor of Psychiatry or Psychological Medicine to Act as a Signatory, 1951.
147 Dr. J. H. Rey, "Discussion on Amenorrhoea and Hirsutism," *Proceedings of the Royal Society of Medicine* 50 (23 January 1957).
148 Ibid. p. 453.

and 'delinquency' during the premenstrual phase.[149] The patients involved in the study were assessed through the taking of daily vaginal smears and urine samples. This was so Rey could analyse the effect of specific hormonal mechanisms on menstrual function and emotional disturbance.[150] The study concluded by claiming that there was a positive relationship between the severity of psychiatric illness and ovarian function.

Not only were female psychiatric patients implicated in the discourse of hormones and PMS, but so too were nonhumans. Following Rey's report, Dr B.T. Donovan discussed the relationship between 'psychogenic amenorrhoea,'[151] a psychologically induced absence of menstruation. Here Donovan drew on animal studies to highlight the mechanisms underlying 'the condition,' claiming that guinea-pigs and rats were in a constant state of ovulation when a large area of the hypothalamus was destroyed. Injecting rats with progesterone would permit the resumption of a 'normal' functioning oestrous cycle.[152]

These ideas of the psychiatrists who studied menstruation helped to contribute to definitions of femininity and female sexuality in the 1950s. With menstruation's vast and unstable repertoire of physical and emotional symptoms, women had to be controlled, and it was the male doctors and biological scientists who implemented this control over female (and animal) bodies.[153] Women were seen by biological science as natural objects of knowledge, similar to the nonhuman in the lab. As Elizabeth Grosz asserts, 'the female body has been constructed not only as a lack or absence but with more complexity, as a leaking, uncontrollable, seeping liquid; as formless flow...' Women's bodies became 'inscribed [with] a mode of seepage.'[154] Therefore these ideas of menstruation intersected with ideas of the nonhuman – both were seen as natural objects of knowledge to be controlled and regulated – a biopolitical animalady. Women, in terms of menstruation and mental health, were diagnosed as abnormal, prescribed treatments, and accordingly construed as 'a conglomeration of attributes to be predicted and controlled along with other natural phenomena.'[155]

149 Ibid.
150 Ibid. p. 453.
151 Dr. B.T. Donovan, "The Hypothalamus and Gonadotophin Secretion," ibid.
152 Ibid. p. 454.
153 Showalter, *The Female Malady*. p. 129.
154 Elizabeth Grosz, *Volitile Bodies: Towards a Coporeal Feminism* (Bloomington: Indiana University Press, 1994). p. 203.
155 Linda Alcoff, "Cultural Feminism Versus Post-Structuralism: The Identity Crisis in Feminist Theory," in *Feminism and Philosophy: Essential Readings in Theory, Reinterpretation, and Application*, ed. Nancy Tuana, Rosemarie Tong (Boulder: Westview, 1995). pp. 434–435.

'The English have landed'[156]: Katharina Dalton's animalady

The most prominent medical texts about menstruation and PMS came from a woman scientist at the time. It was the work of British general practitioner and endocrinologist Katharina Dalton which set the tone for the links between PMS and madness in mid-twentieth century Britain.[157] What Dalton did was to construct an argument about the pre-menstrual woman as being centred entirely around the function of their reproductive organs. She traced a dividing line between normality and abnormality at certain times of the month. Her research focused on the effect's PMS had on women's physiology, women's tendency to commit violent crime, their productivity at work and school, and the propensity for more women to be admitted to psychiatric hospitals at the peak of their ovulatory period.[158] In her 1960 *British Medical Journal* article, she declared:

> The adverse effect of menstruation on the normal school work of 217 menstruating girls, aged 11 to 17 years, is evidenced by the finding that one in every four girls had a fall in weekly mark during the premenstruum followed by a rise after menstruation. It is appreciated that in times of stress the premenstrual symptoms are increased. It would appear, therefore, that on occasions of important examinations the *handicap* imposed by menstruation will be proportionately increased. About one girl in six in any examination entry will be in her premenstruum and thus at her lowest intellectual ebb. *While zealots campaign assiduously for equality of the sexes, Nature refuses to grant equality even in one sex.*[159]

For Dalton, nature was indeed separate from culture; women and girls were part of nature. They were adversely affected by their menstrual cycles, and they were biologically a very different species to that of men. Dalton further explained the links between PMS and physical violence in her popular book of 1964 *The Premenstrual Syndrome* where she suggested that the monthly hormone imbalance and the 'handicap' of menstruation may make the woman deceitful:

---

156 The phrase 'The English have landed' is a French euphemism for being on your period. See: Barnett, *Period*. p. 281.
157 Zahra Meghani, "Of Sex, Nationalities and Populations: The Construction of Menstruation as a Patho-Physiology," in *Menstruation: A Cultural History*, ed. Andrew Shail, Gillian Howie (Hampshire: Palgrave Macmillan, 2005). p. 131.
158 Raymond Greene, Katharina Dalton, "The Premenstrual Syndrome," *British Medical Journal* 4818 (1953): 1007–1013. Katharina Dalton, "Menstruation and Acute Psychiatric Illness," ibid. (1959). "Effect of Menstruation on Schoolgirls' Weekly Work," *British Medical Journal* 1, no. 5169 (1960): 326–328; "Menstruation and Crime," *British Medical Journal* 2, no. 5269 (1961): 1752–1753.
159 "Effect of Menstruation on Schoolgirls' Weekly Work." p. 328. [my italics].

All too often the patient herself is not fully aware of the distress caused by her periodic tantrums and it is the husband or social worker who first stresses the need for treatment. When a woman demonstrates bruises as signs of her husband's cruelty it is well to remember the possibility that these may be spontaneous bruises of the premenstruum and it is wise to enquire about the date of her last menstruation.[160]

Katharina Dalton contributed to the medical construction of women as being naturally abnormal and deceitful.[161] By responding to women's pain and distress in a manner that understood their causes in biologically and hormonally charged ways, this implied the cures of the condition as bringing the body back to a state of normality.[162] And so this form of control over the female body did not necessarily contribute towards women's emancipation but rather subjected it to a mechanistic physiology.[163]

Animals and women were natural objects of knowledge that needed to be controlled and managed, even standardised. The sexism and speciesism implicit in mid-twentieth-century British endocrinology and reproductive science stems from ideologies about sex roles, and the positivist/technocratic logic of human domination over nature.[164] To change the semiotics of animal experimentation into one of scientific welfarism, contributed to the creation of a discourse of care towards the nonhuman which had notions of domination hidden within it. The very representation and language of science were changed to enable more subtle modes of control to be had over 'natural' bodies.

Its 'shark week!'[165] Bloody monstrous bodies of the late-twentieth century and beyond

From 1970 onwards, Katharina Dalton's writings on PMS gained widespread attention. She wrote many accessible articles in the popular press, in academic journals and authored her books for both lay audiences and medical professionals; connecting the role of hormones to women's emotional instability. Yet, it was with the general public that her work gained the most ground and tacit acceptance.[166] Even though at the time, there was

---

160 *The Premenstrual Syndrome* (London: William Heinemann Medical Books Limited, 1964). p. 94.
161 Anne Fausto-Sterling, *Myths of Gender: Biological Theories About Women and Men*, 2nd ed. (New York: BasicBooks, A Division of HarperCollins Publishers, Inc., 1992). p. 95.
162 Ibid.
163 Haraway, *Simians, Cyborgs, and Women: The Reinvention of Nature.* pp. 26–27.
164 Ibid. p. 67.
165 'Shark week is a euphemism for being on your period, see: Barnett, *Period.* p. 280.
166 Esther Rome, "Premenstrual Syndrome (PMS) Explained through a Feminist Lens," in *Culture, Society and Menstruation*, ed. Virginia Oleson; Nacny Fugate-Woods (London: Hemisphere Publishing Corporation, 1986).

an overwhelming lack of scientific evidence connecting the role of hormones to the changing psychological and physiological conditions associated with the menstrual cycle.[167] What Dalton did in the 1970s was to help facilitate the widespread cultural acceptance of PMS and the role of the menstrual cycle in explaining women's sudden alterations in mood. Furthermore, aiding in its rationalisation.[168]

In her 1964 book *The Premenstrual Symptom*, Dalton stipulated the psychological and somatic symptoms of PMS, including, lethargy, irritability, depression, epilepsy, headaches and constipation.[169] One particular psychological sign was 'nymphomania' or the insatiable desire for sex. *Al lá Selye*, Dalton explains women's increase in their sex drive as abnormal and a symptom of PMS:

> A young psychopathic girl was brought for treatment after she had been out all night on several occasions "following the boys" and her adoptive parents then realised that these occasions only occurred during the premenstruum. Gray found some form of sexual disorder in 39 per cent of his 38 sufferers from the premenstrual syndrome.[170]

This pathologising of a young girl and her desire for sex helped to foment contemporary attitudes towards women and their periods. In her 1978 book *Once a Month*, Dalton asserts that these 'images' of menstruating women, as having an abnormally high libido and behaviourally are 'fickle, changeable, moody and hard to please' are a direct result of the 'ebb and flow of the menstrual hormones.'[171] These discourses enfolded women within the realm of the natural and controlled by her hormones. This is despite the fact that recent studies have not demonstrated the link between changes in mood and the cyclical rise and fall of 'female hormones.'[172]

Thanks to Dalton, the 'animal within' all women in the pre-menstrual phase became a dominant cultural trope of the mid-late twentieth century. Furthermore, solidifying women's experiences as one of biopsychiatric distress, emotions are conceptualised as illnesses and in need of control – women must be tamed.[173] Foucault called this the 'hysterisation of women's bodies,' a strategic accord, whereby the process of the feminine body is

---

167 Ann Oakley, *Sex, Gender and Society* (Abingdon: Routledge, 1981).
168 Fausto-Sterling, *Myths of Gender: Biological Theories About Women and Men*.
169 Dalton, *The Premenstrual Syndrome*. pp. 7–14.
170 Ibid. p. 9.
171 Katharina Dalton, *Once a Month: Understanding and Treating PMS*, 6th ed. (Nashville: Hunter House Publishers, 1999). p. 11; p. 103.
172 Denise Russell, *Women, Madness & Medicine* (Cambridge: Polity Press, 1995). p. 65.
173 Lisa Cosgrove, Bethany Riddle, "Constructions of Femininity and Experiences of Menstrual Distress," *Women and Health* 38, no. 3 (2003): 38.

analysed, qualified and disqualified (does this ring any bells with the treatment of lab animals? It should).[174]

To be female is to be 'Othered,' a polluted body that has specific consequences. What this suggests is that this 'Otherness' facilitates fear and loathing of the bleeding body, one which becomes scientised to deal with this difference.[175] We at once become like the experimental animal, included, to be analysed and categorised; excluded because of our difference. Agamben's exclusive inclusion operates at the level of the body, the level of difference and 'Otherness.'

It was in the early 1980s when women's abject bodies became the focus of attention for the courts of law and mass media. In 1981 Sandie Smith and Christine English walked free from court on account of their PMS.[176] Sandie Smith was charged with two counts of threatening to kill a policeman, and of possessing an offensive weapon. She had a previous conviction of the manslaughter of a nineteen year old girl whom she stabbed and of which she had been on probation. Christine English killed her partner by running him over in a car.[177]

The British tabloid newspapers *The Daily Mirror* and the *Daily Express* sensationalised the court cases of the two women. Yet, it is in this reporting that we can get to understand the intricate patriarchal discourses at play which demonstrate the entanglement of women and animals as abject 'Others,' with pathologically suspect bodies. The press drew judges' comments from both court cases, representing the women as unstable beings needing medical intervention:

> Tragic Barmaid Sandie Smith walked free from court yesterday after a judge decided that the *"ravaging animal"* in her could be tamed at last. "My nightmare is over" said Sandie, who is driven *wild* by premenstrual tension every 20 days unless she receives careful doses of the drug progesterone.[178]

The impulse to kill and harm others marks the women as a 'ravaging animal' who is 'wild' during her pre-menstrual phase. The only cure is the medically sanctioned injection of hormones, and this was the hormone progesterone. For Christine English, newspapers reported the story in a similar way to the

---

174 Foucault, *The History of Sexuality Vol 1: The Will to Knowledge*.
175 Valerie Hay, Andrea Egan Sophie Laws, *Seeing Red: The Politics of Pre-Menstrual Tension* (London: Hutchinson and Co. Ltd., 1985).
176 Joan Chrisler, Karen Levy, "The Media Construct a Menstrual Monster: A Content and Analysis of Pms Articles in the Popular Press," *Women and Health* 16, no. 2 (1990): 89–104.
177 Sophie Laws, *Seeing Red: The Politics of Pre-Menstrual Tension*.
178 Richard Wright, "The End of My Nightmare," *Daily Express*, Tuesday 10 November 1981. p. 3.

Smith case, with the Daily Mirror running a special one page spread on the 'illness' of PMS:

> Two women walked free this week from different courts after they had killed. Both had been suffering severely from a very real illness with both a physical cause and a name – pre-menstrual tension. When it strikes, women are liable to lash out at their kids, scream at their husbands, crash the car and feel like they just can't cope. In extreme cases they may turn to crime, become violent, even commit suicide.[179]

This 'impulse' to kill in both women is reduced down to their biologically urges, because PMS was, as the *Daily Mirror,* quoting Katharine Dalton, said 'a hormonal disease which affect[s] the mind.'[180] It seems, court judges and newspaper journalists alike did not consider the women's broader socio-economic milieu. The socio-legal system was united in explaining away the women's violence only as a result of her hormones, with the *Mirror* exclaiming 'there is mounting evidence to show that, at certain times of the month, and for no other reasons, some women can go berserk.'[181] If only, as Barbara Jackson of the *Mirror* advised, the women could have convinced their man and doctor that they have a hormonal problem; thereby resulting in taking daily doses of progesterone in the form of the pill to control their feral behaviour.[182] Female violence is reduced to biology. As we have seen, the popular press often referred to the women, and incidentally, to the menstrual cycle and PMS as 'raging beasts,' 'raging animals' and another interesting animal metaphor: 'the taming of the shrew inside of you.'[183]

Only the pathologisation of women's bodies can calm the animal within. This can be done by having regular check-ups with the doctor and ingesting synthetically synthesised hormones. Women's bodies, like the nonhuman animals of the laboratory, are pathologically out of control and need regulating and containing – reduce that stress! During the 1980s, women's lives and the lives of animals of the laboratory became entwined in hegemonic discourses about 'natural' bodies needing treatment and 'care.' Yet, this negative trope did not go unnoticed. Journalist Anna Raeburn of *Cosmopolitan* magazine wrote an article in the May 1980 edition entitled 'On Women as Guinea-Pigs':

> In general, I don't regard men as my persecutors, but sometimes a situation arises where I cannot help but feel that I'm just some sort of

---

179 Barbara Jackson, "That Time of the Month," *Daily Mirror*, 12 November 1981. p. 9.
180 Peter Kane, "The Tension That Made a Woman Kill," ibid., 11 November. p. 1.
181 Ibid. p. 3.
182 Jackson, "That Time of the Month." p. 9.
183 Joan Chrisler, "Hormone Hostages: The Cultural Legacy of PMS as Legal Defence," in *Charting a New Course for Feminist Psychology*, ed. Lynn H. Collins, Michelle R. Dunlap, Joan C. Chrisler (London: Praeger, 2002). p. 242.

screen for them to project their dreams onto, *a chunk of meat they're experimenting with*, particularly when I consider the world of medicine and the might of pharmaceutical companies.[184]

Raeburn elicits a feeling of metaphorical similarity between being a woman in contemporary society and feeling like a dead animal. Feminist Carol Adams calls this intersection of women and animals the absent referent, whereby the bodies of women are often metaphorically treated as dead animals – pieces of meat – the nonhuman animal is literally missing but very much present in the metaphor.[185] Here we have an explicit example in Raeburn's articles about the medicalisation of women's bodies and their intersections with nonhuman animals. She discusses a range of medical treatments from the contraceptive pill, to anti-morning sickness drugs and Valium[186]:

> Far more women take more Valium than men, and for years it has been regarded as the "mother's little helper" of The Rolling Stones song. But was it withdrawn? Is it restricted? Rarely. It keeps us quiet you see… With your help I can try to prevent a few more frightened women from feeling like the laboratory animals we're all so sorry for.[187]

Recall the quote from the 2014 *Home Office guidance* about sedating laboratory animals to reduce their stress, and a striking similarity between the lives of women and lab animals is revealed. The *Guidance* advises the administration of: '…medication where appropriate, such as *sedatives, tranquilisers*, analgesics or anaesthetics…'[188] to nonhuman animals to reduce their stress. It seems that women are not the only ones that need to be kept quiet.

'Mad cow disease'[189]: The classification of PMS as a mental disorder, 1994–present

The idea that women are like 'ravaged animals' when they are premenstrual gained official clinical recognition in 1994. The American Psychiatric Association included PMS or 'Premenstrual Dysphoric Disorder' (also known as Late Luteal Phase Dysphoric Disorder) in the appendix of their

---

184 HHC [DBV/30/15], Records of the British Union for the Abolition of Vivisection, Press cuttings, 1932–1993. Anna Raeburn on Women as Guinea-Pigs, *Cosmopolitan*, May 1980. [Emphasis added.]
185 Carol J Adams, *The Sexual Politics of Meat* (Oxford, U.K.: Polity Press, 1990).
186 HHC [DBV/30/15], Records of the British Union for the Abolition of Vivisection, Press cuttings, 1932–1993. Anna Raeburn on Women as Guinea-Pigs, *Cosmopolitan*, May 1980.
187 Ibid.
188 Office, "Guidance on the Operation of the Animals (Scientific Procedures) Act, 1986." p. 36. [Emphasis added.]
189 A Finnish euphemism for PMS, see: Barnett, *Period*. p. 281.

Diagnostic and Statistical Manual of Mental Disorders (DSM-IIIR, DSM-IV).[190] This classified it as a psychiatric disorder but one which required further study before its inclusion as an 'official' diagnostic category.[191] Feminists both within and outside the medical sphere debated the usefulness of this decision for women; with some seeing it as further patriarchal entrenchment of the disordered female body and others claiming that it would allow women to be taken more seriously.[192]

The latest edition of the DSM (DSM-5) awards Premenstrual Dysphoric Disorder (PMDD) full diagnostic category and receives the exalted status of a full-blown psychiatric disorder.[193] It stipulates seven criteria for the diagnosis of PMDD (from A to G). The definition encompasses both psychological, cognitive and somatic factors including mood swings, irritably or anger, depression and anxiety, 'feeling overwhelmed or out of control,' increased interpersonal conflicts, and lack of concentration or interest in usual activities.[194] In the book *DSM-5 Made Easy: The Clinician's Guide to Diagnosis* by U.S. Professor of Psychiatry James Morrison, it emphasises the seriousness of the condition:

> The consequences of PMDD can be serious: Such a patient could experience mood symptoms during an accumulated 8 years of her reproductive life. Some patients may be unaware how markedly their anger and other negative moods affect those around them, and may suffer from severe depression; perhaps 15% attempt suicide. Yet, the typical patient doesn't receive treatment until she is 30, sometimes even later. Symptoms may be worse for older women, though menopause offers a natural endpoint (duration is sometimes extended by hormone replacement therapy). Overall, this condition ranks high amongst the seriously underdiagnosed mental disorders.[195]

The emphasis is placed on psychological symptoms of mood and how women who experience such a disorder can negatively affect other people in their personal and social life. The ageing process, with the onset of menopause, seems to satiate women's moods as it offers a 'natural endpoint.'

---

190 Chrisler, "Hormone Hostages: The Cultural Legacy of PMS as Legal Defence."
191 Kendler, "A Dsm Insiders' History of Premenstrual Dysphoric Disorder."
192 Susan Markens, "The 'Problematic of Experience' a Political and Cultural Critique of PMS," *Gender and Society* 10, no. 1 (1996): 42–58; Chrisler, "Hormone Hostages: The Cultural Legacy of PMS as Legal Defence."
193 Liisa Hantsoo, C. Neill Epperson, "Premenstrual Dysphoric Disorder: Epidemiology and Treatment," *Current Psychiatry Reports* 17, no. 11 (2015): 87.
194 American Psychiatric Association 5th ed. American Psychiatric Publishing; Arlington: 2013., *Diagnostic and Statistical Manual of Mental Disorders*, 5th ed. (Arlington: American Psychiatric Publishing, 2013). p. 625.4.
195 James Morrison, *Dsm-5® Made Easy: The Clinician's Guide to Diagnosis* (New York: Guilford Press, 2014). p. 146.

To codify women as suffering from PMDD, the clinician has to obtain two prospective ratings of two menstrual cycles, then 'what you as a clinician decide to do with this is, of course, your business.'[196]

The advice from Morrison is embellished with a case study of a woman named Amy Jernigan, who visits her GP requesting a professional diagnosis of PMDD. Her subjective experiences are listed with regards to her moods, anger and irritably with the people around her '4–5 days' before her period. Her background is noted, level of education and relationship to her 'anti-feminist mother' who may have had the disorder too – thus, emphasising the genetic transmission of the disorder. The vignette ends with a description of Amy declaring 'I hate being the feminist with PMS—I feel like a walking cliché.'[197] A discussion then follows that places her symptoms into the DSM-5 criteria for PMDD. The language used in this segment of Morrison's book, and as we have seen so far, the description behind most discussions on any form of PMS, focuses on the negative experiences.[198] Anger is not part of women's nature (even if you are a feminist cliché!), it is instead, something that needs controlling and requiring medical surveillance. Jacquelyn Zita calls this aspect of medical control of menstruating bodies a form of '"protective" secondary citizenship,'[199] a paternalistic form of 'care' and welfare over female bleeding bodies who are deemed lesser to males in society.

Hormones as the casual factor for distress once again come to haunt the bleeding body. Contemporary aetiology links the role of hormones to the biological contributors of the central nervous system, genetic factors and interestingly, stress.[200] Stress and the hormonal fluctuations during the luteal phase of the menstrual cycle (when symptoms of PMS appear) have been linked to the higher occurrence of Post-Traumatic Stress Disorder (PTSD) in women during the reproductive years. It is thought that women show a higher heart rate and more excessive responses to stress; with 'hormone and neurosteroid fluctuations [contributing] to PTSD symptom development, particularly since premenstrual symptoms and PTSD symptoms are somewhat similar.'[201]

---

196 Ibid. p. 147.
197 Ibid. p. 148.
198 Jacquelyn N. Zita, "The Premenstrual Syndrome: "Dis-Easing" the Female Cycle," *Feminism and Science 2* 3, no. 1 (1988): 77–99.
199 Ibid. p. 79.
200 Hantsoo Liisa, C. Neill Epperson, "Premenstrual Dysphoric Disorder: Epidemiology and Treatment."
201 Walter Busuttil, "Psycholoigcal Trauma and Post-Traumatic Stress Disorder," in *The Female Body in Mind: The Interface between the Female Body and Mental Heatlh*, ed. Mervat Nasser, Karen Baistow, Janet treasure (Hove & New York: Routledge, 2007). p. 41.

Contemporary animaladies: Rats with PMDD and fluoxetined women

And so it seems, Hans Selye's notions of stress plague us again. The hormonal basis of women's animalady is explained in terms of the amount of progesterone, estrogen and allopregnanolone (ALLO) – a naturally occurring steroid that acts on the brain – during the premenstrum. Animal studies have been used to substantiate the occurrence of PMDD as a result of a decrease in ALLO. Studies include the use of male mice by manipulating their behaviours to induce anxiety and depression[202]; socially isolating rats just after weaning and generating stress through administering a 'foot shock'[203]; and by making rats complete a forced swim test and restricting food intake to create chronic stress to determine the rate of neurosteroid activity.[204] This is despite the lack of evidence linking chronic stress and ALLO response as a symptom of PMS.[205]

This focus on the connection between the brain and the regulation of hormone activity in the etiology of PMDD was also the focus for Polish pharmacological researchers Tomasz Schneider and Piotr Popik. Their experiment was an evaluation of 'estrous cycle-dependent irritability' in female rats.[206] For Schneider and Popik, it was hoped that this study would help to account for the effect of antidepressants on the rats PMDD expressed behaviour in terms of the pre-menstrual symptom of irritability. To test their hypothesis, the authors wanted to measure the burying behaviour of the rats at specific points during the estrous cycles. Schneider and Popik chose marbles as they are 'non-noxious' agents. Furthermore; the marble-burying test is a standardised test that has been characterised as a model for demonstrating anxiety and compulsive behaviour in mice. Schneider and Popkik developed a modified version to try out on rats, claiming[207]:

> Marble-burying behaviour is one of the few models that exhibit sensitivity to the majority of antidepressants and employs testing that does not involve severe stress… [This] model is focused on estrous cycle-dependent

---

202 M. Nelson, G. Pinna, "S-Norfluoxetine Microinfused into the Basolateral Amygdala Increases Allopregnanolone Levels and Reduces Aggression in Socially Isolated Mice," *Neuropharmacology* 60, no. 7–8 (2011): 1154–1159.
203 M. Serra et al., "Social Isolation Stress and Neuroactive Steroids," *Eur Neuropsychopharmacol* 17, no. 1 (2007): 1–11.
204 J. Evans et al., "Allopregnanolone Regulates Neurogenesis and Depressive/Anxiety-Like Behaviour in a Social Isolation Rodent Model of Chronic Stress," *Neuropharmacology* 63, no. 8 (2012): 1315–1326.
205 Hantsoo Liisa, C. Neill Epperson, "Premenstrual Dysphoric Disorder: Epidemiology and Treatment."
206 Tomasz Schneider, Piotr Popik, "An Animal Model of Premenstrual Dysphoric Disorder Sensitive to Antidepressants," *Current Protocols in Neuroscience* 46, no. 1 (2009): 9.31.1–9.31.10.
207 Ibid.

irritability, which has been found in human epidemiological studies to be the single most frequently reported symptom of PMDD.[208]

This experiment is relevant to us for two reasons: firstly, it demonstrates the historical continuity of the transmutation of experimental animal bodies with those of female human bodies in the analysis of PMS. Secondly, it highlights the historical persistence of the concept of stress as a patriarchally induced psychologically experience for women and animals. This stress can only be cured by pharmacological intervention; and as an experimental practice first explored by the UFAW.

Throughout the article, the authors do emphasise the importance of not creating stress in the rats, and the study was approved by their Institutional Animal Care and Use Committee (IACUC). This makes sure that the experimenters follow 'officially approved procedures for the care and use of laboratory animals. The IACUC is a product of the European Union regulations on experimental animals, which at the time of the experiment would have been EU Directive 86/609/EEC. Now, the IACUC falls under EU Directive 2010/63.[209] It directly relates to the use of the '3R's and legal guidance regarding the care of animals of the laboratory. For example, the authors recommend avoiding:

> Creating any kind of additional stress during the test. Stress (noise, presence of other people, turning on the lights) leads to immobility and freezing behaviour and may profoundly influence the results. Animals should be well handled before starting the experiment.[210]

Schneider and Popik also stipulate the cages of confinement and various accoutrements that run alongside standard laboratory rat keeping:

> House the animals in groups of four or five per cage, at a controlled temperature of 21° to 22°C, humidity (40% to 50%), and reversed 12 hour light/12 hour dark cycle (lights off at 10:00) for at least 2 weeks before starting evaluation of the estrous cycle phases. Standard lab chow and water should be freely available. Conduct experiments between 11:00 and 14:00, i.e. during the dark phase. Mark females' tails with permanent non-toxic black marker. Red-light lamps are used to see the rats in the dark. *Rats cannot see red light; the authors typically use six 25-W red bulbs: three over the home cages and three over the test cages.*[211]

---

208 Ibid. (n.p).
209 Council of the European Union, "Directive 2010/63/EU of the European Parliament and of the Council of 22 September 2010 on the Protection of Animals Used for Scientific Purposes," *Official Journal of the European Union* (2010).
210 Schneider and Popik, "An Animal Model of Premenstrual Dysphoric Disorder Sensitive to Antidepressants." (n.p.).
211 Ibid. (n.p.).

The size of the cages had to be 47 cm in length by 27 cm in width and 15 cm depth. White noise was used to drown out any stress-inducing sounds, and this was also present in the testing room/cages. Here single rats were placed at two points during their oestrous cycle – proestrus and metestrus – and after ten minutes were returned to their group cage. The scientists then counted how many marbles they had buried. If part of the experimental group who had received an injection of antidepressant, the number of marbles buried was an indication of how efficacious the antidepressant was in reducing irritability – the fewer the marbles, the lesser the stress. Smear tests were given to determine what phase of the oestrous cycle the rats were in. It was revealed that 'female rats show aggressive behaviour during the first few days of the collection of a virginal smear. During subsequent days they become calmer. Rats should be well handled before the experiments.'[212]

The study concluded by arguing:

> The proposed model appears to have construct validity derived from similarity in the underlying mechanisms, i.e., increased sensitivity to changes in ovarian hormone levels in a subgroup of female rats and in women suffering PMDD. In addition, it is characterised by the face validity derived from phenomenological similarity between marble-burying behaviour in the model and irritability in PMDD patients, as well as from the fact that the described phenomenon affects only a fraction of subjects (both rats and women). Finally, the model appears to fulfill criteria of predictive validity, derived from similarity in response to treatment in the model and human condition. Tentatively this model may be used to study the neuroendocrine mechanisms triggering premenstrual irritability, and the detailed mode of action of antidepressants when used for PMDD.[213]

This recent study of PMDD in rats demonstrates the confluence of animals, women and stress in the biomedical community. Laboratory animal stress and female human stress in the guise of PMS offers insight into biopolitical animaladies. Animal studies to determine hormonal fluctuations is the crucial component in determining the biological origin of PMDD. The medical profession once again justifies women's erratic behaviours as being a result of their 'raging hormones.'[214] The scientific and cultural accounts of PMS rest on understandings of the female body as a 'problem' needing to be fixed. Helen Malson and Mervat Nasser explain that these conceptualisations

---

212 Ibid. (n.p.)
213 Ibid. (n.p.)
214 Linda Gannon, "The Impact of Medical and Sexual Politics on Women's Health," *Feminism & Psychology* 8, no. 3 (1998): 285–302; Markens, "The 'Problematic of Experience' a Political and Cultural Critique of PMS."

of women's pre-menstrual bodies mean that an estimated 5–95% of women who have periods are rendered 'unreliable, intellectually debilitated, accident-prone, mentally unstable and violent.'[215] In other words, the vast majority of women, regardless of cultural or social context, are unstable because of their bleeding bodies.

I have just given a flavour of studies which illustrate this systemic oppression of women and animals. The pathologisation (and animalisation) of women's bodies by biological and medical science is a way to control women and further entrench violent domination over nonhuman animals. As Malson argues, the female reproductive body is always constructed as Other within the patriarchal order. This is done through the animalisation of women's bodies whereby the reproductive body is construed dualistically, and therefore in opposition to the rational mind. As Malson observes 'it is animal-like – 'cow-like' – uncontrolled and excessive.'[216] Stress – in any guise- is the historically contingent category which links these unholy bodies together in a biopolitical Möbius knot.

Conclusion

This chapter has documented the historically contingent links between women and animals in biomedical science and its experimental practices. This was illustrated by an analysis of the constituent discourses of stress and PMS. Hans Selye's notion of stress paved the way for the rise of laboratory animal welfare in Britain from the mid-twentieth century onwards, and correlatively, situated the bleeding female body within narratives medical welfare. Together, animals and women's bodies combined to produce a marginalised 'Other' that needed to be controlled and restrained as a result of their noncompliance. What we have here is a biopolitical animalady.

Bibliography

American Psychiatric Association. *Diagnostic and Statistical Manual of Mental Disorders*, 5th ed. Arlington: American Psychiatric Publishing, 2013.
Adams, Carol J. *The Sexual Politics of Meat*. Oxford, U.K.: Polity Press, 1990.
Agamben, Giorgio. *Homo Sacer: Sovereign Power and Bare Life*. Stanford: Stanford University Press, 1998.

---

215 Helen Malson, Mervat Nasser, "At Risk by Reason of Gender," in *The Female Body in Mind: The Interface between the Female Body and Mental Health*, ed. Mervat Nasser, Karen Baistow, Janet Treasure (Hove & New York: Routledge, 2007). p. 9.
216 Helen Malson, "Anorexic Bodies and the Discursive Production of Feminine Excess," in *Body Talk: The Material and Discursive Regulation of Sexuality, Madness and Reproduction*, ed. Jane Ussher (London and New York: Routledge, 1997). p. 237.

Alcoff, Linda. "Cultural Feminism Versus Post-Structuralism: The Identity Crisis in Feminist Theory." In *Feminism and Philosophy: Essential Readings in Theory, Reinterpretation, and Application*, edited by Nancy Tuana, Rosemarie Tong. Boulder: Westview, 1995.

Barnett, Emma. *Period*. London: HarperCollins Publishers Ltd, 2019.

Bell, Susan. E. "Gendered Medical Science: Producing a Drug for Women." *Feminist Studies*, 21, no. 3 (1995): 469–500.

Birke, Lynda. *Feminism, Animals and Science: The Naming of the Shrew*. Buckingham, UK: Open University Press, 1994.

———. "Telling the Rat What to Do: Laboratory Animals, Science and Gender." In *Gender and the Science of Difference: Cultural Politics of Contemporary Science and Medicine*, edited by Jill A. Fisher. NJ: Rutgers, The State University, 2011.

Birke, Lynda, Arnold Arluke, Mike Michael. *The Sacrifice: How Scientifc Experiments Transform Animals and People*. West Lafayette, IN: Purdue University Press, 2007.

Bruley, Sue. *Women in Britain Since 1900*. Hampshire and New York: Palgrave, 1999.

Burch, R.L., W.M.S. Russell. *The Principles of Humane Experimental Techinque*. London: Methuen & Co LTD, 1959.

Busuttil, Walter. "Psycholoigcal Trauma and Post-Traumatic Stress Disorder." In *The Female Body in Mind: The Interface between the Female Body and Mental Heatlh*, edited by Mervat Nasser, Karen Baistow, Janet treasure, 41–56. Hove & New York: Routledge, 2007.

Chrisler, Joan. "Hormone Hostages: The Cultural Legacy of Pms as Legal Defence." In *Charting a New Course for Feminist Psychology*, edited by Lynn H. Collins, Michelle R. Dunlap, Joan C. Chrisler, 238–252. London: Praeger, 2002.

Special Correspondent. "Adaptation to Stress: Conference of Behavioural Scientists." *British Medical Journal* 2, no. 5092 (1958): 382–384.

Dalton, Katharina. "Effect of Menstruation on Schoolgirls' Weekly Work." *British Medical Journal* (1960): 326–328.

———. "Menstruation and Acute Psychiatric Illness." *British Medical Journal* 1 (1959): 148–149.

———. "Menstruation and Crime." *British Medical Journal* 1 (1961): 1752–1753.

———. *Once a Month: Understanding and Treating Pms*. 6th ed. Nashville: Hunter House Publishers, 1999.

———. *The Premenstrual Syndrome*. London: William Heinemann Medical Books Limited, 1964.

Dalton, Katharina, Raymond Greene. "The Premenstrual Syndrome." *British Medical Journal* 4818 (1953): 1007–1013.

Donovan, B. T. "The Hypothalamus and Gonadotophin Secretion." *Proceedings of the Royal Society of Medicine* 50 (1957): 455–456.

Duxbury, Catherine. "Of Monkeys, Men and Menstruation: Gendered Dualisms and the Absent Referent in Mid-Twentieth Century British Menstrual Science." *Journal of Historical Sociology* 32, no. 1 (2019): 94–107.

Evans, J., Y. Sun, A. McGregor, B. Connor. "Allopregnanolone Regulates Neurogenesis and Depressive/Anxiety-Like Behaviour in a Social Isolation Rodent Model of Chronic Stress." [In eng]. *Neuropharmacology* 63, no. 8 (Dec 2012): 1315–1326.

Fausto-Sterling, Anne. *Myths of Gender: Biological Theories About Women and Men*. 2nd ed. New York: Basic Books, A Division of HarperCollins Publishers, Inc, 1992.

———. *Sexing the Body: Gender Politcs and the Construction of Sexuality*. 2nd ed. New York: Hachette Book Group, 2020.

Fine, Cordeila. *Testosterone Rex: Unmaking the Myths of Our Gendered Minds*. 2nd ed. London: Icon Books Ltd, 2018.
Foucault, Michel. *The History of Sexuality Vol 1: The Will to Knowledge*. 5th ed. London: Penguin Books Ltd., 1998.
Fox-Keller, Evelyn. "Language and Ideology in Evolutionary Theory: Reading Cultural Norms into Natural Law." In *Feminism and Science*, edited by Evelyn Fox-Keller, Helen E. Longino. Oxford, U.K.: Oxford University Press, 1999.
Frank, Robert. The Hormonal Causes of Premenstrual Tension. *Arch NeurPsych*. 1931;26(5): 1053–1057.
Gannon, Linda. "The Impact of Medical and Sexual Politics on Women's Health." *Feminism & Psychology* 8, no. 3 (1998): 285–302.
Grosz, Elizabeth. *Volitile Bodies: Towards a Coporeal Feminism*. Bloomington: Indiana University Press, 1994.
Gummett, Philip. *Scientists in Whitehall*. Manchester, U.K.: Manchester University Press, 1980.
Hantsoo, Liisa, C. Neill Epperson. "Premenstrual Dysphoric Disorder: Epidemiology and Treatment." *Current Psychiatry Reports* 17, no. 11 (2015): 87.
Haraway, Donna. *Primate Visions: Gender, Race, and Nature in the World of Modern Science*. New York: Routledge, 1989.
———. *Simians, Cyborgs, and Women: The Reinvention of Nature*. London: Free Association Books, 1991.
Hinchcliffe, Steve, Kristin Asdal, Tone Druglitrø, ed. *Humans, Animals and Biopolitics: The More-Than-Human Condition*. Edited by Smanatha Hurn, Chris Wilbert, Multispecies Encounters. Oxon: Routledge, 2017.
Jackson, Barbara. "That Time of the Month." *Daily Mirror*, 12 November 1981, 9.
Jackson, Mark. *The Age of Stress: Science and the Search for Stability*. Oxford, U.K.: Oxford University Press, 2013.
———. "The Pursuit of Happiness: The Social and Scientific Origins of Hans Selye's Natural Philosophy of Life." *History of the Human Sciences* 25, no. 5 (2012): 13–29.
Jordanova, Ludmilla. *Sexual Visions: Images of Gender in Science and Medicine between the Eighteenth and Twentieth Centuries*. Wisconsin: The University of Wisconsin Press, 1989.
Kane, Peter. "The Tension That Made a Woman Kill." *Daily Mirror*, 11 November 1981, 1, 3.
Kendler, Kenneth, Peter Zachar. "A Dsm Insiders' History of Premenstrual Dysphoric Disorder." In *Philosophical Issues in Psychiatry III: The Nature and Sources of Historical Change*, edited by Kenneth S. Kendler, Josef Parnas, 350–370. Oxford, U.K.: Oxford University Press, 2015.
Kirk, Robert G.W. "The Invention of the "Stressed Animal" and the Development of a Sceicne of Animal Welfare, 1947–1986." Chap. 9, In *Stress, Shock and Adaptation in the Twentieth Century*, edited by David Cantor, Edmund Ramsden. Rochester, NY: University of Rochester Press, 2014.
Kirk, Robert G.W. "Between the Clinic and the Laboratory: Ethology and Pharmacology in the Work of Michael Robin Alexander Chance, C. 1946–1964." *Medical History* 53 (2009): 513–536.
Lawrence, Jon. "Paternalism, Class and the British Path to Modernity." In *The Peculiarities of Liberal Modernity in Imperial Britain*, edited by Simon Gunn, James Vernon. California: California Press, 2011.
Laws, Sophie, Valerie Hay, Andrea Egan. *Seeing Red: The Politics of Pre-Menstrual Tension*. London: Hutchinson and Co. Ltd., 1985.

Levy, Karen, Joan Chrisler. "The Media Construct a Menstrual Monster: A Content and Analysis of Pms Articles in the Popular Press." *Women and Health* 16, no. 2 (1990): 89–104.

Longino, Helen E. *Science as Social Knowledge: Values and Objectivity in Scientifc Inquiry*. Princeton, New Jersey: Princeton University Press, 1990.

Malson, Helen. "Anorexic Bodies and the Discursive Production of Feminine Excess." In *Body Talk: The Material and Discursive Regulation of Sexuality, Madness and Reproduction*, edited by Jane Ussher, 223–245. London and New York: Routledge, 1997.

Markens, Susan. "The "Problematic of Experience" a Political and Cultural Critique of Pms." *Gender and Society* 10, no. 1 (1996): 42–58.

Marks, Lara V. *Sexual Chemistry: A History of the Contraceptive Pill*. New Haven and London: Yale University Press, 2001.

Meghani, Zahra. "Of Sex, Nationalities and Populations: The Construction of Menstruation as a Patho-Physiology." In *Menstruation: A Cultural History*, edited by Andrew Shail, Gillian Howie. Hampshire: Palgrave Macmillan, 2005.

Merchant, Carolyn. *The Death of Nature: Women, Ecology and the Scientific Revolution*. New York: Harper & Row Publishers Inc., 1983.

Morrison, James. *Dsm-5® Made Easy: The Clinician's Guide to Diagnosis*. New York: Guilford Press, 2014.

Nasser, Mervat, Helen Malson. "At Risk by Reason of Gender." In *The Female Body in Mind: The Interface between the Female Body and Mental Health*, edited by Mervat Nasser, Karen Baistow, Janet Treasure. Hove & New York: Routledge, 2007.

Nelson, M., G. Pinna. "S-Norfluoxetine Microinfused into the Basolateral Amygdala Increases Allopregnanolone Levels and Reduces Aggression in Socially Isolated Mice." [In eng]. *Neuropharmacology* 60, no. 7–8 (Jun 2011): 1154–1159.

Oakley, Ann. *Sex, Gender and Society*. Abingdon: Routledge, 1981.

Office, Home. "*Guidance on the Operation of the Animals (Scientific Procedures) Act, 1986.*" edited by Home Office. London: Crown Copyright, 2014.

Oudshoorn, Nelly. *Beyond the Natural Body: An Archeology of Sex Hormones* London: Routledge, 1994.

Perretta, Gemma, Bryan Howard, Timo Nevalainen, ed. *The Cost Manual of Laboratory Animal Care and Use: Refinement, Reduction, and Research*. Boca Raton: CRC Press, Taylor and Francis Group, 2011.

Plumwood, Val. *Feminism and the Mastery of Nature*. London: Routledge, 1993.

Probyn-Rapsey, Fiona. "Review Article: Multispecies Mourning: Thom Van Dooren's Flight Ways: Life and Loss at the Edge of Extinction by Thom Van Dooren." *Animal Studies Journal* 3, no. 2 (2014): 4–16.

Probyn-Rapsey, Fiona, Lori Gruen. "Distillations." Chap. Introduction In *Animalmaladies: Gender, Animals, and Madness*, edited by Lori Gruen, Fiona Probyn-Rapsey, 1–8. New York & London: Bloomsbury Academic, 2019.

Ramsden, Edmund, David Cantor, ed. *Stress, Shock and Adaptation in the Twentieth Century*. Rochester, USA: University of Rochester Press, 2014.

Repo, Jemima. *The Biopolitics of Gender*. New York: Oxford University Press, 2016.

Rey, J. H. "Discussion on Amenorrhoea and Hirsutism." *Proceedings of the Royal Society of Medicine* 50 (1957): 453–460.

Ricardo Costeira, Karla A Lee, Benjamin Murray, Colette Christiansen, Juan Castillo-Fernandez, Mary Ni Lochlainn, Joan Capdevila Pujol, Iain Buchan, Louise C Kenny, Jonathan Wolf, Janice Rymer, Sebastien Ourselin, Claire Steves, Timothy

Spector, Louise Newson, Jordana Bell. "Estrogen and Covid-19 Symptoms: Associations in Women from the Covid Symptom Study." https://www.medrxiv.org/content/10.1101/2020.07.30.20164921v3.

Riddle, Bethany, Lisa Cosgrove. "Constructions of Femininity and Experiences of Menstrual Distress." *Women and Health* 38, no. 3 (2003): 37–58.

Rippon, Gina. *The Gendered Brain: The New Neuroscience That Shatters the Myth of the Female Brain*. London: Penguin, 2019.

Roberts, Celia. *Messengers of Sex: Hormones, Biomedicine and Feminism*. Cambridge: Cambridge University Press, 2007.

Rome, Esther. "Premenstrual Syndrome (Pms) Explained through a Feminist Lens." In *Culture, Society and Menstruation*, edited by Virginia Oleson, Nacny Fugate-Woods, 145–152. London: Hemisphere Publishing Corporation, 1986.

"The Royal Society." https://royalsociety.org/about-us/history/.

Russell, Denise. *Women, Madness & Medicine*. Cambridge: Polity Press, 1995.

Said, Edward. *Orientalism*. 5th ed. London: Penguin Classics, 2003.

Sani, Angela. *Inferior: How Science Got Women Wrong and the New Research That's Rewriting the Story*. London: 4th Estate, 2017.

Scheman, Naomi. "Though This Be Method, yet There Is Madness in It: Paranoia and Liberal Epistemology." In *Feminism and Science*, edited by Evelyn Fox-Keller, Helen E. Longino. Oxford, U.K.: Oxford University Press, 1999.

Schneider, Tomasz, Piotr Popik. "An Animal Model of Premenstrual Dysphoric Disorder Sensitive to Antidepressants." *Current Protocols in Neuroscience* 46, no. 1 (2009): 9.31.1–9.31.10.

Seán T. Anderson, Garret A. FitzGerald. "Sexual Dimorphism in Body Clocks." https://science.sciencemag.org/content/369/6508/1164.

Selye, Hans. "The General Adaptation Syndrome and the Diseases of Adaptation." *Journal of Clinical Endocrinology* 6, no. 2 (1946): 117–230.

———. *The Story of the Adaptation Syndrome Told in the Form of Informal, Illustrated Lectures*. Montreal Canada: Acta Inc, Medical Publishers, 1952.

———. "Stress and the General Adaptation Syndrome." *British Medical Journal* 1, no. 4667 (1950): 1383–1392.

———. *The Stress of Life*. 2nd ed. New York: McGraw-Hill, 1976.

Serra, M., E. Sanna, M. C. Mostallino, G. Biggio. "Social Isolation Stress and Neuroactive Steroids." [In eng]. *Eur Neuropsychopharmacol* 17, no. 1 (2007): 1–11.

Showalter, Elaine. *The Female Malady*. 17th ed. London: Virago Press, 1985.

Stamp-Dawkins, Marian. *Animal Suffering: The Science of Animal Weflare*. Bungay: The Chaucer Press Ltd, 1980.

Strange, Julie-Marie. "'I Believe It to Be a Case Depending on Menstruation': Madness and Menstrual Taboo in British Medical Practice, C. 1840–1930." In *Menstruation: A Cultural History*, edited by Andrew Shail, Gillian Howie. Hampshire: Palgrave Macmillan, 2005.

Selye, Hans. "Stress and the General Adaptation Syndrome." *British Medical Journal*, no. 4667 (1950): 1383–1392.

Tanner, James M., ed. *Stress and Psychiatric Disorder: The Proceedings of the Second Oxford Conference of the Mental Health Research Fund*. Oxford, U.K.: Blackwell, 1960.

Taskin, Bismee. "Female Sex Hormone Could Offer Protection against Covid, Says Study by King's College London." https://theprint.in/india/female-sex-hormone-could-offer-protection-against-covid-says-study-by-kings-college-london/477348/.

Taylor, Nik, Heather Fraser. "Women, Anxiety, and Companion Animals: Towards a Feminist Animal Studies of Interspecies Care and Solidarity." Chap. 10. In *Animaladies: Gender, Animals and Madness*, edited by Lori Gruen, Fiona Probyn-Rapsey, 155–71. New York & London: Bloomsbury Academic, Bloomsbury Publishing Inc., 2019.

Union, Council of the European. "Directive 2010/63/EU of the European Parliament and of the Council of 22 September 2010 on the Protection of Animals Used for Scientific Purposes." *Official Journal of the European Union* (2010).

Ussher, Jane. *Women's Madness: Misogyny or Mental Illness?* Hemel Hempstead: Harvester Wheatsheaf, 1991.

Viner, Russell. "Putting Stress in Life: Hans Selye and the Making of Stress Theory." *Social Studies of Science* 29, no. 3 (1999): 391–410.

Wadiwel, Dinesh Joseph. *The War against Animals*. Leiden & Boston: Brill Rodopi, 2015.

Wadiwel, Dinesh Joseph, Matthew Chrulew. "Introduction: Foucault and Animals." In *Foucault and Animals*, edited by Matthew Chrulew, Dinesh Joseph Wadiwel. Leiden & Boston: Brill, 2017.

Worden, Alastair N, ed. *The Ufaw Handbook on the Care and Management of Laboratory Animals*. Edited by Alastair Worden. 1st ed. London: Bailliere, Tindall And Cox, 1947.

Wright, Richard. "The End of My Nightmare." *Daily Express*, 10 November 1981.

Zita, Jacquelyn N. "The Premenstrual Syndrome: "Dis-Easing" the Female Cycle." *Feminism and Science 2* 3, no. 1 (1988): 77–99.

Section III
Conclusion
21st century compassion fatigue

7 Conclusion

As I finish writing this book, Britain has officially left the EU, is in its third lockdown due to coronavirus and the government has sanctioned the use of a dangerous pesticide that kills bees.[1] Couple this with the devastating impact of climate change: coastal erosion, flooding, vanishing sea birds and hotter summers,[2] and what we have here to borrow the term from scholar of human ecology Andreas Malm, a chronic emergency.[3]

This destruction of the world as we know it has been transformed by a particular set of social relations: Capitalism. Jason Moore calls this era the Capitalocene: since Capitalism's advent, domination over nonhuman 'others' has become unprecedented and is fomented further by its advance under neoliberalism.[4] The list of veritable troubles above reveals that they all, in one way or another, involve the domination of nonhuman animals and nature in the Capitalocene. The coronavirus is a zoonotic disease that originated from nonhuman animals kept on a wet market in China; one of the main drivers of climate change is habitat destruction and biodiversity loss[5] and pesticides are tested on nonhuman animals before being approved for use.[6]

In Britain in 2019, 3.4 million experiments were conducted on animals, and the majority (93%) involved the use of mice, fish and rats.[7] This is

---

1 Mattha Busby, "Government Breaks Promise to Maintain Ban on Bee-Harming Pesticide," *The Guardian*, 2021.
2 Friends of the Earth, "How Is Global Warming Affecting the UK?," https://friendsoftheearth.uk/climate-change/how-is-global-warming-affecting-the-uk.
3 Andreas Malm, *Corona, Climate and Chronic Emergency: War Communism in the Twenty-First Century* (London: Verso, 2020).
4 Jason Moore, "The Rise of Cheap Nature," in *Anthropocene or Capitalocene? Nature, History, and the Crisis of Capitalism*, ed. Jason Moore (Oakland CA: PM Press, 2016).
5 Malm, *Corona, Climate and Chronic Emergency: War Communism in the Twenty-First Century*.
6 Health and Safety Executive, "Vertebrate Testing," https://www.hse.gov.uk/pesticides/pesticides-registration/applicant-guide/vertebrate-testing.htm. To test pesticides on animals, applicants for a licence to conduct *in vivo* tests have to have evidence that there is no alternative.
7 Home Office, "Annual Statistics of Scientific Procedures on Living Animals Great Britain 2019," ed. Home Office (London, 2020). https://www.gov.uk/government/collections/statistics-of-scientific-procedures-on-living-animals.

DOI: 10.4324/9780429461644-8

undoubtedly to increase next year, due to the amount of research conducted to find a vaccination to immunise the human population against Covid-19. We can assume then, that the fight for the abolition of animal experimentation is far from over, but what is to be done? In Simon Springer's words, the only option is to 'fuck neoliberalism, yep fuck it. Neoliberalism sucks. We don't need it.'[8]

Environmental sociologists Diana Stuart and Ryan Gunderson argue that there are two interconnected drivers of damaging human–animal relations. First, 'the subjection of life/nature (including animals) to capital accumulation,' they call this 'capital's ethos.' Second, 'the instrumentalisation of nature (including animals),' which they call 'domination ideology.'[9] I have hoped to track this couplet of domination capitalism and violent human–animal relations throughout this book. With a focus on animal experimental science after World War II, I have shown how such a science has become attuned to the public's emotional demands while silently still engaging in a 'business as usual' approach towards nonhuman animals. Over the last 70 years, this response from science changed the discourse of animal testing by internalising the rhetoric of welfare into its practice and legal regulation.

In this book, I have shown that such welfarist discourses of care in the laboratory are historically contingent and highly political, rather than stemming from an ethical or moral praxis. This book has aimed to challenge existing understandings of animal experimentation and place contemporary practice in its historical context. In this book, I have sought to:

- Historically trace the development of laboratory animal science from 1945 to present. We all have used animals as a means to end. This is most definitively the case in laboratory science, whether in war, medicine or disease. The legal framework allows experimentation to continue at an unprecedented rate and drawing on Foucault; we can make sense of it in terms of governmentality and regulation over nonhuman bodies which renders them powerless.
- Demonstrate how the construction of scientific knowledge through nonhuman animals creates subject–object binaries, which have powerful and detrimental consequences for nonhuman animals. This objectification of nonhumans has resultant power–knowledge *effects* that reinforce the continuation of specific kinds of scientific knowledge and its associated masculinist ontology of positivism.

8 Simon Springer, "Fuck Neoliberalism," *ACME: An International Journal for Critical Geographies* 15, no. 2 (2016): 285–292.
9 Diana Stuart, Ryan Gunderson, "Human-Animal Relations in the Capitalocene: Environmental Impacts and Alternatives," *Environmental Sociology* 6, no. 1 (2020): 69.

- Explore how the *effects* of these power–knowledge relations are gendered and have implications for (and intersections with) other subjugated groups in British society, particularly, women. I have investigated how animal experimentation in Britain still unconsciously enforces Cartesian dualisms, which, as a consequence, are gendered.

This book has again added to the wealth of evidence that underlies our violent relations with nonhuman animals. These power relations are driven by our insatiable desire to consume and generate wealth; in other words, animal experimentation has accelerated under Capitalism and so too has the domination and degradation of the natural world.[10] For anarchist ecologist Murray Bookchin, domination has occurred at two levels, the material and subjective. He calls this saturation of the entire lived experience 'epistemologies of rule.'[11] This particular form of governance fostered the development of patriarchy and a selfish disposition in societies' rulers. It is no surprise then, that what I have documented in this book, illustrate how these dominance hierarchies are inherently gendered. Women are man's antithesis, the opposite of rationality and the abject 'Other' unto which scientists can study her reproductive body, regulated and controlled. Like nonhuman animals' bodies, women's bodies are seen as a commodity and utility to be classified, medicalised and exploited. The great Marxist thinkers, Theodor Adorno and Max Horkheimer, discuss woman's status in capitalist society and say:

> Women have no personal part in the efficiency on which this civilisation is based…Woman is not a being in her own right, a subject. She produces nothing but looks after those who do; she is a living monument to a long-vanished era when the domestic economy was self-contained. The division of labour imposed upon her by man brought her little that was worthwhile. She became the embodiment of biological function, the image of nature, the subjugation of which constituted that civilisation's title to fame.[12]

Women and animals are intrinsically and epistemologically interlinked. With women represented as the 'image of nature.'[13] that at the same time animalises her and devalues nonhuman animals.

---

10 Moore, "The Rise of Cheap Nature," Gunderson, "Human-Animal Relations in the Capitalocene: Environmental Impacts and Alternatives."
11 Murray Bookchin, *The Ecology of Freedom: The Emergence and Dissolution of Hierarchy* (Edingburgh UK: AK Press, 2005). p. 159.
12 Theodor Adorno; Max Horkheimer, *Dialectic of Enlightenment*, 4th ed. (London: Verso, 2008). pp. 247–248.
13 Bookchin, *The Ecology of Freedom: The Emergence and Dissolution of Hierarchy*. p. 193.

In this book, three main themes emerge from the narratives about animal experimentation and gender – all related to the notion of domination in the Capitalocene. They are the animal body as a presupposed object; knowledge production and power relations: the authorising gaze and; gendered science and knowledge production. What follows is an exposition of each theme to conclude the book.

Animal body as presupposed object

I have shown how this creation of active objects (or in Foucauldian terms: docile nonhuman bodies) is facilitated through the techniques of welfare promulgated by the UFAW since the mid-twentieth century. This was initially done to create economics of efficiency in laboratory human–animal relations: reducing wastage of animals, improving their physical and psychological health to make experiments more valid and housing animals in clean conditions. Through the mechanisms of laboratory human–animal relations, the idea of welfare increases the animal body's utility. Therefore, it increases the power humans have over nonhuman bodies, establishing 'in the body the constricting link between an increased aptitude and an increased domination.'[14] In other words, scientific welfarism creates healthier animals, but in doing so, increases regulation, control and domination over nonhuman bodies to ensure their healthiness is fit-for-purpose. Historically, animal bodies have always been seen as objects, ultimately lent to their further objectification. Structured by the discourse of stress examined in Chapters 5 and 6, the laboratory's actual material spaces, as we saw, are gendered places and heavily disciplined spaces of care and welfare. After the Second World War, women were recommended as perfect for laboratory assistant or 'nurse' to the animals. Then, the 'feminine became subsumed by the masculine in all but its unconscious symbolism.'

Knowledge production and power relations: The authorising gaze

As was discussed in Chapter 5, one way of managing animal bodies and behaviour was through the scientists' gaze. This gaze over the laboratory animal has been structured over the years by the UFAW and Laboratory Animals Bureau's work. Laboratories and nonhuman animals became standardised in mid-twentieth century Britain via the circulation of the UFAW's discourses of care towards the laboratory nonhuman. If we look back to Chapter 6 and the nonhuman animals' role in forming a medical conceptualisation of 'stress,' the gaze over their living bodies became essential to delineate the very symptoms of this condition.

---

14 Michel Foucault, *Discipline and Punish: The Birth of the Prison*, 4th ed. (London: Penguin Books Ltd, 1991). p. 138.

The scientists' examined the gaze over the dead animal body in Chapter 4, exercised in the post-mortems conducted during the biological weapons trials by Porton Down Chemical and Biological Research Establishment. Strict adherence to a post-mortem technique was required, which equipped the scientists with a way to conceptualise disease as a fundamental components of weapons of war weapons of war. As I argued in this chapter, the post-mortem acted as an exercise of power over nonhumans that was grounded in the socio-political and helped establish a military-*animal*-industrial complex in mid-twentieth century Britain. The animal body, subjected to the scientists' gaze, became divided and separated into sections, each aspect representing a piece rather than the whole of the nonhuman. In this chapter, I drew on Lisa Johnson's Foucauldian inspired *discourse of lines* to elucidate the complex power–knowledge relations between the animals, scientists, the British military and the broader socio-historical context in the creation of the military-animal-industrial complex.[15]

This gaze over nonhuman animals helps to entrench a standardised view of them and creates a docile body, yet still objectified. It is only through the scientist's gaze that the status of nonhuman animals changed, and a whole set of discourses and practices surrounding laboratory animals became established after 1945. Nonhuman bodies have been 'rewritten,' with the judiciary's help and their relations with various scientific bodies (see Chapters 1 and 2), so science can continue its practices. This has meant a shift to more 'humane' methods in laboratory human–animal relations, as was evidenced in Chapters 5 and 6.

Gendered science and knowledge production

Throughout most of the chapters, I have argued that laboratory animal science is gendered and helps create gendered power–knowledge relations. Both animals and women are subjected to the male gaze, and as a result, are objectified and used to *generate* knowledge and powerful discourses about the world. As evidenced in Chapter 4, animals were used to create biological weapons and in Chapter 6, with the discourses of pre-menstrual stress. The effect of this gaze is one that exemplifies power–knowledge relations notably, in the philosophical underpinnings of science and jurisprudential ones in law. For instance, implicit in the methodologies of biological warfare trials and the jurisprudence of the Animals (Scientific Procedures) Act, 1986 was the reliance on Cartesian dualisms that render women and animals on one side of a dualistic divide, and that entrenched their inferiority to that of the human male. As we can see, there are links between scientific knowledge and legal knowledge creation.

---

15 Lisa Johnson, *Power, Knowledge, Animals* (Basingstoke: Palgrave Macmillan, 2012). pp. 56–62.

Likewise, it is worthy of note that through the male gaze and the creation of such binaries, laboratory animals are individualised and recognised as having individual 'personalities.' This too is a form of disciplinary power over bodies that combine with the laboratory's spatial layout, the result of which was that nonhuman animals, become even more subjugated in the relations of power–knowledge. This individualisation via the male gaze creates subject–object binaries. These binaries are inherently masculine and rest on the philosophical assumptions of positivism.

Power over both animals and women is regulated through different yet comparable techniques. This ties to power–knowledge relations that discursively construct bodies through techniques pervasive in modern society. The power–knowledge of laboratory animal science discourses shows that gendered disciplinary power can be articulated through the very performance of science and its enunciation of an objective reality through the paradigm of positivism.

Positivism and the resultant power–knowledge relations promote the masculine worldview at the expense of the feminine.[16] Animal experimentation upholds this notion, even at the UFAW's declaration of its rejection of Cartesianism in the 1950s! Science in Britain still pursues the positivist methodology, which, as Foucault claims, instils upon social life a particular arrangement of knowledge about the world,[17] creating a set of classifications about nonhumans, replete with psychological, physiological and social characteristics. These classificatory mechanisms that included acknowledging psychological dimensions in animals ensure that they continue to be used in experiments.

The very methodological approach used to test on animals further entrenches this classificatory knowledge about them. Positivism rests upon *a priori* assumptions that ultimately:

> delimit[ed] the totality of experience [of] a field of knowledge, define[d] the mode of being of the objects that appear in that field, provides man's [sic] everyday perception with theoretical powers and defines the conditions in which he can sustain a discourse about things that is recognised to be true.[18]

Initially, this power–knowledge derived from the state's experts and enabled a transformation of the laboratory animal (and woman). It also provided the basis of laboratory animal science in post-war Britain and its twenty-first century operation. As we have seen, this rests upon the dualistic

---

16 It is worthy of note that I am speaking of the masculine and feminine as historical, social constructs, not in an essentialised manner. See introduction for 'note on terminology.'
17 Michel Foucault, *The Order of Things*, 11th ed. (Oxon and New York: Routledge, 2008). p. 172.
18 Ibid. p. 172.

assumptions of the doctrine of positivism, to subjugate bodies and make them docile. This is most noticeable in discussions of pain in Chapters 1–3 and its changing legal definition during the formulation of the Animals (Scientific Procedures) Act, 1986; and how this parallels women's legal standing in contemporary society. I called this the power–pain nexus.

For the most part, this book has documented the nature of laboratory human–animal relations since 1945 and demonstrated that animals played an integral part in state science and structuring ideas concerning gender roles in Britain. The gendered aspect of science Britain is bifurcated: first, science itself is masculinist (through its ontological and epistemological underpinnings, and methodologies), and second via its outcomes which have detrimental effects on those deemed extraneous to masculinity, in this case, animals and women. Consequently, I hope I have rendered visible the cultural and social nature of science, and how the creation of laboratory animal science was far from objective but drew on the social norms and values of contemporary Britain. Overall power–knowledge relations and their effects on nonhuman animals and other subjugated groups in society have been the main focus of this work. With this study, I respond to other feminist histories of science that have neglected to consider the significant role of nonhumans within this history and have overlooked the crucial developments in Britain's scientific culture.

So, what is to be done?

Earlier on in the chapter, I quoted Simon Springer's call to 'Fuck neoliberalism.' To end animal experimentation and its patriarchal accoutrements, we must indeed fuck it right off. But how do we go about doing this? Taking stock from the climate and environmental movements of the last 40 years or so, I advocate for non-violent direct action reinvigoration. Coupled with a greater collectivity of social movements that reach out to each other and participate in conjoined action and thinking. The anti-capitalist movements, the climate change movements, Black Lives Matter, women's and LGBQT+, and animal rights activists must work together to overthrow a system that affects all life on earth. Joined-up thinking and action will only make us stronger, it will help us build alliances and have allies that can help pressurise governments to make changes for the better and influence the public sphere. To paraphrase the climate activist Greta Thunberg's words, our house is on fire, and we need to do something, now. Right now.

Bibliography

Bookchin, Murray. *The Ecology of Freedom: The Emergence and Dissolution of Hierarchy*. Edinburgh UK: AK Press, 2005.
Busby, Mattha. "Government Breaks Promise to Maintain Ban on Bee-Harming Pesticide." *The Guardian*, 2021.

Earth, Friends of the. "How Is Global Warming Affecting the UK?" https://friendsoftheearth.uk/climate-change/how-is-global-warming-affecting-the-uk.

Executive, Health and Safety. "Vertebrate Testing." https://www.hse.gov.uk/pesticides/pesticides-registration/applicant-guide/vertebrate-testing.htm.

Foucault, Michel. *Discipline and Punish: The Birth of the Prison*. 4th ed. London: Penguin Books Ltd, 1991.

———. *The Order of Things*. 11th ed. Oxon and New York: Routledge, 2008.

Gunderson, Diana, Ryan Stuart. "Human-Animal Relations in the Capitalocene: Environmental Impacts and Alternatives." *Environmental Sociology* 6, no. 1 (2020): 68–81.

Horkheimer, Theodor, Max, Adorno. *Dialectic of Enlightenment*. 4th ed. London: Verso, 2008.

Johnson, Lisa. *Power, Knowledge, Animals*. Basingstoke: Palgrave Macmillan, 2012.

Malm, Andreas. *Corona, Climate and Chronic Emergency: War Communism in the Twenty-First Century*. London: Verso, 2020.

Moore, Jason. "The Rise of Cheap Nature." In *Anthropocene or Capitalocene? Nature, History, and the Crisis of Capitalism*, edited by Jason Moore, 78–115. Oakland CA: PM Press, 2016.

Office, Home. "Annual Statistics of Scientific Procedures on Living Animals Great Britain 2019." edited by Home Office. London, 2020.

Springer, Simon. "Fuck Neoliberalism." *ACME: An International Journal for Critical Geographies* 15, no. 2 (2016): 285–292.

Index

1876 Cruelty to Animals Act 15, 22–25, 35, 40, 48, 100, 133–134, 141, 165
1983 White Paper 50–51
1985 White Paper 53–54, 56

abuse towards women 1, 75, 78–80; *see also* women
Adams, Carol J. 4, 83, 119, 125, 189
Adorno, Theodor 205
Advisory Committee on Animal Experiments 48
Agamben, Giorgio 79, 174–175
agentic beings 48
Allington Farm 108
allopregnanolone (ALLO) 192
androgen 177
animaladies 7, 158–159, 183–185; contemporary 192–195; in post-war era 176–179
Animal Aid 52
animal complement 99
animal-dependent breeding 123
animal-dependent science 50, 152
animal enclosure 145; cage 145–146; pen 146; run 146; stall 146
animal experimentation: law in Britain 3–4, 6, 13, 22, 30; rationalising 50–56
animal experimentation at Porton Down CBDE 89–93; biological warfare and the state 96–98; experiments and production of knowledge 111–112; gender, warfare and nonhuman animals 93–96; gendered violence towards nonhuman animals of war 117–119; no peace for animals 103; Operation Cauldron 105–108; Operation Harness 103–105; Operation Negation 105–111; Operation Ozone 108–111; Operation X 98–100; post-mortem 112–117; power, knowledge and crown immunity 100–102
animal house, standardisation of 133, 136
animal/human dualism 82
Animal-Law 70
Animal Liberation (Singer) 37
animalmaladies 158–159
animal morality 166
Animal Rights movement 37
animals: behaviour of 33; economic commodity 17; legal welfarism 17; as property 17; sentience 67; suffering 174; violence towards 17
Animals (Scientific Procedures) Act (ASPA), 1986 6, 14–16, 43, 48, 50, 56–59, 62, 69, 80, 123, 130, 140–142, 153, 170, 174, 209
Animal Suffering: The Science of Animal Welfare (Dawkins) 172
animal welfare 36, 68, 80; considerations 18; lobbyists 54; movement 25
Animal Welfare (Sentencing and Recognition of Sentience) Draft Bill 68
Animal Welfare Year, 1976 37
anthrax 98, 104
Anthropocene 158
anthropomorphism 139
anti-cruelty penalties 68
anti-discrimination law 79
anti-personnel anthrax bomb 97
Antivivisection and Animal Defence Society 26
anti-vivisection groups 52, 102
anti-vivisection movements 23–25, 77
Asdal, Kristin 50
atomic weapon testing 98
attitude towards animals 65

Attlee, Clement 129
autopsies 114–115

Bacharach, A. L. 131
Bacon, Francis 94, 124
Bacterium tularense 107, 110, 118
Bakare-Yusuf, Bibi 81–82
Balls, Michael 52
Balmer, Brian 90
Ben Lomond 115
Bentley, Judy 92
Bikini Atoll 99
biodiversity loss 203
biological bomb 103; testing on Guinea-pigs 117; testing on monkeys 117
Biological Research Advisory Board (BRAB) 97
biological warfare 96–98, 207
biological weapons (B. W.) 96–98, 103–108
biopolitical animalady 183
biopolitical violence 18
biopolitics 18
biopower 20
Birke, Linda 4, 145
Blair, Tony 62
Bookchin, Murray 205
Bowlby, John 137, 161
breeding cages 149
breeding females 150
Brexit 59–69
British animal experimentation law 13–16; 1876 Cruelty to Animals Act 23–25; animals into politics, 1979–1981 37–38; Laboratory Animals Protection Bill, 1979 38–40; legal strategy of sentience 16–20; post-war anti-vivisection revival and Littlewood enquiry 25–27; property and pastoral power 20–23; Protection of Animals (Scientific Purposes) Bill, 1979 40–42; stress, distress and psychological pain in nonhuman laboratory animals 29–35; UFAW, role of 27–29
British Anti-Vivisection Society 99
British liberalism 3
British Union for the Abolition of Vivisection (BUAV) 26, 37
Brown, Wendy 7, 78
Brucella suis virus 105, 119
Brucella viruses 98
brucellosis 104

Burch, R. L. 165, 167–168, 175
Butler, Judith 8–9
BVA 52
B. W. *see* biological weapons

cages 138
Calley, Darren 13
Cameron, David 66, 69
Cannon, Walter B 161
capitalism 79, 203, 205
Capitalocene 203
care 61
cartesian dualism 31, 81
Cartesianism 208
casual autopsies 114
central nervous system 191
Chamberlain, Ronald 27
Chance, Robin Alexander 164–165
Chemical and Biological Defence Research Establishment (CBDE) 89
chemical and biological warfare 90
Christian pastorate 20
Chrulew, Matthew 48
Churchill, Winston 60, 108
Cobbe, Francis Power 102
Code of Practice (CoP) 142–143
CoE's Treaty Series 123 60
Cold War 7, 110
Committee for the Reform of Animal Experiments (CRAE) 38
compassion fatigue: defined 2; severity, factors affecting 2
consumer capitalism 46
Container Technologies 126
contraceptive pills 176
Convention for the Protection of Vertebrate Animals 170
Convention on the Elimination of All Forms of Discrimination Against Women of 1979 (CEDAW) 74
Cooperation in Science and Technology (COST) 143, 151
Council of Europe (CoE)'s convention 15, 49, 141
Covid-19 1, 74; and female sex hormones 178–179; zoonotic disease 203
COVID-19 vaccination 1; mice in the research for 2
CRAE alliance 52–53
Crenshaw, Kimberlé 76
Crown Prosecution Service 79
cruelty 26–27

Cruelty to Animals Act, 1876 6, 50–51, 100–101
Cruelty to Wild Animals Act of 1951 33

Dale, Henry 28
Dalling, T. 32–33
Dalton, Katharina 184–189
Darnton, Robert 89
Darwin, Charles 166
Dawkins, Marian Stamp 171–174
Defence Research Policy Committee (DRPC) 97
degrees of freedom 42, 146
department of Experimental Animals 15
Derrida, Jacques 8
Descartes, Rene 94, 124
Despret, Vinciane 139
discipline 20
discomfort 33
domestic abuse and risk of harm to women 75
Domestic Abuse Bill in 2020 78–79
domination 64
domination ideology 204
Donovan, B.T. 183
Down, Porton 7
Druglitrø, Tone 50
DSM-5 Made Easy: The Clinician's Guide to Diagnosis (Morrison) 190
Duxbury, Catherine 14

Economic Community (EEC) 60
economic liberalism 3, 46
Ede, James Chuter 26
Edgerton, David 91–92
EEC Directive 60
Ellison, Rachel 2
Elston, Mary Ann 77
English, Christine 187
Environment, Food and Rural Affairs Select Committee 68
Equality Act 2010 80
estrogen 192
estrous cycle-dependent irritability 192
Ethical Review Body (ERB) 62
European Communities (EC) 59
European Convention on Human Rights 59
European Convention on the Protection of Animals in Experiments and Other Scientific Procedures 37
European Treaty Series 123 15

European Union (EU): Directive 86/609/EEC, 1986 15, 18–19, 62–63, 70; Directive 2010/63 on the Protection of Animals 13–14, 16, 18, 59, 65, 70, 142–143
experience of pain 13
experimental animals 55
Extraneous to Britain 15

female; *see also* gender; women: containment 145; sex hormones 177, 181; sexuality 183; violence 188
Femicide Census 79
feminine/female *see* gender
Fildes, Paul 96
Foucault, Michel 5, 14, 20, 22, 47–48, 111; apparatuses of security 58; self-mortification 42; submission 42–43
Fox-Keller, Evelyn 167
FRAME 52
Francione, Gary 17, 32
Frank, Robert T. 180
free market 46
free trade 3
French, Richard D. 14
Fry, Peter 40–41

gender: based violence 78, 117–119; female human and laboratory nonhuman bodies 124–125; 'feminine' (the mother) 132; intersectional nature of animals, science and 8; and power of unconscious 125–128; violence towards nonhuman animals of war 117–119; warfare and nonhuman animals 93–96
general adaptation syndrome (GAS) 160–161, 167, 170, 181–183
genetically modified (GM) experimental animals 150
genetic factors 191
Giffard, John Anthony Hardinge 37
Gove, Michael 68
governmentality 6, 14, 20, 22, 47–48, 50; forms 48; nonhuman 69–71
Great Apes, ban on use 62
Grosz, Elizabeth 124, 183
Gruen, Lori 4, 158
guinea-pigs 95, 104, 107–108, 111, 113; autopsy 117; parts 116–117
Gunderson, Ryan 204

habitat destruction 203
Halsbury, Lord 38–39
Halsbury Bill 41, 48

214 Index

Halsbury Select Committee Bill of 1980 51–52
Hampson, Judith 56
Handbook on the Care and Management of Laboratory Animals (UFAW) 27, 123, 129–140, 164–166
Haraway, Donna 4–6
Henderson, David 97
Hinde, Robert 161
Hindle, Edward 131
Hobsbawm, Eric 3
Hollands, Clive 38, 52, 54–56
homeostasis 161
Horkheimer, Max 205
Hormone Replacement Therapy 179
hormones 191; dimorphism 179; female sex 177; male sex 177
Houghton, Lord 38, 52
housing and care 143
human 74; animal relationships 61, 94, 134, 204; dignity 74; dominance hierarchies 18, 30; killing techniques 63; psychosocial factors in workplace 2–3
Humane Experimental Technique (Hume) 167
Hume, C. W. 27, 131, 167
Hunt, Lynn 3
hyper-reductionism 92

infant and caregiver act 127–128
inhumanity 169
Institutional Animal Care and Use Committee (IACUC) 193
institutionalisation of welfare 56–59
International Committee on Laboratory Animals (ICLA) 134
intersectional nature of animals, science and gender 8
intersectional oppressions 76

Johnson, Boris 69
Johnson, Lisa 111, 207

Keynesianism 46–47
Kind Killing 34
King, Angela 125
Kirk, Robert 136, 164
Klein, Naomi 4

Laboratory Animals Bureau (L.A.B.) 129, 206
Laboratory Animals Protection Bill 39–40

laboratory spaces and gendered places 123–124; 3 Rs 128–130; female human and laboratory nonhuman bodies 124–125; gender and power of the unconscious 125–128; laboratory animal becomings 145–152; legalisation and standardisation of laboratory container technologies 140–145; nonhuman laboratory animals 136–140; Post-war legitimation of laboratory animal science 128–130; rationalisation of laboratory spaces and 3Rs 141–145; spaces of segregation 130–136
Lacan, Jacques 127
landing ship tanks (L.S.T) 103
Lane-Petter, William 28, 133–134, 138, 140, 145, 153, 165
Late Luteal Phase Dysphoric Disorder 189
Lee, Wendy Lynne 81, 83
legal welfarism 17
liberalism 3
licensing system for scientists 15, 23, 36, 42, 54, 57; project licence 55
Liddell, Howard 161–162
Lind-af-Hageby, Lizzy 26
Lisbon Treaty 67
Littlewood, Stanley 29
Littlewood, Sydney 29
Littlewood Report of 1965 22–23, 49–50, 53, 69, 141; committee 39; recommendations 35–36
Lord Cohen of Birkenhead 28
Losurdo, Domenico 3
Lucas, Caroline 67
Lynch, Michael 139–140

Maastricht Treaty 59
MacKinnon, Catharine 7, 76, 78, 80, 83
male sex hormones 177
Malm, Andreas 203
Malson, Helen 194–195
mass autopsies 114
Medawar, P. B. 165
Medical Research Council (MRC) 28, 96, 129, 142
menstrual disorders 157–158
menstruation 177–179
menstruation, adverse effect of 184
Mental Health Fund 161
mental ill-health in women 7, 157
mental sufferings 33

mice 108, 111, 138
Microbiological Research Department (MRD) 97
military-animal-industrial complex (MAIC) 90, 125
mind-body dichotomy 167
Ministry of Supply (MoS) 97
Mobilisation Against the Government White Paper 52
monkeys 104, 107, 113–114, 138
Moore, Jason 203
Morrison, James 190–191
Morton, J. D. 89, 106, 110
mother–child dyads 162

Nasser, Mervat 194
National Antivivisection Society 52, 99
National Canine Defence League 99
National Health Service 25
Negation 108, 118
Nembutal injection 114
neoliberalism 3, 46
neoliberal laboratory 'care' 46–47; Advisory Committee Report, 1981 48–49; Animals (Scientific Procedures) Act, 1986 56–59; British regression to nationalism 59–66; Europe and Brexit 59–69; governmentality 47–48; institutionalisation of welfare 56–59; nonhuman governmentalities 69–71; rationalising animal experimentation 50–56
Newsome, Joseph T. 2–3
Nixon, Rob 4
Noble, Dennis 171
Nocella, Anthony 92
nonhuman animals 8; act 128; contingent categories 112; discourses of welfare 22; mental suffering 33; trials, used for 112
nonhuman governmentalities 69–71
nonhuman laboratory animals 48
no peace for animals 103
normativity of killing 114
Noske, Barbara 92

oestrogen 177
oestrous cycle 194
Ogden, Thomas 124
Operation Cauldron 105–109, 112
Operation Harness 98, 102–105, 109
Operation Negation 105–112
Operation Ozone 108–111
Operation X 98–100

pain: defined 53; and distress 175; indescribability of 82; infliction of 81; legal regulation of 24; nonhuman animals, to encapsulate 16; states of suffering 33; theorisation of 174–176
Pain Condition 24, 30–31, 34, 42, 51, 53–54, 63, 99, 141
Painless Killing 34
Palmer, Clare 22
Pasteurella Pestis 105, 107
pastoral power 6, 14, 20–21, 42, 47, 50, 70; biopolitics 21; individualised knowledge 21; responsibility 21; self-mortification 21; of state 21; submissive 21
pathogen-free laboratory animals 133
pathogens testing 105
pathologise menstrual disorders 157
Pavlov, Ivan 162
Peggs, Kay 64
pesticides 203
phylum Chordata 49
physical violence 184; *see also* pre-menstrual stress
PMS *see* pre-menstrual stress
polycarbonate 150
polyphenylsulfone 150
polysulfone 150
pontoon 106
Popik, Piotr 192
Porton Down CBDE, animal experimentation at 89–93, 207; biological warfare and the state 96–98; experiments and production of knowledge 111–112; gender, warfare and nonhuman animals 93–96; gendered violence towards nonhuman animals of war 117–119; no peace for animals 103; Operation Cauldron 105–108; Operation Harness 103–105; Operation Negation 105–111; Operation Ozone 108–111; Operation X 98–100; post-mortem 112–117; power, knowledge and crown immunity 100–102
positivism 95, 208
post-mortem 112–117
post-traumatic stress disorder (PTSD) 2, 191
power 22
power, knowledge and crown immunity 100–102
power–knowledge relations 208

Power–Pain Nexus 7, 80–83
premenstrual dysphoric disorder (PMDD) 189–190, 194
pre-menstrual stress (PMS) 157, 179–181, 184–185; *see also* women, animals and stress and PMS; irritability 192
pre-menstrual syndrome 7
Premenstrual Syndrome, The (Dalton) 184, 196
premenstrual tension 180
Principles of Humane Experimental Technique 176
privatisation 3, 46
Privy Council order 77
Probyn-Rapsey, Fiona 7, 158
progesterone 177, 192
project licence 55
protected animal 65
Protection of Animals (Scientific Purposes) Bill, 1979 40–42, 49
psychiatric disorder 190
psychodynamic energies 128
psychological notions of wellbeing 13

rabbits 111, 138
Raeburn, Anna 188
rats 138, 194
Rees, Merlyn 37
Research Defence Society (RDS) 28, 140
Rey, Joseph Henry 182
rights of women and animals 4
Ritvo, Harriet 15
Royal Army Medical Corps. 133
Royal Commission on Vivisection 22, 25
Royal Society for the Protection of Animals (RSPCA) 28–29, 37; animal experimentation committee 38; reformation of 1876 Act 52
royal society's ethical working party on animal experiments 170–174
Russell, W. M. S. 130, 166–168, 175
Ryder, Richard 24–25, 36–38, 40

sacred animals 174–176
Salter, Colin 92
Samson, Colin 4
SARS-CoV-2 1
Scarry 81–82
Scarry, Elaine 81
schizophrenia 176
Schmidt, Ulf 90
Schneider, Tomasz 192

Scientific Basis of Kindness to Animals, The 28
Scottish Antivivisection Society 52
Seamer, John 52
security 20
self-mortification 33, 35, 42
Selye, Hans 159–164, 167, 170, 176, 181–183, 195
sentience 70
sentient beings 13, 16, 66
sex discrimination in Britain 79
sex hormones 177–179
sexism 80–81, 92
sexual cycle of the lower animals 181
sexual dimorphism 179
sheeps 105
Shell-Shock 159
Singer, Peter 37
Smith, Sandie 187
social hierarchies 78; animate–inanimate 76; human–animal 76; male–female divisions 76
Sofia, Zoë 124, 126, 135, 146, 152
speciesism 92
species-specific testing 19
Springer, Simon 204, 209
standardisation 132
Starling, Ernest 177
Story of the Adaptation Syndrome, The (Selye) 164
stress 7, 33, 160–161; hormonal fluctuations 191; in laboratory animals 160; Selye's concept 164
Stress of Life, The (Selye) 181
Stuart, Diana 204

Taylorism 115
Techniplast 150
technologies of gender 126
testosterone 177
Thatcher, Margaret 3, 38, 46; neoliberal agenda 46–47
Three Rs (Replacement, Reduction and Refinement) 25, 56, 62, 130, 142–143, 157, 169, 175
Thunberg, Greta 209
Tories 52
Tory paternalism 46
toxicity tests 59
Treaty of Rome 60
Treaty on the Functioning of the EU (TFEU) 67
tularemia 104

UK Independence Party (UKIP) 66
U.N. Declaration of Human Rights (UNDHR) 74
Universal Declaration of Human Rights 74
Universities Federation for Animal Welfare (UFAW) 25–28, 42, 53, 123, 130–132, 169, 179, 206

Vaccinia Virus 108
Venezuelan Equine Encephalomyelitis 108, 110–111
Victims of Science (Ryder) 37
Vinter, Jean 34
violence towards animals 117–119
virulent plague *see Pasteurella Pestis*
virulent virus 119
vivisection 42; continuation and intensification 42; industrial-complex 56; law for 15, 24

Wadiwel, Dinesh Joseph 17–18, 20, 35, 48, 64
weapons of mass destruction 91
Weed, Elizabet 152
welfare of nonhuman animals 13–14
welfare of nonhuman laboratory animals 65
welfarist approach to laboratory animals 3
Whitelaw, William 36, 52
Wilder-Kofie, Temari 2–3
Williams, Bernard 171
Winnicott, Donald 124
women: animalisation of body 195; in capitalist society 205; domestic abuse and risk of harm to 75; fluoxetined 192–195; health and mental health 176; hormones 176; legal dehumanisation 76; 'natural' disposition to motherhood, housework and marriage 95; neurotic women 176–177; pain and distress 185; pathologisation of body 195; pre-menstrual bodies 195; sex-appropriate behaviour 176; sexism and violence towards women 75; sexual intercourse 176; structural interrelationship between animals and 76; suffering 78
women, animals and stress and PMS 157–158; animaladies 158–159; animaladies in post-war era 176–179; animal welfare, beginnings in 164–166; bloody monstrous bodies 185–189; contemporary animaladies 192–195; domestication and subordinatios 158–159; general adaptation syndrome 159–164; Katharina Dalton's animalady 184–185; kindness to animals 167–170; mad cow disease 189–191; PMS 179–181; PMS as mental disorder 189–191; rats with PMDD and fluoxetined women 192–195; royal society's ethical working party on animal experiments 170–174; sacred animals 174–176; Selye's female derangement 181–183; UFAW Handbook 159–164
women's subjugation and speciesism in legal system 74–77; animals and legal rights 77–80; domestic abuse and risk of harm to 75; power–pain nexus 80–83
Worden, Alastair 27, 131
Working Women's Organisations 95

Zita, Jacquelyn 191
zoonotic disease 203

Printed in the United States
by Baker & Taylor Publisher Services